Signs of God

Miracles and their Interpretation

MARK CORNER
Charles University, Czech Republic

ASHGATE

Published by
Ashgate Publishing Limited
Gower House
Croft Road
Aldershot
Hampshire GU11 3HR
England

Ashgate Publishing Company
Suite 420
101 Cherry Street
Burlington, VT 05401-4405
USA

Ashgate website: http://www.ashgate.com

British Library Cataloguing in Publication Data
Corner, Mark
  Signs of God : miracles and their interpretation
  1. Miracles
  I. Title
  231.7'3

Library of Congress Cataloging-in-Publication Data
Corner, Mark.
  Signs of God : miracles and their interpretation / Mark Corner.
      p. cm.
  Includes bibliographical references and index.
  ISBN 0-7546-4029-9 (hardcover : alk. paper)—ISBN 0-7546-4030-2 (pbk. : alk. paper) 1. Miracles. I. Title.

  BT103.C67 2005
  231.7'3—dc22

2004021057

ISBN 0 7546 4029 9 (HBK)
ISBN 0 7546 4030 2 (PBK)

Typeset by Manton Typesetters, Louth, Lincolnshire, UK.
Printed and bound in Great Britain by MPG Books Ltd, Bodmin, Cornwall.

Contents

Contents

Preface

This book began, oddly enough, as a satire. It was a story about a woman who claimed to be Christ coming for a second time. Certainly the character in the story bore some resemblance to Jesus of Nazareth. She performed miracles, courted controversy and was killed.

Good or bad, the satire was unpublishable. General publishers found that it had too much theology; theological publishers found that it had too little. But Ashgate took the trouble to suggest that it was rewritten as an academic book, with parts of the satire used for purposes of illustration. I would like to thank Sarah Lloyd at Ashgate for her encouragement in this respect.

In the end I jettisoned the satire and wrote a work of theology, though the former has left its mark on part of one chapter. However, I do not think that the point of the original work has been lost. I was trying (among other things) to challenge the view that the twenty-first century is less credulous than the first or less likely to believe in miracles (not to mention less likely to be unkind to someone like Jesus of Nazareth). I have always been struck by Nineham's use of the quote by C.G. Darwin that 'London in 1750 was far more like Rome in A.D. 100 than like either London or Rome in 1950' (Nineham 1978: 55). Though there are obvious ways in which that historical generalization is true, I think that Nineham is profoundly wrong in the assumption that qualitatively different cultural and social assumptions somehow shield the 'modern' age from the 'ancient'. He seems to know neither the scepticism of the ancients nor the superstition of the moderns. But rather than address this issue directly, I think that it has been much better to have addressed it indirectly, by focusing on the question of miracles and attempting to discuss them in their theological, historical and philosophical aspects. In order to make the text as digestible as possible, I have divided it into three sections corresponding to these different aspects.

I am very conscious of the fact that this book tries to cover a great deal, but even more conscious of what it has left out. It limits its discussion of miracles outside Christianity, and even inside Christianity its perspective is obviously restricted. Even so I tried to cover as much as possible, because I consider that the question of miracles is central to Christian thought. 'Once upon a time', wrote Franz Rosenzweig, 'miracles were no embarrassment to theology, but on the contrary its most effective and reliable confederate' (1985: 93). Thought needs to be given to the reasons why that is no longer the case. It seems to me that the idea of miracles cannot be left cordoned off like a terminally ill patient in the corner of the hospital ward, as if this is the one doctrine that cannot somehow be repaired or adapted in a modern secular world. Hence, insofar as I have tried to show the importance of miracles, I have perhaps ranged too far with them; but for the reason cited above, perhaps my faults in this respect can be regarded as the faults of my virtues.

Since I left the UK in 1992, when universities there were beginning to suffer the sort of decline so brilliantly analysed in Professor R.H. Roberts' recent *Religion, Theology and the Human Sciences* (2002: 86–110), I have had the good fortune to teach at the Charles University, Prague, where despite operating in a second language the students have been able to discuss philosophical and theological questions with ease. I owe much to them for my ideas. I should also like to thank former colleagues and friends who have kept in touch with me since leaving England, particularly Professor Christopher Rowland, who has not ceased to encourage me in developing views which I suspect are rather different from his own. Finally, I should like to mark a continuing debt to the late Professor Donald MacKinnon, whose lectures of thirty years ago continue to inspire so many of us in our thinking and writing.

Prague
June 2004

PART I
MIRACLES IN
PHILOSOPHICAL
PERSPECTIVE

Chapter 1

What is a Miracle?

One of the best ways of seeing how difficult this subject can be is to try to define a 'miracle'. I will consider several definitions in this chapter before outlining the one I propose to adopt in this book. This should be borne in mind in later chapters, where what I am arguing may well apply to miracles in some senses of the term but not others.

A Miracle as a Wonderful Event

It would be possible to define a miracle simply as a wonderful event. Take the following common phrases or sentences which contain the word 'miracle': 'China's economic miracle'; 'a miracle of modern science'; 'every time a baby is born, the miracle of life is renewed'. In none of these cases is any violation or transgression of a law of nature asserted. The emphasis in these examples is more upon the extraordinary impact of nature itself in its day-to-day working, whether nature is expressed in terms of laws that are economic, technological or biological.

The etymology of the word 'miracle' supports this interpretation. It comes from the Latin 'miraculum' meaning an object of wonder (cf. 'mirus', wonderful and 'mirari', to wonder). It would be possible to consider many things 'objects of wonder' – sunsets, mountain peaks and Shakespeare plays could all come into this category.

The 'wonderful event' view of miracle can be found in the writings of the Protestant theologian Friedrich Schleiermacher (1768–1834). Schleiermacher considers the subject of miracles in his magnum opus *The Christian Faith*. At the root of his theology is the idea of a 'religious self-consciousness, by means of which we place all that affects or influences us in absolute dependence on God' (quoted in Smart 1962: 328). This self-consciousness, however, is not awakened by miracles understood as violations of the laws of nature. Far from it; the laws of nature express the wonders of a creation which is divinely ordained, and to violate them would amount to violating or invading God's own work. If anything, therefore, miracles understood as transgressions of the laws of nature would weaken rather than strengthen the human person's consciousness of God.

Schleiermacher's Romantic sensibilities are such that piety is awakened by nature taking its proper course, not by its being interfered with. Where we have a true knowledge of nature, we reject any idea that God would 'invade' God's own work. Nature is always more honoured in the observance than the breach. In sum, 'It can never be necessary in the interest of religion so to interpret a fact that its

3

dependence on God absolutely excludes its being conditioned by the system of nature' (quoted in Smart 1962: 335). The 'miraculum', the object of wonder, is always something natural, and if this object is singled out it is simply because of the response it evokes.

Schleiermacher's theology has been identified with a view of miracle as a religious name for an event. Though this will not do as a bald summary of Schleiermacher, it rightly shows that the theologian believed miracles concerned a religious response to the natural rather than the irruption of the supernatural.

Sometimes miracles are interpreted in terms of a religious response to the natural which is located at the level of ethical behaviour rather than feeling. Take the following interpretation of Jesus' famous feeding of the five thousand. The interpretation argues that the five loaves and two fishes are effectively what people will initially admit to having. However, the combination of Jesus' teaching and his charismatic presence inspires people to give up what they had been saving for themselves. The 'miracle' thereby becomes the act of sharing, overcoming the human tendency to hoard and act selfishly. This interpretation (I am not here debating its rights and wrongs as exegesis of the text, or even the thorny question of *how* to debate the rights and wrongs of any exegesis), like the others I have mentioned, rejects the idea of any transgression of the laws of nature; but the 'object of wonder' is understood here in terms of a moral rather than (or perhaps as well as) an emotional response.

As with Jesus' miracles, contemporary miracles can also be interpreted in this light. Someone who goes on a pilgrimage to Lourdes, for instance, might argue that the 'real' miracle is the sense of community and acceptance among people who are ordinarily given up as 'hopeless cases'. Instead of being an irritation to doctors and hospital managers, showing up the limited capacities of the former and straining the financial resources of the latter, the pilgrims are honoured as those who find special favour with Christ. They cease to be a 'problem' to the rest of society. This meaning can be found in the gospels also, in the acceptance given to lepers and the refusal to treat them as social outcasts. The modern world likes to think that it has moved beyond such attitudes in its treatment of the sick and dying, but of course it has not.

There is one very important aspect to miracles that the 'wonderful event' definition does bring out, and that is the fact that miracles must be beneficial and have some religious significance. This is the reason, as I discuss later, why the philosopher Thomas Hobbes could not see a talking cow as a 'miracle'. Moreover, it suggests that miracles are either acts of God or acts carried out in the name of God. There are implications for the biblical understanding of 'miracle' here, which I discuss in Chapter 6 on the miracles of Jesus. What, for instance, of those miracles which are called 'punitive' because they bring someone harm rather than benefit? What about the 'signs and wonders' which, according to Mark 13:22, various 'impostors' will be able to carry out in Christ's name? These are difficult questions, but the position I shall take is that only God or God's followers (using God's power, not their own) can perform a miracle and that the world can only be a better place for a miracle having been performed. This will mean that my definition will not exclude the question of the effect and purpose of a miracle. It will not concentrate simply upon its being an event with no natural explanation.

I would claim that my position can be defended as in line with the thinking of the New Testament. The word 'miracle', as I have already suggested, comes from the Latin word 'miraculum', with the emphasis upon causing wonder. But the New Testament has a slightly different emphasis. Of those words that might be equivalent to 'miraculum' in Greek, 'thauma' appears nowhere in the New Testament, 'thaumasion' appears only in Matthew 21:15 and 'paradoxon' appears only in Luke 5:26. The word 'teras', which means evoking wonder and astonishment, is found many times in the New Testament, but it is usually partnered by a term which stresses the religious significance of what happens – commonly 'semeion' meaning sign or 'dunamis' meaning act of power. The most frequent New Testament phrase of all (in English) is 'signs and wonders'. In other words the emphasis is not simply upon something impressive but something religiously significant. A talking cow is merely a wonder. A miracle must also be a sign. It seems to me that this is a point recognized by Schleiermacher and must not be forgotten as we try to reach a different definition.

Whatever its merits, I have ruled out the definition given by Schleiermacher as inadequate. As I discuss in Chapter 9, for instance, I do not think that the 'resurrection' of Jesus can be defined as an expression of resolve or commitment on the part of his disciples to continue the work of their former leader. I do not believe that the 'Che lives' interpretation will do. For that reason, I am going to look at some other definitions of 'miracle', though there is no reason why 'miracles' in these other senses that I am about to describe cannot happen alongside 'miracles' as (in the true sense of the word) awe-inspiring events.

Miracle and Coincidence

The following example shows a slightly different understanding of 'miracle'. Suppose a news item refers to someone having a 'miraculous' escape after days lying under rubble in the aftermath of an earthquake. The news report probably does not mean to imply that concrete became feather-light or that human beings suddenly developed a bodily frame with the resistance of steel. What is implied is that the human body has strong *natural* powers of resistance under stress and that there are often air pockets inside the mountains of detritus formed by collapsed masonry. The result can be a welcome piece of good fortune when someone survives trapped for days. 'Miracle' here seems to mean something like 'extraordinary stroke of luck'. This is presumably what BBC World implied on 8 July 2003, concerning a report that a 2-year-old boy had survived a plane crash in the Sudan. The reporter made the comment: 'If so, it's a miracle.' He did not, I think, mean to imply that God had somehow suspended the laws of nature in order to protect the child from death. He meant that the child had been lucky enough to survive without any such suspension. In theological terms, the reporter probably had in mind something more like 'providential care' than 'miraculous interference'.

R.F. Holland's definition of 'miracle' as 'an extraordinary coincidence of a beneficial nature interpreted religiously' (1989: 53) appears closest to the examples given above concerning survivors of earthquakes and plane crashes. Holland cites the example of a child playing on a railway line and becoming entangled in the tracks when an express train is due. At the moment the train approaches, the driver decides to practise an emergency stop. The train just stops in time and the child is freed. Another older example which an earlier generation often used was the nine days of complete calm during the evacuation of British and French troops from Dunkirk in 1940.

However, whilst Holland offers an example of a 'miracle' which does not necessitate any transgression of the laws of nature, his argument does seem to go further in terms of direct divine involvement or some special act of God than Schleiermacher's does. To return to the example above: don't those who call Dunkirk a 'miracle' mean something more than that it was just a 'lucky escape'? Isn't there an implication, when people refer to the 'miracle of Dunkirk', that God somehow acted to 'hold off' any impending storm?

Or take Holland's example, the case of the train driver braking in front of the child. Doesn't calling it a 'miracle' imply that God somehow acted to 'make' the driver practise an emergency stop? Suppose God simply observed the train driver making an emergency stop and felt pleased about it – would that be enough to call it a miracle? It is not clear that it would. We feel that God must 'do' something. God must somehow 'put it into the mind of' the driver that he or she should practise an emergency stop. The idea behind these 'coincidences' is that God acts in some special way – to still the storm or stop the train.

Compare another miracle often referred to where the sea is concerned – the parting of the Red Sea. It would seem obvious that in this case there is some 'special act of God' that clears a pathway for the Israelites between the waves. Some would see this as something different from the miracle at Dunkirk. However, it could be argued that the case of the Red Sea and the case of Dunkirk are not so disparate as they might at first appear. In both cases people think of the Deity acting in such a way that the workings of nature do not follow the course they would have followed had God *not* acted.

Isn't this the case also when reference is made in the news to the survivors of earthquakes and other natural disasters? Even in popular usage, where some would argue that the currency of 'miracle' is severely debased ('his shot on goal was a bloody miracle!'), there may be a sense that God acts in a particular way, for instance by protecting the child in an air pocket under the rubble. This does not mean that the rubble suddenly became feather-light or that the child could suddenly live without breathing. It means that the air pocket was in the right place at the right time to help the child. It is in this sense that many people who speak of their 'miraculous escapes' do think of a special act of divine providence keeping them alive, and therefore mean something more than the commentator who describes a lucky goal on the football pitch as miraculous.

The conclusion would seem to be that both the Red Sea and Dunkirk require a special act of God. They could be distinguished as follows. It could be said that in the Red Sea case God does something nature could never do. In the Dunkirk case, God does something nature could have done but in this particular instance it is God rather than nature who does it. The miraculous survivors of earthquakes or oncoming trains are in the 'Dunkirk category'. But even if this distinction is accepted, it doesn't alter the fact that in *both* cases God acts in some specific way.

The suggestion I am making is that even Holland's definition, which speaks of 'an extraordinary coincidence of a beneficial nature interpreted religiously', cannot avoid the idea of some special divine action. It can perhaps avoid the idea of that 'special divine action' transgressing natural laws. It can be an act of God which exploits these laws rather than bypassing them. But it is still an act of God. In some way or other, even where no law is broken, God 'does something' and does not merely 'spectate'.

Some modern interpretations of 'chaos theory' and the uncertainty principle try to weave these apparent coincidences into the overall design of the universe. By some gentle 'touch on the tiller' millions of years earlier, God somehow manages to determine 'coincidences' far in advance of their happening without having to 'break into' the system God has created. I find such suggestions confusing, but will discuss this in detail in later chapters. I remain convinced that for a 'lucky' escape to be a 'miraculous' escape, God must specifically act to facilitate it or bring it about.

God's Actions as Interventions

Some philosophers of religion, such as Swinburne and Mackie, use the term 'intervention' to describe this special act of God. Thus J.L. Mackie writes that 'a miracle occurs when the world is not left to itself, when something distinct from the natural order as a whole intrudes into it' (1982: 20). But there is a danger implicit in this notion of 'intervention'. It implies that human beings ordinarily inhabit a self-sufficient universe which they interpret and manage of their own accord. Occasionally, however, perhaps because of a particular threat to this universe or a particularly deserving victim within it, God will break in from outside and rearrange it. Not too often, however, or those inside that universe might give up trying to sort their own lives out and simply summon God to solve their problems for them.

The image of the created universe as an ordinarily self-sufficient whole which occasionally necessitates a little benign interference from outside is a pervasive one. The world is like a children's playground with God on the outside keeping a watchful eye in case things get out of control. Ordinarily, the Deity will let things run their course. On occasion, however, the divine being has to 'intervene'.

It seems to me that this image is seriously misleading concerning God's relation to the universe. If God 'occasionally intervenes' in the world, that implies that the Deity ordinarily stands apart from it. Occasional presence implies ordinary absence. It suggests that the universe is a self-sufficient entity which is looked down upon by a divine observer 'from above'. It is for this reason that I prefer to use the term 'special act of God' to define 'miracle' rather than 'act of divine intervention'. In Chapters 3 and 4 I develop this point further.

To speak from a purely Christian point of view (though this must be true of other religions as well), raising one aspect of Christian belief inevitably draws in others. The notion of God 'intervening' in the world has implications for the understanding of other aspects of Christian doctrine.

Take the notion of 'creation'. Some interpretations of the world as God's 'creation' move in the direction of imagery which presents the universe as a self-sufficient entity which the Deity can then interfere with (or not) in a miraculous way. God 'creates' something which is 'seen to be good' and is then coaxed in the right direction by its Maker through a series of external interventions – messages, threats, acts of violent destruction or of assistance – all of them coming 'from beyond' as part of God's tireless efforts to housetrain humanity.

A self-sufficient universe of this sort is presented by one of the most famous images of the world as God's creation, that of William Paley (1838) with his watchmaker analogy. Paley asks us to imagine someone out for a walk who comes across a watch lying on the ground. They are unsure what this object is, but from its intricate design they are clear that it is not a natural object. Such craftsmanship demands a craftsman. Paley wants us to respond to the natural universe as the walker responded to the watch. The universe is too intricate 'just to be'. It must have a maker.

Such an 'argument from design' to the existence of God raises many questions which are not part of this discussion. What is being commented on here is the fact that Paley's way of seeing the universe is another example of viewing it as a 'thing outside God'. Discussions proceed on the basis that the universe, like a watch, is a self-sufficient entity, and the question then becomes one of whether there really exists a God 'outside' it who made it. Arguments about miracles similarly abound with images of the Maker of the watch intervening to 'repair it' or 'put it right' or 'wind it up'. Unsurprisingly, it is often pointed out that the better the watch, the less in need of service it will be. A perfect watch would require no interference. Miracles therefore become evidence of God's imperfect craftsmanship!

But is this imagery helpful? Or is it the case that it deceives more than it enlightens? I have argued that it is necessary to think in terms of a 'particular action' of the Deity which may or may not 'transgress natural law'. But does this notion of a 'particular action' in turn require us to think in terms of some kind of 'external intervention' by God, benign or otherwise, in the affairs of the universe, as so many of those who write about miracles and other aspects of Christian theology do? I would argue that it does not require us to do so and that doing so anyway only serves to sow confusion about other aspects of Christian doctrine.

It is possible to describe miracles in such a way as to avoid this sense of a normally absentee God who occasionally turns up to 'set things right' or at least help them along. It could be emphasized instead that God is never apart from the world, that the Deity is, after all, described as 'omnipresent' and that this attribute must obviously entail a constant presence. The relation of the created universe to the Creator is less like that of finished pot to the potter than like that of a tune to the singer. The craftsman that brought the pot into being is separate from it. Once formed, the pot could survive the absence or even the death of the potter. But the tune can only last as long as the singer chooses to sing. At any moment the singer could choose to sing no more and the tune would disappear (this analogy, which comes from the early church period, did not have to consider cassettes and recording studios). The dependence of the created universe upon the Creator, this argument goes, is a constant and absolute one.

If God's relation to the created universe is viewed in these terms, then miracles are not acts of occasional interference by God in a world from which the Deity is ordinarily absent. God is always present, sustaining the universe in being. It would be best to say that God is always involved with the universe, but God's involvement takes different forms. Performing miracles may be one of those forms.

The Problem of Laws of Nature

Any definition of 'miracle' runs up against the problem of 'laws of nature', what they are and whether or not miracles 'violate' or 'transgress' them. Such questions form a recurring theme of this book. What I want to do now is to discuss a couple of very different approaches to the problem.

In Chapter 11, where I discuss miracles in various non-Christian religious traditions, I cite the example of al-Ash'ari in Islam. Al-Ash'ari rejects the notion of secondary causes as inhibiting God's power; everything that happens is therefore directly willed by God. There is no universe created and then left to run 'of its own accord'. Instead, the universe is being recreated at every instant of time. Human action is an illusion and all change is brought about directly by God's decree.

Al-Ash'ari adopts a position of perpetual divine intervention because he thinks it would be insulting to God's power to adopt a different viewpoint. Each moment of history, he argues, is effectively a new creation, a direct act of God. Merely to suppose that it was brought about by preceding conditions, using some theory of causation, is to interpose some other agency between God and creation. To al-Ash'ari, God's creation is a series of actions conceived atomistically in which whatever God wills comes into being. A 'law of nature', precisely because of the word 'law' which seems to be prescribing how changes are to be made, violates this notion of direct divine action.

Al-Ash'ari's position is a reaction against 'law' as something constraining, a 'Thou shalt not'. He sees the idea of laws of nature as an insult to the Deity, a 'Keep off the Grass' sign held up to the face of the omnipotent God. But the laws of nature do not have to be understood as prescriptive. Suppose we agree with al-Ash'ari that God's creation is a series of specific divine actions. Do these actions take place according to any pattern? Commentators like R.C. Zaehner (1971: 186) support the idea that they do. God's actions follow a certain 'custom' – chosen by

God alone, of course. Then may we not, avoiding the word 'law' which might suggest prescribing to God how God must act, describe what otherwise might be called 'the laws of nature' as something like 'customary divine behaviour'? And if that is acceptable, we might then want to speak of another category of divine action called 'uncustomary behaviour'. Both God's customary and uncustomary forms of behaviour would be determined entirely according to God's will, but the distinction between the two types of behaviour would still be a useful one. What I am suggesting is that even in al-Ash'ari's terms it may be possible to retain an equivalent of the distinction between 'providence' and 'miracle' in Christian theology.

Al-Ash'ari's sensibilities appear to be the precise opposite of Schleiermacher's. For Schleiermacher, I have suggested, the laws of nature express the wonder of a creation which is divinely ordained, and to violate them would amount to violating or invading God's own work. Rather than it being an 'insult' to God for the laws of nature to be binding, it is here an 'insult' for them to be anything else. We find writers like Peacocke and Polkinghorne, discussed in detail later, viewing 'special divine actions' in a similar manner, as forms of tampering which diminish the divine product. Thus it is possible to find views which consider God undermined both by being compelled to observe the laws of nature and by being compelled to displace them.

The fact that the argument about what 'honours God ' can be interpreted in both ways illustrates that the argument is hardly a decisive one. It depends upon language and point of view. It seems to me perfectly possible to argue that God could choose to combine a form of activity which was in accordance with laws of nature – the general divine action (GDA) which constitutes God's continuous work of creation – with instances of specific divine action (SDA). There remains an argument about how to make sense of SDA, of course, but I see no compelling argument in the view that SDA would be too 'insulting' to God's handiwork.

As for al-Ash'ari, we have already seen how reworking the language might make a combination of SDA and GDA acceptable to him. One final point on this, however, is that a position of constant and exclusive SDA, in which not only does all change come by God's decree through a series of direct actions, but there is no observable pattern or (to use Zaehner's word) custom in the way these actions take place, would effectively abolish miracles. This is what Lawton means when he says 'nothing could be called miraculous when anything could happen' (2002: 240), or Rosenzweig when he says that 'in a wholly miraculous world, wholly without law, an enchanted world … the individual miracle could hardly strike one as a miracle' (1985: 95). Miracles need laws of nature in order to stand out themselves as actions which, whether they are rare or frequent, cannot ever be the only form of divine action. There could be laws of nature without miracles; but there could not be miracles without laws of nature.

Problems in Recognizing a Miracle

In his book *Religion and the Decline of Magic*, Keith Thomas discusses something he calls the 'weapon salve' (1971: 225). This consisted in the belief that a wound could be cured through anointing the weapon that caused it. At first sight this might seem to involve belief in a miracle, as indeed for some people it did. But for others it represented no more than science, and reflected the 'laws of nature'. Robert Fludd saw it as 'an entirely commendable attempt to harness the invisible forces he believed to be pulsating through the natural world' (Thomas 1971: 304). In other words it was a scientific procedure. To his clerical opponent, William Foster, the parson of Hedgerley, however, it was 'diabolical' and its inventor, Paracelsus, was what Thomas calls 'a monstrous conjuror working outside the bounds of nature'. But this was because the university training of a parson was more likely to be Aristotelian, involving the claim that nothing could work at a distance. Action at a distance had to involve some kind of diabolical (or divine) suspension of the laws of nature. To the Neoplatonist Fludd, on the other hand, action at a distance was perfectly conceivable. Foster's science was simply too small.

It is fascinating to find precisely this argument in the discussion of Isaac Newton's laws of motion between the philosopher Leibniz and Newton's disciple Samuel Clarke. Leibniz and Newton had already fallen out over who could claim credit for inventing calculus, but the argument here concerns Leibniz' rejection of the very foundations of Newtonian mechanics. Leibniz insists that what Newton refers to is a 'miracle' since it is simply not possible for one thing to affect another 'at a distance'. He has Parson Foster's problem with the weapon-salve. If God causes a body 'to move free in the ether round about a certain fixed centre, without any creature acting upon it', he claims, 'I say, it could not be done without a miracle; since it cannot be explained by the nature of bodies' (Vailati 1997: 11–12). It is a 'supernatural thing', he claims, for one thing to affect another at a distance.

Clarke responds that bodies may attract by 'invisible and intelligible means', but he knows that Leibniz will not accept gravitation as a scientific principle. So he tries another tack in order to challenge Leibniz' insistence upon the miraculous. He points out that this attraction between bodies happens 'regularly'. A miracle, on the other hand, must be 'unusual'. Leibniz is unimpressed by this, for 'then monsters would be miracles', so Clarke has to qualify his definition. A miracle must not only be unusual but it cannot be the 'rare effect of usual causes', that is to say akin to an eclipse or a monstrous birth, which Clarke calls a 'prodigy'.

However, it is precisely Leibniz' refusal to see gravitational attraction in terms of any 'usual causes' that has led to the claim concerning miracles. Clarke is therefore forced to hang his rejection of the miraculous entirely upon the fact that such attraction is a regular event. 'Did man usually arise out of the grave, as corn grows out of seed sown', he points out, 'we should certainly call that natural.'

Whatever the merits of Leibniz' rejection of Newton's laws of motion, his scepticism towards Clarke seems justified. Imagine someone who finds the laws of aerodynamics unacceptable in the way Leibniz finds Newton unacceptable. That person claims that heavy objects simply can't stay up in the air, the way Leibniz claims that there can be no action at a distance. When asked about air travel, our sceptic replies that planes are being maintained (at least in most cases) in the air by a divine miracle – a miracle that has been repeated so often by a merciful God concerned about passenger safety, that it has been misconstrued as a natural law. Can our sceptic's position really be undermined simply by saying that miracles can't happen all the time?

It seems to me not. The sceptic has to be shown how the laws of aerodynamics work. It certainly does look peculiar that huge lumps of metal can rise into the air and stay there, but a study of the flow of air around objects and the way in which lift, thrust and drag can act as counters to gravitation can provide a scientific explanation of why planes rise into the air and stay there for thousands of miles. Clarke may have lacked the means to have provided such a scientific explanation in his own day, since many of the discoveries that could throw light upon action at a distance (for instance those emerging from the important research of Robert Boyle in the late seventeenth century into the nature of gases and establishing that air has weight) were only in the process of being developed.

Of course the sceptic may not be convinced by these explanations and insist on a miracle. But to say with Clarke that it can't be a miracle because it happens all the time seems to me wrong. I would argue that it can't be a miracle for other reasons. These may involve the fact that there is no plausible natural explanation, or a willingness to associate a natural but coincidental event with an act of God. Often, as the Leibniz–Clarke correspondence shows, there will be an argument as to what constitutes a natural explanation. There are moments when an explanation seems counter-intuitive (gravitation, aeronautics), and at such times it may take a while to win support. If we are eventually persuaded of the explanation, this is not because it is a mere description of an observed regularity, but because it enables us to see how things work in a way we couldn't see before.

I concede the argument that the laws of nature do not stay the same and that there may be disagreement concerning what those laws are. Neoplatonist and Aristotelian worldviews clashed in the seventeenth century, and as a result one side saw a miracle where the other saw nature at work. Ironically, there is a case to be made that in the modern day too close an attachment to the Newtonian worldview is holding science back: at the time, however, Newton was seen as a revolutionary. 'Action at a distance' was the quantum mechanics or the theory of relativity of the seventeenth century – something counter-intuitive and liable to make people uncomfortable in contemplating it. Nowadays it has the status of a 'received view' and an orthodoxy which, if anything, holds back further scientific progress.

Definition of 'Miracle'

In the course of this chapter I have considered the idea of a 'miracle' as an emotionally and/or morally uplifting event. It is the merit of the 'wonderful event' definition that it points out the failings of an approach to miracles which sees them as acts of divine 'intervention', as if God is only involved with the world when God performs miracles. When the poet Gerard Manley Hopkins remarks that the world is charged with the glory of God, when Schleiermacher's Romantic perspective calls a miracle 'the religious name for an event' or when J.L. Mackie chooses to entitle his book on arguments for and against the existence of God *The Miracle of Theism* (1982), they are all correct insofar as they imply that the physical universe itself, or for that matter the lives of ordinary human beings within it, are never apart from God. The sense in which it can be said that 'life itself is a miracle' is the sense in which God is never absent from the world but eternally sustains it. There is no absent Deity making occasional visits; there is an ever-present Deity who varies the divine modus operandi in relation to the world. The 'wonderful event' definition also influences my own in that I shall assume that a miracle must come from God (whether or not a malevolent supernatural force or forces exist), must be beneficial and must be religiously significant.

Even so, I have been unwilling to accept the 'wonderful event' definition. It is true that I have not given reasons for such a rejection in this chapter, but I hope that I can justify this on the grounds that the 'wonderful event' definition effectively removes most of the problems associated with advocating the case for miracles in a modern 'scientific' age. By insisting on a more difficult approach I can perhaps be forgiven for (initially) riding roughshod over an easy one.

I have been drawn instead to a definition of a miracle as a 'special' or 'immediate' divine action. Of course that only makes sense if there are other sorts of divine action which are not immediate (which are 'mediated'), and I have accepted that this distinction must be made. However, it seems to me that neither those who argue only for SDA (for example al-Ash'ari), nor those who argue only for GDA (for example Peacocke) make their case. I consider these views in more detail in Chapters 11 and 4, respectively. The point here is that I know that my definition must maintain the existence of two forms of divine action, which the two acronyms above help to distinguish.

I have conceded that whilst a miracle involves the absence of a natural explanation, it is impossible to know for certain that a natural explanation *is* absent. There may be disagreements concerning the laws of nature themselves, as I have tried to illustrate in the case of the weapon-salve and the ideas of Newton. As I discuss in detail in the following chapter on Hume, what some people claim to be a miracle might be the working of an as yet undiscovered natural law. A person who recovers unexpectedly from cancer, for instance, might in fact have recovered quite naturally. When the disease is better known, cases of what is now called 'spontaneous remission' may be explicable according to principles which medical science has yet to uncover. It is therefore always possible that what appears to be an instance of God working directly, rather than through secondary causes, may in fact be a case of secondary causes operating in a manner which we do not yet recognize.

However, the fact that one cannot be certain of something doesn't entail that it cannot be the case. Unfortunately, many religious people feel such a need to cling to certainty, that they jettison any argument that will provide them with less. As I discuss in Chapter 9 on the resurrection of Jesus, this presumption has unfortunate consequences.

The theist sometimes arrives at a definition which presumes that ordinarily the Deity works through 'second-order' or created causes, which make things happen in accordance with the laws of nature. In the case of miracles, however, this second-order causation is absent. Things happen because of God alone. Miracles on this view represent an occasional *absence*, not an occasional presence, an absence of the influence exerted by the created order willed into being and constantly sustained by God. God is always present and always active in the world, but usually the divine power operates through intermediary causes. In the case of a miracle, however, the intermediary drops out and the activity is God's alone. This is roughly speaking the position that can be associated with the Thomist tradition (the tradition based upon the teachings of Thomas Aquinas), though Aquinas himself makes further distinctions that are not made here (*Summa contra Gentiles* III, 101, 2–4).

As we will see in the course of this book, the question of how God operates without intermediary causes needs careful examination. I am not convinced that Aquinas' definition is as useful as it seems. Earlier in this chapter I considered a definition which sees miracles in terms of divinely willed coincidences. However, I argued that these events still require, in order to be significant, a special act of God. God may make use of rather than override the laws of nature in producing an effect (for example nine days of calm sea at Dunkirk), but this means more than that God simply observes it happening. I would suggest that the 'coincidence' view of miracle does not actually let us off the hook of explaining what a 'special act of God' is. Indeed, the coincidence view reminds us of something that it is easy to forget, namely that the problem is not so much of whether or not God 'violates' a law of nature, but precisely how God connects with the world in any 'special divine action', whether or not the laws of nature are transgressed. Recent work on the subject, as I discuss later, struggles for this very reason to make sense of what Austin Farrer (1967: 65) called the 'causal joint' between God's actions and that of human beings or the natural processes of the world.

Indeed I do not see why the believer in miracles as 'coincidences', faced with the question 'How did God stop a storm in the English Channel in June 1940?', is challenged by anything less difficult than the believer in miracles as 'violations' of natural law who has to explain how God parted the Red Sea. In fact, though the 'coincidence' theorist is supposed to believe that God 'exploits' rather than 'overrides' laws of nature, it seems to me that in both cases God can be said to be 'overriding' them. As we will see in Chapter 3, the problem may be one of how we conceive of God acting in the world.

I will therefore define a 'miracle' as a special or immediate act of God, as opposed to God's continuous work of creating and sustaining the world. The result of this act will be beneficial and religiously significant.

Doubtless this definition has its faults, but at least it enables us to have some instrument for assessing the arguments that have emerged in the philosophical, biblical and religious traditions which we will now consider.

Chapter 2

Hume and Miracles

Probably the most famous philosophical consideration of miracles comes from the eighteenth-century Scottish philosopher David Hume. Hume is generally associated with a sceptical position on the subject of miracles, one which claims that it is always more plausible to think that those claiming to have seen a miracle are either deceived or lying than to suppose that a miracle took place. Wouldn't it be more sensible, even for someone believing that they are in the process of witnessing a miracle, to conclude either that they are deluding themselves or that they are confused by what they see? Reading Hume seems to have successfully embedded in the minds of many the idea that whilst a miracle is logically possible, it is always unreasonable – it is almost a case of 'intellectual bad manners' – to believe that one has taken place. This chapter will consider Hume's position in detail, and will pick up on a point discussed in the first chapter, namely the sense in which one person's 'miracle' may be another person's undiscovered (or unrecognized) law of nature.

The Unreliability of Witnesses

Hume offers a number of reasons for his sceptical position. First, he argues that miracles are not well-attested. Those who claim to have seen them do not contain sufficient numbers of. …

> … men of such unquestioned good sense, education and learning, as to secure us against all delusion in themselves; of such undoubted integrity, as to place them beyond suspicion of any design to deceive others; of such credit and reputation in the eyes of mankind, as to have a great deal to lose in the case of their being detected in any falsehood; and at the same time attesting facts, performed in such a public manner, and in so celebrated a part of the world, as to render the detection unavoidable.[1]

The question of attestation is interesting, because it throws up a number of issues and perhaps prejudices concerning the reliability of witnesses. It is at the very least arguable whether 'men of education and learning' are any less credulous than those without it. The 'good sense' which Hume talks about could have been as evident in a Galilean fisherman as in, for instance, a highly paid official with a good knowledge of Latin in the service of Pontius Pilate. The notion of 'undoubted integrity' is also difficult. In one sense it is, of course, impossible to meet this requirement. Hume is right to suggest that we cannot say whether, for instance, the disciples of Jesus possessed 'undoubted integrity', when the biblical records are the only evidence of their existence and provide very little information about their personalities – and what is provided, in the case of Judas and Peter, for instance, hardly suggests flawless characters. But in another sense Hume is obviously making an impossible demand. Undoubted integrity arguably exists nowhere – how confidently, for instance, could one use this phrase of anyone living today? We believe or disbelieve testimony by weighing evidence that never comes to us with the impregnable badge of authenticity which Hume seems to demand. 'Credit and reputation in the eyes of mankind' seems to be a similarly strange notion. Credit when, and for whom? Credit and reputation have often been the hallmark in their lifetimes of people later shown to have been congenital liars. The idea that they should have a lot to lose by lying might seem appropriate, but does this mean that people always tell the truth or that they are very careful about the way they lie? People with a lot of credit to lose arguably show a greater, not a lesser, propensity for lying.

The notion of a 'celebrated part of the world' is also questionable. Eighteenth-century England (or Scotland) was arguably as full of superstition as eighteenth-century India. Of course the modern reader tends to interpret Hume's criterion as referring to their present day as opposed to the distant or even the eighteenth-century past. The present age is supposedly 'scientific' unlike the 'superstitious and credulous' primitives who lived two millennia ago. Such a view is highly dubious, as I discuss elsewhere in this book. It was perfectly possible for a sceptical Joseph to interpret his wife's pregnancy as evidence of adultery in the first century, just as it is perfectly possible for a highly sophisticated twenty-first-century person of 'good education and learning' to be an avid reader of horoscopes and refuse to travel on Friday 13th.

These arguments could equally well be applied against a further objection Hume offers in this part of his *Enquiry*. He points out that reports of miracles 'are observed chiefly to abound among ignorant and barbarous nations' or have been passed down to more civilized societies by 'ignorant and barbarous ancestors'. Not only does this beg questions about the intellectual and moral 'progress' of humanity, but it presumes that credulity is inversely proportional to technological and scientific progress. The very fact that such progress has created and indeed is the object of much credulity suggests that this is a highly questionable account of human 'development', though one characteristic in many ways of the eighteenth-century 'Enlightenment'.

In short, whilst Hume is correct to suggest that miracles are not (and indeed never can be) attested in such a way that what people report is so overwhelmingly persuasive that they cannot but be believed, there is much to be questioned in his manner of measuring reliable testimony. Poor first-century fishermen were no more likely to distort the truth than wealthy, educated and respected citizens of the third millennium.

Miracles as a Means of Proving Religion True

There is another part of the quotation above which must be discussed. This is the notion of 'attesting facts, *performed in such a public manner*, and in so celebrated a part of the world, as to render the detection unavoidable' (my italics). For it is perfectly true that many of the miracles of Jesus, for instance, did not take place before thousands of people who might be expected to apply their sceptical minds to what was being shown them. Some are certainly described as 'public events', such as turning the water into wine at the wedding in Cana; others, such as certain healing miracles, take place with no one else knowing besides the person cured. Not only that, but in some cases the biblical text records Jesus explicitly requesting that a miracle *not* be made public. We also find him refusing a 'sign' to the Pharisees. In the case of Christianity – for it is only the miracles of Jesus being referred to here – it would seem highly unlikely that they are meant somehow to demonstrate Christ's credentials. Yet that was the belief of a number of people writing in or shortly before Hume's day.

Hume would have been well aware of a school of thought which tried to argue that the miracles (and prophecies) in the Bible provided 'proof' of Christ's claims about himself. Davies quotes the example of Samuel Clarke in his Boyle lectures of 1705, where he claims that 'The Christian religion is positively and directly proved, to be actually and immediately sent to us from God, by the many infallible signs and miracles, which the author of it worked publicly as the evidence of his Divine Commission' (1993: 210). Against this view, Hume quite rightly saw that miracle and prophecy provided the shakiest of foundations for establishing the truth of the Christian faith. The argument that these miracles were witnessed centuries ago by people who might have been confused, might have been lying and might have simply been credulous fools is perfectly valid, and is an effective challenge to any assumption that miracles and prophecies somehow 'prove Christianity true'.

I would take issue as much with the position of Samuel Clarke as with that of David Hume. Indeed, I would argue that to an extent the one provoked the other. Hume's scepticism about miracles was encouraged by the claims of Clarke and others that miracles had a potential for 'proving Christianity true'. Certainly the New Testament writers themselves were convinced that Jesus' life and works, including the miracles, represented the fulfilment of prophecies made in the Hebrew Bible (Old Testament). But this did not mean that they thought the Bible could be used in order to provide some kind of mathematical certainty that the miracles occurred.

Such 'proof', I would argue, was not the point of Jesus' miracles. They were not performed like conjuring tricks before a mass audience of sophisticated and sceptical people because they were never intended to 'prove' anything. The answer to the Pharisees' demand for a 'sign' is 'No'. There is no dive from the temple into the supporting arms of angels. Though 'doubting Thomas' (another disciple of dubious character) sees the wounds made by the nails on the cross, he is reminded that those who 'do not see' and yet believe are better than he (John 20:29). None of this, it goes without saying, establishes the authenticity of these texts. But it does establish the fact that whether or not they happened Jesus' miracles are not intended to put his claims beyond doubt. There is no attempt at all to rally the sort of audience of the great and the good that Hume seeks; indeed it is explicitly rejected. Miracles don't create faith; if anything, the biblical text prefers to say that faith creates miracles (I devote a whole chapter later to the miracles of Jesus where these points are developed further).

Moreover, looking elsewhere in Hume's *Essay* it is not clear that his standards of evidence could ever be satisfied. Swinburne cites the philosopher's comments about the miracles attributed to the famous Jansenist Abbé Paris. Hume says that 'many of the miracles were immediately proved upon the spot, before judges of unquestioned integrity, attested by witnesses of credit and distinction, in a learned age, and on the most eminent theatre that is now in the world' (Wollheim 1963: 215). No credulous primitives these! Not even the Jesuits, sworn enemies of the Jansenists, are able to disprove these miracles. 'Where shall we find such a number of circumstances agreeing to the corroboration of one fact?' asks Hume rhetorically (Wollheim 1963: 220), and yet the overwhelming evidence of 'reliable and trustworthy' sources is of little avail in convincing him. 'What have we to oppose to such a cloud of witnesses, but the absolute impossibility or miraculous nature of the events which they relate? And this surely, in the eyes of all reasonable people, will alone be regarded as a sufficient reputation' (Wollheim 1963: 220). Thus Hume's position turns into that of the French philosopher Denis Diderot, an almost exact contemporary, who claimed that if the entire population of Paris assured him that a man had been raised from the dead, he would not believe a word of it.

As Swinburne comments, 'here the credibility of the witnesses in terms of their number, integrity and education is dismissed, not as inadequate, but as irrelevant' (1970: 16). Miraculous is now synonymous with 'absolutely impossible'. It becomes clear that the lack of credible witnesses is a distraction from some more fundamental objection which we have yet to tease out.

The Lure of the Marvellous

Hume's next objection to the credibility of the miracle accounts concerns a human tendency to believe what is 'marvellous'. 'The passion of surprise and wonder, arising from miracles, being an agreeable emotion, gives a sensible tendency towards the belief of those events from which it is derived.' Now it is true that there is a certain attraction towards believing extraordinary things. Mackie (1982: 15) cites flying saucers. One might equally cite the unquestioning embrace of every new technological or scientific 'breakthrough', from understanding the secrets of ageing to mapping out the origins of the universe. Here there is a clear inclination towards credulity, which feeds off the often contradictory statements of the scientific establishment much as an earlier worldview fed off the ideas of the theological establishment.

But there is an opposite 'human tendency' too. There is an 'agreeable emotion' of scepticism, which gives a sensible tendency towards *dis*belief. There are credulous believers who accept anything new, and there are credulous (in their own way) *dis*believers who reject anything different. It is surely just as possible to argue that people prefer the security of what they know and the regular, predictable course of events than that they are longing for 'surprise and wonder'. In fact it is often observed that people are 'taken by surprise' when extraordinary events happen (for example events in the political realm like the fall of the Shah in Iran or even the collapse of communism in 1989) precisely because they have become embedded in a way of thinking that refuses to countenance anything new.

Once again the suspicion is that Hume's argument rests on an implicit assumption that 'primitive' people were so desperate to see a miracle that in the end they forced themselves to witness one. The idea is not so much that 'we' long to be surprised but that 'they', with their primitive, hand-to-mouth existence, must have longed for some 'wonder' all the time. As we have already seen, this is questionable. Both the first and the twenty-first centuries had and have their sceptics and their credulous believers.

Miracles in Different Religious Traditions

The next argument used by Hume is that the miracle reports of one religion are contradicted by those of others. This is an argument which proceeds from an assumption that the world's religions are in a state of constant conflict (I examine views on miracles within a range of religions outside the Christian tradition in Chapter 11). Not all people would accept that. Mackie, for instance, seems content to respond that since all religions worship the same God in different ways, it is possible that all their accounts of miracles are true and are not mutually exclusive. Certainly the degree of mutual acceptance between religions, including acceptance of each other's miracles, often goes unappreciated. Not all Christians, for instance, recognize the high value which Islam puts upon Jesus, including acceptance of the miracle of the Virgin Birth, something which has troubled many a Christian Bishop of Durham.

Swinburne is surely technically correct in arguing that evidence for a miracle wrought in one religion is only evidence against the occurrence of a miracle wrought in another 'if the two miracles, if they occurred, would be evidence for propositions of the two religious systems incompatible with one another' (1970: 60). He is also correct when he goes on to argue that most alleged miracles 'would show at most the power of a god or gods and their concern for the needs of men, and little more specific in the way of doctrine' (1970: 61). Thus a 'Christian' miracle and a 'Hindu' miracle, precisely because in most cases neither is carried out in order to prove what Swinburne calls 'the specific details of their systems', may be perfectly compatible with one another.

However, there may be something intellectually complacent about a general religious amnesty in which everybody's miracles are declared true. To take the example of Christianity. In John's gospel, a man who has had his sight restored comments that 'never since the world began has it been heard that any one opened the eyes of a man born blind. If this man were not from God he could do nothing' (John 9:32–3). Of course it can be said that this is a particular author's slant and that there is no 'competition' among the founders of religions to perform the most miracles. But it is difficult wholly to exclude the idea that each religion claims for its particular founder a unique miracle-working capacity. It is unlikely that believers in a particular religion will find it easy to accept the miracles claimed by all the others. It has to be admitted that some claims concerning miracles may be false.

But this is not necessarily a problem for the theist. Agreeing to the proposition that not all reports of miracles are true does not require one to agree that they are all false. Some may be true and others false. Some reports of Christ's miracles may be true and others false – this may be a problem for those who believe that every part of the Bible must be 'infallible', but for many if not most Christians such selectivity will be perfectly acceptable.

Moreover, most biblical scholars studying Christian origins would argue that there were other Jews making very similar claims, even messianic ones, to those of Jesus during his lifetime. There were other sects (Christianity was effectively a Jewish sect at the time) pointing to the miracle-working powers of their leaders. You don't have to go to other religions, in other words, to find a rash of different claims about miracles; you can find them within the same religious tradition at a time of political and religious ferment. Yet the Christian 'sect' was the one that survived. The argument that this might have something to do with the fact that Jesus' miracle-working powers were shown to be genuine, despite all the *claims* being made by others at the time, may be more plausible than the idea that miracles were being performed all over the region – let alone the rest of the world. The man whose sight was restored may have a point, as by implication does Hume. There are too many claims concerning miracles for them all to be true. There are limits to the debasement of the currency.

The 'Raising' of Elizabeth I

I have argued that Hume's scepticism appears effective as a means of undermining the idea that miracles somehow 'prove Christianity true'. Indeed there is some evidence that this was the *point* of Hume's scepticism. Confronted by what might now be seen as the shallow Deism of Samuel Clarke and others purporting to show that the miracles of Jesus were somehow an irrefutable demonstration of his divine status, Hume was bound to be sceptical. His position was that 'a miracle can never be proved so as to be the foundation of a system of religion' (Wollheim 1963: 223).[2] This is something that most people, including most believers in miracles, could surely agree upon.

However, to suppose that supporters and opponents of Hume could settle the matter here would be naive. In the eyes of many commentators Hume goes much further in his scepticism about miracles. We have already seen this implied by

Hume's own comments dismissing the claims of the Jansenist Abbé Paris, despite the apparently overwhelming evidence concerning his miraculous powers.

We may turn to a rather less compelling example of miracles than that of the Abbé Paris, namely Queen Elizabeth I (in Chapter 12 I consider a fictitious 'resurrection' in the modern day which might also be considered in this context). If historians were all to describe the resurrection of Elizabeth I, Hume explains, he would feel bound to consider their reports a product of deliberate deceit, given that they were referring to 'so signal a violation of the laws of nature' (Wollheim 1963: 223). Once again it seems that criteria such as the reliability of the witnesses is irrelevant rather than simply inadequate.

This lack of interest on Hume's part in his own criteria is unfortunate, because the criteria are not unimportant. Suppose, for example, we were seriously to consider the idea of Elizabeth I's resurrection. We would find that even during her lifetime there were attempts to associate her with supernatural powers, and in particular to link her with the Virgin Mary. England's 'Elizabethan Settlement' ruled out a return to the Catholicism of Elizabeth's half-sister, but the Catholic faith remained popular in many parts of the country, as did the ritual traditions associated with it, particularly those connected with the Virgin Mary. There were efforts to make the Virgin Queen an alternative focus for the Mariological longings of the masses.

On the other hand, most historians now see Elizabeth's decision not to marry as political, a product of the experience of Mary's disastrous marriage to Philip II. And her virginity they tend to see as a convenient myth which was of undoubted benefit to a ruler attempting to survive on the throne as a Protestant in a (still, arguably) largely Catholic nation. Hume is quite right – if contemporary historians started making claims about the assumption (let alone the resurrection) of Elizabeth the 'unspotted lily', they simply wouldn't be believed. But they would fail to persuade not only because of a common reluctance to accept 'signal violations' of the laws of nature, but also because people could offer a clear political explanation for why these stories might have been deliberately invented and spread by her supporters at the time.

In the case of Jesus' resurrection such explanations at the historical level may not be so clear-cut. This is not just a question of witnesses – there may have been a few, or there may (as one of the gospels records) have been several hundred. It is a question of context and historical judgement. Is Jesus of Nazareth, like Elizabeth, a ruler in need of a few miracles in order to establish his authority? Or does he prefer to play down their significance? Then there are practical historical issues such as why the body was not produced by his opponents in order to demonstrate that it had not been 'raised'.

Nobody can find in the weighing of historical evidence a conclusive argument for or against the resurrection of Jesus. The body could have been stolen or 'lost', or perhaps it *was* produced but the fact has remained unrecorded. These will always remain possibilities. History can only deal in probabilities at best. Nevertheless, it can fairly be said that the historical evidence can be considered in both cases, and in the case of Jesus' resurrection can be said to have proved more persuasive, on the whole, than in the case of Elizabeth's.

Yet this level of discussion is not one which interests Hume. Weighing the evidence in the case of various claims about miracles is not important to him. As Swinburne says, he considers the credibility of witnesses irrelevant rather than insufficient. He does so because he formulates a 'sceptical rule' which effectively rules out belief in any miracles whatsoever. I shall now turn to this 'sceptical rule'.

Hume's Sceptical Rule

This rule claims that it is *always* more plausible to believe that the witnesses to a miracle lied or were deceived than that this 'signal violation of the laws of nature' took place. In Hume's own words cited above from the famous chapter on miracles in his *Enquiry*, 'No testimony is sufficient to establish a miracle unless the testimony be of such a kind, that its falsehood would be more miraculous than the fact which it endeavours to establish' (Wollheim 1963: 211). The implication is that if the fact one is trying to establish is a miracle, that is to say a 'violation of the laws of nature', then the testimony cannot in *any* circumstances be sufficient to establish it. That is why Hume is uninterested in the testimony even when it is (apparently) overwhelmingly strong, as in the case of the Abbé Paris.

There are two ways in which Hume's argument can be challenged. One denies that any miracle violates a law of nature. So the answer to Hume's 'so signal a violation' of the laws of nature is that there is no violation. The other challenge claims that even if a miracle *is* a violation of the laws of nature, it can't be ruled out on those grounds alone.

The first argument, namely the one which claims that miracles do not break the laws of nature, is one that we shall consider in detail in Chapter 3. What I will concentrate upon here is the second argument, which I believe is sufficient in itself to refute Hume's position.

Hume himself defined 'miracle' as 'a transgression of a law of nature by a particular volition of the Deity or by the interposition of some invisible agent' (Wollheim 1963: 211). The second position accepts this definition. Here I am following Richard Swinburne in his adoption of the definition that a miracle is 'a violation of a law of nature by a god' (1970: 11).

It is important to recognize that in one sense Hume, the supreme empiricist, is perfectly willing to concede the possibility that a 'law of nature' may be violated. In the argument concerning the character of these 'laws', Hume would accept that they are human summaries which generalize about the way things behave, but contain no 'must' in the sense of saying that things cannot conceivably behave in any other way. There is a uniformity in nature which makes it possible to generalize about the way things behave, but there is no *requirement* that they behave in this way. This is the danger involved in talking about 'laws' – for laws (though of course they may, in a legal sense, be broken) prescribe. Laws of nature do not prescribe, they *de*scribe, to none more so than to Hume himself, who is seen as embodying an empirical tradition which insists upon this very point.

Thus Hume is seen as the pre-eminent exponent of the 'regularity theory of causation'.[3] By this is meant the view that a law of nature, such as one of the kind that argues 'a causes b', is no more than a generalization about the behaviour of a and b. It is not a claim concerning any 'necessary connection' between a and b making it unavoidable that b follows from a. It expresses an exceptionless regularity. Day by day the sun rises and so far as we know has always risen, but for Hume there is nothing in the nature of things to 'compel' it to rise tomorrow.

Therefore Hume's case against miracles is not that they never do happen or never could happen, but only that we never have good reason for believing that they have happened.

The difficulty for the theist, however, is that this is hardly a 'but only'. For to establish that whilst miracles are theoretically possible there is very little reason to believe that they happen is still a very strong position against miracles. Demonstrating that a miracle is 'logically possible' becomes something of a Pyrrhic victory for the theist, if as a matter of fact it is never plausible to accept that one has taken place. This is why in order to make room for miracles some challenge has to be made to Hume's rule that it is always more plausible to believe that the witnesses were deceived or lying than that a miracle took place.

Marvels and Miracles

Hume is prepared to concede that 'marvels' occur, as opposed to 'miracles'. But Hume is clear that a 'marvel' and a 'miracle' are different things. In the case of 'marvels', such as the freezing of water as it must appear to someone who has only known a hot climate, or (another example he gives) total darkness over the face of the earth lasting eight days (Wollheim 1963: 209–10), something occurs that is contrary to what experience tells them should happen. What they see is contrary to the laws of nature as they know them. But this does not mean the same thing as 'violating' the laws of nature.

Sometimes it is argued that were it never to be plausible that laws of nature were violated, then none of the significant leaps forward in scientific progress, the 'paradigm shifts' that involve breaking with an established pattern of interpretation, would ever have been made. But these 'scientific leaps forward' do not quite represent the same thing as 'transgressions' of the laws of nature. In the case of 'marvels' it is true that one law is broken, but only because another has been found. The law of gravitation gives way to the law of relativity. In the case of miracles, all laws have to give way. Even in the case of quantum theory, where some have argued that all laws give way, they give way to a theory of random behaviour which is itself a kind of law. But where a miracle is concerned we are asked to believe not that we need a better law but that we will never find one.[4]

An example mentioned in the last chapter illustrates this well. Suppose someone is suffering from terminal cancer. They pray and are prayed for. A well-known healer comes to see them. Then they recover. Three options now present themselves. One, that the cancer was misdiagnosed. In this case, we need no new law of nature in order to explain what happened. Two, that it was correctly diagnosed but that we know so little about cancer that we have not yet managed to arrive at the scientific law which explains apparently spontaneous regressions. Had we the access to this knowledge, we would have been able to explain exactly why this patient recovered and another didn't. In this case, we do not yet have the law of nature in order to explain what happened, but one day we will arrive at it. Today, it is a 'marvel' (according to Hume's understanding). Tomorrow it will be the instance of a natural law. The third option is that God intervened and destroyed the cancer. This requires us to believe not only that we don't have the scientific knowledge to explain what happened now, but that we could never have it. There is no undiscovered law of nature which could make sense of this event, and a million years of further refinements in our medical understanding will be unable to produce it. Hume's point is that it is always more reasonable to believe that one of the first two options applies than to believe the third.

However, the problem for Hume's position is this. It is clear that there is a difference between a 'miracle' and a 'marvel', as I have tried to illustrate. But it is also clear that in the case of either *the testimony has to be believed before there is any point in analysing what has happened.* If someone dying of cancer gets out of their hospital bed, walks home and announces that they've been cured, there may well be an argument about whether this was a false diagnosis, a publicity-seeking trick, an instance of spontaneous regression illustrating the limits of medical knowledge or a special act of God (a miracle). But most of the people engaged in that argument will be willing to agree that a person dying of cancer returned home in good health. Otherwise the argument can hardly take place at all, and it certainly cannot establish a 'marvel' any more than it can establish a 'miracle'.

If Hume wants a 'sceptical rule', then it cannot be that it is always more reasonable to believe that the witnesses were deceived or lying than that a miracle occurred. It can only be that it is always more reasonable to believe that there exists some kind of natural explanation which in the present state of our scientific knowledge we are not privy to (a marvel) than that there is no natural explanation at all (a miracle). Once again I will use an example in order to illustrate what this position might look like.

Suppose I was walking through a cemetery and saw a grave opening up and a body rising up out of it. What would I think? If I did think about what had happened rationally and didn't just run off in a panic, I'd probably consider that it was a practical joke. Or I might think I was hallucinating. Half an hour later, recovering from my experience, I might ask myself whether I'd seen anybody at all or had just been deluded. Perhaps my memory was now playing tricks on me. I was remembering something that never happened. And so on.

Perhaps I had a camera with me and took a picture – but what would even that prove when I got the print back of someone crawling out of the earth? Perhaps I might have had the presence of mind to capture the person, take them back to my house and compare them with photographs (if they existed) of what they looked like in 1756 when they died. But that will prove nothing. Perhaps they speak the English of Hume himself or Edward Gibbon – but that could merely show the elaborate preparation that went into producing this hoax. Let us go even further (and of course most witnesses to an alleged miracle won't have the chance to gather as much evidence as this) and suppose that we have taken the person who emerged from the grave to a laboratory and can now subject them to a DNA test. Even then it is possible to argue that someone has managed to clone a replica of the original body from a piece of their decaying tissue. Such a thing is very unlikely (some would say 'impossible') given the present state of scientific knowledge, but is it *less* likely than that a person rose from the dead? I might consider that it is *less* likely that some scientists have kept their advances a secret, perhaps so that they can go on researching. Faced with the alternative of believing that a person rose from the dead, I might choose instead to believe that extraordinary scientific advances had taken place which the general public knew nothing about. In other words, I would adopt the view that I had witnessed a 'marvel', not a 'miracle'. There existed laws of nature which could explain it, but I didn't yet know what they were.

Even in the case where I myself witness a miracle (thereby bypassing the problem of the credibility of witnesses, except insofar as I have to believe myself as a witness), I cannot be sure that one has taken place. I can always find an alternative explanation to a miracle in terms of an undiscovered law. In the example above I could, for instance, claim that superior intelligences from outer space had landed in the cemetery and created a clone through their superior technical skills. But once I go this far in my explanation, can I still justify my position in terms of its greater 'plausibility' than belief in a miracle?

Whatever the evidence, it is always possible to claim that something other than a miracle has taken place – a point I tried to establish in the last chapter. But is it always 'more reasonable' to do so? That is a much more difficult proposition. It seems to me that it is grounded upon a presupposition about the innate unbelievability of miracles which Hume, from his empiricist perspective, is the last one to be entitled to make. If I consider a miracle about as likely as the arrival of aliens from outer space, then even if I were to witness a person rising from the dead (as in the example given above), I would decide that on the balance of probability what I had witnessed (including the subsequent DNA test) was an example of the superior scientific prowess of people I'd never seen or heard of. But it is difficult to see how that would automatically be more 'reasonable' than believing in a miracle. Rather, I would argue with Swinburne (himself citing William Paley's critique of Hume in the preface to *A View of the Evidences of Christianity*) that 'in describing the improbability of miracles, he suppresses all those circumstances of extenuation, which result from the knowledge of the existence, power and disposition of the Deity' (1970: 69).

Conclusions

To sum up this chapter. In the first section I questioned some of the presumptions behind Hume's attack on the reliability of witnesses to miracles. A recurring theme of this book is to question the idea that 'primitive' people fell for every miracle on offer, whilst 'modern' people have grown up enough to reject them. However, I argued that Hume's scepticism is effective as a means of undermining the idea that miracles somehow 'prove Christianity true', and agreed with the verdict that 'a miracle can never be proved so as to be the foundation of a system of religion'.

I then went on to consider Hume's 'sceptical rule' which effectively rules out belief in any miracles whatsoever, by arguing that it is *always* more plausible to believe that the witnesses to a miracle lied or were deceived than that some 'signal violation of the laws of nature' took place. By comparing the resurrection of Jesus to that claimed for Elizabeth I, I pointed out that there are a host of considerations involved in assessing claims about miracles which have nothing to do with the issue of transgressing laws of nature but rather with weighing historical evidence. These should not be forgotten or omitted from consideration, though of course they cannot ever amount to a proof one way or the other. In Chapter 9, with reference to Jesus' resurrection, I defend the importance of the historian's evidence, even though it must always fall short of proof.

I then looked at two approaches to challenging Hume on the point concerning 'signal violations' of the laws of nature. One argues that a miracle does not, in fact, violate any law of nature. I did no more than mention this argument, but the next chapter will give it more thorough consideration. The other approach agrees that miracles *do* violate laws of nature. However, it argues that Hume cannot argue that it is always more reasonable to believe that witnesses lied or were deceived than that the event happened. For if he does so argue, he will have to rule out 'marvels' too, since in both cases (marvel and miracle) there has to be agreement about what took place (someone emerged from a grave, huge numbers of loaves and fishes suddenly appeared, a blind man could see again) before one sets about trying to establish how it could be explained.

I concluded by arguing that it is, of course, always possible to explain what has happened in terms of hitherto undiscovered laws – for instance ones that have been kept secret or have been discovered by superior intelligences from outer space. But I do not see why, while possible, it should be considered more 'reasonable' to adopt such an explanation – least of all if you take the sort of view Hume does about the priority of empirical evidence. It might therefore be argued that there is no reason to rule out belief in miracles as less credible in all circumstances than error or deceit on the part of witnesses.

In his book *Miracles*, C.S. Lewis ([1947] 2002) makes the point that miracles are particularly appropriate to the 'biblical God', because unlike some kind of 'great spiritual force', the God of the Judaeo-Christian tradition is one whose nature and purposes are revealed through the performance of particular actions, of which miracles are an example. Though I have been at pains to argue that belief in God's continuous creative and sustaining presence must not be forgotten in the stress upon special miraculous actions which are sometimes termed examples of divine 'intervention', it is clearly the case that the God of the Bible (and the God of certain other religious traditions too) is revealed through certain key events which are described by believers as acts of God. I shall now consider these 'acts of God' and whether a concept of 'miracles' can be sustained in their terms.

Notes

1 This and the following quotations from Hume on the subject of the reliability of testimony to miracles are taken from his *Enquiry Concerning Human Understanding*, Section X 'On Miracles', reprinted in Wollheim (1963), pp. 205–29. The text exists in several editions. Richard Wollheim's useful collection of Hume's writings on religion (1963) also includes *The Natural History of Religion* and the *Dialogues Concerning Natural Religion*. The text has also spawned a great deal of secondary literature. S. Tweyman (1996) provides a selection of responses to Hume. David Johnson (2000) provides an interesting challenge to Hume's arguments.
2 The view advanced by Antony Flew (1961), chapter VIII.
3 For a useful discussion of this, see Levine (1989).
4 Swinburne adopts Ninian Smart's useful definition of a 'miracle' as 'an occurrence of a non-repeatable counter-instance to a law of nature' (1970: 26). A repeatable counter-instance would show that the law needed to be modified; a non-repeatable counter-instance shows that any exceptions to the operation of a law cannot be accounted for by arriving at a new and better law. But the key point must be that in principle – where miracles are concerned – no better law can ever be found. A marvel encourages the search for a law of nature which takes account of what has been hitherto unknown; a miracle is intended to rule out such a search.

Chapter 3

Miracles and Acts of God

The notion of an 'act of God' is not just a quaint means of eluding responsibility beloved of insurance companies. It is fundamental to Jewish, Christian and other forms of religious belief about God and the means by which God is made known to human beings. In the next two chapters I shall develop the idea of a miracle as a 'special or immediate act of God', proposed at the end of the first chapter. I will do so by considering the general question of what constitutes 'acts of God'.

'Acts of God' in Biblical Exegesis

Christians have often claimed that they learn about God because of God's active self-disclosure (revelation). The Bible, they argue, is less the history of humanity's efforts to understand the divine being, than the history of God making God known to the world through a series of actions. This was the point of view expressed by the so-called 'biblical theology' movement some fifty years ago. It laid stress upon the absolutely fundamental significance of a God who acts. *God Who Acts* was, indeed, the title of G. Ernest Wright's work in 1952. In this work, subtitled *Biblical Theology as Recital*, Wright defines 'biblical theology' as 'the confessional recital of the redemptive acts of God in a particular history' (1952: 13). In his view it would be more appropriate to call the Bible a record of the acts of God than (for instance) an account of the intellectual or even moral striving of humanity, though these may be part of the human response to those acts.

Of course the biblical theology movement was only one strand of Christian thinking. However, the idea of a 'God who acts' crept – sometimes surreptitiously – inside other more radical streams of thought as well. Consider, for instance, the position outlined by the famous New Testament scholar Rudolf Bultmann in his essay 'New Testament and Mythology' at around the same time as Wright's book (the essay first appeared in English in 1953; it was published in the original German in 1947). Bultmann refers to a 'pre-scientific' worldview which describes changes coming about on earth through miracles, special acts of God which appeared to usurp or ignore the laws of nature. According to Bultmann this is something that we find unacceptable nowadays. These laws of nature are not only laws the modern world takes for granted, but the edifice upon which it has erected the whole scientific-technological sweep of its success. This is a world of wirelesses (Bultmann's formulations of modern technology already sound terribly dated) and washing machines. Those who live and work in such a world simply cannot revert to a primitive mindset. They must interpret these 'acts of God' in other terms.

31

It is interesting to examine exactly what, in Bultmann's view, constitutes the 'different worldview' of the biblical writers. He says that they presumed some kind of three-decker universe, earth being in the middle, heaven above and hell beneath. Communication between the different storeys was managed by strange creatures – angels and demons – which make no sense, he says, to us today. Nor, according to Bultmann, does Jesus himself make sense when he is described as 'ascending' or 'descending' between storeys. There can be no perforating influence on the part of divine (or devilish) wonder-workers operating from above or below.

'Demythologisation' becomes the process by which, in Bultmann's view, the kerygma (the essential preached message of the New Testament) is stripped of what he believed to be alienating features representing a different worldview and is then repackaged in terms that make this kerygma acceptable to us. This second part of the process might suggest that 'remythologisation' was a better term, but Bultmann insists that it is not a case of one mythology being replaced by another. The kerygma which was once expressed in terms of myth is now expressed in terms of existential truths about our dependence on God's grace. As the British existentialist theologian John Macquarrie put it in his *Principles of Christian Theology* a generation after Bultmann:

> The way of understanding miracle that appeals to breaks in the natural order and to supernatural interventions belongs to the mythological outlook and cannot commend itself in a post-mythological climate of thought. The traditional conception of miracle is irreconcilable with our modern understanding of both science and history.
>
> (1977: 13)

Our 'modern understanding' of science and history has apparently drawn the net too tightly for God to enter with 'actions', and though the reference is to miraculous actions it is difficult to see how this can fail to apply to *any* acts of God. To use jargon, God cannot be a player on the world scene.

Banishing God in this way, however, causes difficulties. Just how is it possible to take the Bible, which many Christians, as we have seen, would describe as a record of God's actions in history, and turn it into a set of existential truths about the human condition? In fact few of these would-be exclusionists, where acts of God are concerned, really go the full distance. Bultmann is the most famous and his is the example that can most usefully be considered. He himself, despite his attempt, as we have seen, to interpret the Bible in terms of the search for authentic human existence, sees that authentic existence as dependent on a unique and decisive act of God. He embraces the existentialist categories of the philosopher Martin Heidegger, yet he also distances himself explicitly from Heidegger and other existentialist philosophers by saying that unlike them the New Testament 'affirms the total incapacity of man to release himself from his fallen state. That deliverance can come only by an act of God' (Bultmann 1972: 27). Hence the notion of an 'act of God' is not swept away but rather affirmed by Bultmann (as was noted by his even more radical critics like Fritz Buri who called for a further act beyond 'demythologisation', that of 'dekerygmatization').[1] There is an act of

God which still remains, an act which Bultmann himself calls 'the crucial distinction between the New Testament and existentialism, between the Christian faith and the natural understanding of being' (1972: 33). He is too much the orthodox Protestant Christian not to want to stress the inability of the human person to find salvation apart from an encounter with God in which the movement is from God to us.

My conclusion would be that Bultmann too wants to speak about an irreducible act of God but, as his more radical critics like Fritz Buri noted at the time, it is very difficult to see what he means by the phrase. The case of Bultmann only highlights the urgent need to know what an 'act of God' – any act of God, miraculous or otherwise – would be like. If we can find both the biblical theology movement and Bultmann sharing a common commitment to an 'act of God', then we obviously need to know what an act of God is. Fortunately, a number of academic scholars involved in biblical exegesis have specifically addressed the issue of what 'God's actions' might be.[2]

SDA and GDA

I want to distinguish between what is called 'special divine action' on the one hand and 'general divine action' on the other. These different conceptions frequently enjoy the acronyms SDA and GDA. GDA is understood to be those actions of God that pertain to the whole of creation universally and simultaneously – effectively God's action in creating and sustaining the world, which Saunders refers to as 'universal steering' (see Saunders 2002: 21–2). SDA, on the other hand, refers to actions of God that pertain to one particular time and place as opposed to another. Among the 'time-and-place-specific' actions of God referred to in biblical and religious traditions would be acts of revelation where God is manifested in particular places or through particular words, in acts such as the parting of the Red Sea, the raising of Jesus of Nazareth from the dead, or particular responses to specific intercessory prayers. These are all specific divine actions which under the definition I gave in the first chapter would be considered 'miracles'.

The question of whether SDAs make sense has troubled many of those who have been involved in biblical exegesis. In an important essay Langdon Gilkey (1961) argued that 'our modern cosmology' had emptied some of the Bible's theological categories, such as 'divine deeds' and 'divine revelations', of what he called their 'univocal' meaning.[3] Here we were, he claimed, possessed of a biblical tradition for which it was fundamental to refer to God as 'speaking' or 'acting' and we didn't even know any more how to interpret these terms. In the rest of this chapter and the next I want to see what can be done about Gilkey's dilemma.

Acts of God as Acts of Human Beings

I want to begin by dealing with two ways of interpreting God's speaking and acting in the biblical narrative that might appear to solve the problem of making sense of the text, without creating the sort of difficulties raised by belief in SDAs. One is to interpret what Gilkey calls 'a vast panoply of divine deeds' in terms not of divine action but of human response. In other words, we might argue that there is only GDA, the 'universal steering' that Saunders talks of and which amounts to a statement that God is the creator and sustainer of the world. But there might also be particular occasions where we recognize this GDA, moments which Ian Ramsey referred to as 'disclosure situations'.[4] What the biblical narrative describes as an act of God on a certain occasion is therefore essentially an act of human beings on a specific occasion, who have what we might call a flash of inspiration concerning the nature of the eternal God. An 'act of God' becomes, in O.C. Thomas's words, simply a 'special sign of God's general providence' (1983: 73). On this view, a particular event highlights what God is eternally like. It is particularly revealing of God's character, in the way that a certain event might disclose to us particularly well what a particular human being was like.

I do not propose to discuss this argument in detail here (it is discussed briefly in Chapter 10). It illustrates that it is possible to interpret the acts of God recorded in the biblical text without a belief in SDA, because what these 'acts of God' really are is said to be acts of men and women. I shall assume in this book that such an interpretation of the biblical text is unsustainable.

More contentiously, I shall assume that a more sophisticated version of this interpretation is also unsustainable. That is the version associated with so-called 'narrative theology'.[5] Narrative theology rightly emphasizes the complexity of the Christian canon as a collection of different forms of literature and indeed different narratives. It seems to me, however, that narrative theology is once again stressing the way in which human communities come to an understanding of themselves in relation to God. Clearly they do so through literary creations that go by various names such as 'story', 'saga', 'legend' and 'narrative', the truth of which may exist at different levels. But these literary creations are still either records of differently layered responses to general divine action or they are a response to SDA. If they are the former, then 'narrative theology' takes us no further than the symbols and 'disclosure situations' described in the previous section. Essentially, it is another way of collapsing an act of God into an act of man or woman.

Supposing, however, we maintain that belief in SDA is an essential ingredient of understanding the biblical narrative, how can we make sense of it? Whenever the concerns over the possibility of SDA arise, the image of 'the modern world' or of 'modern cosmology' as offering a closed system, which God can no longer 'act within', appears to intrude upon the discussion. This is the way in which Gordon Kaufman discusses the issue in his contribution to O.C. Thomas's aptly named *God's Activity in the World: The Contemporary Problem* (1983). He points out that the success of modern science in describing, controlling and predicting events in the natural order is due to the discovery of ways of discerning and formulating 'fundamental structural regularities obtaining between events (laws of nature)'. The success of science in this respect 'makes it increasingly difficult even to conceive what an event occurring somehow independently of this web might be' (Kaufman 1983: 145). The image of impenetrable webs suggests some kind of closed system that shuts out external intervention. At the same time, a number of other scholars reaffirm the notion that without such 'intervention' the claims of theism (or at least of the Christian version of it) are unsustainable. As Walter Kasper would have it, 'The God who no longer plays an active role in the world is in the final analysis a dead God' (1984: 24).

Human Action and Divine Action

The best way to move forward, in such circumstances, may be to build up an idea of what constitutes action and then try to reach some understanding of 'divine action'.[6] It is clear that many of the writers on the subject of SDA adopt the image of a 'closed continuum' of cause and effect which God has somehow to 'penetrate' in acting. I have already given the example of Bultmann, who specifically portrays God's action as an alien power disrupting the continuum of events. But it is also clear that any discussion of *human* actions (leaving acts of God completely out of account for the moment) has to consider whether this 'continuum' is broken.

The issue concerns the question of 'free will' and 'determinism' which is a philosophical issue irrespective of belief about God. We know that human beings can be seen both as causally structured organisms, whose movements are a series of neurophysiological sequences, and as centres of free decision in the determination of at least some of their actions. As Thomas Tracy (1990) points out, it is possible to answer the question of why my arm went up in terms of muscle contractions or in terms of an intention to make contact with a friend. What he calls the 'physiological story' provides a causal explanation; the 'intentional action story', on the other hand, provides reasons for the agent's action of raising an arm. We use both 'categories of explanation' and there is no need, in his view, for one to conflict with the other.

Now it might be further argued that this understanding of human actions provides a means of understanding divine actions too. It could be said that God's agency doesn't have to somehow elbow its way into the 'web' or 'continuum' of creaturely causes, any more than human agency does. God does not need to find a 'gap' in order to get in, just as a human being doesn't need to find a 'gap' in the neurological explanation of an arm being raised. The automatic processes of bodily life can coexist with the reality of intentional actions in a human being. In a similar way, the argument goes, the worldwide operation of natural processes can coexist with the reality of intentional actions on the part of God.

This argument was put forward in the nineteenth century as part of the reaction to eighteenth-century Deism and the desire for a God who was 'immanent' as well as 'transcendent'. Trench argued the point in his *Notes on the Miracles of Our*

Lord in 1862, when he claimed that a miracle was an example of a lower law being put out of action by a higher. In typical nineteenth-century terminology what he called the 'mechanic' was superseded by the 'dynamic', the chemical by the 'vital', and the physical by the 'moral'. He concluded that a miracle was akin to a person lifting an arm against the law of gravity. What is interesting about Trench is that he rejects the idea of a miracle as an instance of God putting aside all secondary laws and acting directly; rather, he sees God as acting according to another and 'higher' law, one that in Lawton's words 'steps out of its concealment' (2002: 144).

The parallel between human and divine actions certainly has a 'with one bound he was free' attraction, in that the concern about restrictive 'webs' and 'nets' disappears. Such 'webs' don't restrict acts of human freedom (at least for those who do not take a deterministic view which denies the reality of human freedom), so why should they restrict acts of God? But things are not, of course, so simple.

The parallel would appear to work best if the physical universe is considered to be God's body, and there are indeed writers such as Grace Jantzen (1984) who seem to be drawn to this view precisely in order to make the parallel work. However, the idea of the universe as God's body is highly questionable. Apart from the issue of whether the universe is a single entity in the way that a body is (what, for instance, constitutes its equivalent of a central nervous system?), the whole analogy smacks of pantheism. Thus we find Langford (1981) distinguishing between GDA and SDA in terms of those things which a body needs to do all the time in order to maintain itself, like breathing, and those things which a body does at particular moments during its life, a particular action such as picking up a pencil. But in that case God's creative activity is not merely something that sustains the universe in being; it is something that sustains God in being. The death of the universe would be the death of God. Creation ceases to be a free act of divine love and becomes, like breathing, an automatic means of survival. God's act of self-giving in creation becomes, on closer inspection, a selfish act, an act of self-preservation. I do not see how the 'world as God's body' position can survive this critique (although, it must be stressed, this is a critique from a Christian perspective; other forms of theism may feel that it is a sustainable point of view).

If the analogy between human actions and divine actions is to be maintained without the idea of the universe as God's body, God's actions have to be those of a disembodied agent. It has to be possible to argue with McLain that 'incorporeality is no barrier to thinking of God literally as an agent who acts in the world' (1990: 151).[7] But even if the idea of a disembodied agent is accepted as coherent, we still require some account of what Tracy calls the 'instrumental substructure' of God's acts. For whilst we might argue that a human being deciding to wave to a friend and the working of muscle contractions in his or her arm may be investigated by separate languages of cause and intention, there is nevertheless an obvious link between the two. If my arm goes upwards in a convulsive jerk, and I am diagnosed as suffering from a disease which prevents me from being able to control my reflexes, then the language of intention ceases to be appropriate in describing what I am doing. My bodily processes only serve my intentions in certain circumstances and under certain conditions. Yet we have somehow to make sense of God as acting through no bodily processes whatsoever.

God's Actions as 'Internal' Actions

This difficulty has inclined some to restrict God's actions so that they only occur 'internally' in the mind rather than 'externally', producing effects in the world. The idea seems to be that God can act in the 'mental arena' without the difficulties which arise if God acts in the 'physical arena'. This makes way for the sort of actions which occur when God, for instance, 'inspires' a prophet, perhaps by enabling the prophet to understand languages which he or she didn't previously know. God acts to 'deliver a message' internally. Another example would be healing miracles which are 'internal to the mind', like exorcisms, and which might be thought to provide less of a problem than 'external' miracles like walking on water.

But it is not clear that this 'body/mind' dichotomy works. For the 'actions' of the mind, just like any other actions, are linked to particular physiological processes. A thought involves a change in the movement of electrons inside the brain, just as the action of raising an arm involves certain muscle contractions in the body. The idea that God can act in our minds, thereby bypassing the difficulties involved when God is said to act in other ways, is a false one.

In his famous *Dialogues Concerning Natural Religion*, Hume points out that 'some small touches, given to Caligula's brain in his infancy, might have converted him into a Trajan'. He goes on to suggest that 'one wave, a little higher than the rest, by burying Caesar and his fortune at the bottom of the ocean, might have restored liberty to a considerable part of mankind'.[8] Hume is surely right to associate these two forms of divine action. Whether God is causing one emperor to have a shipwreck or another to change his personality, either action requires divine intervention to alter the physical processes at work in the world.

There is, however, one difference, which is well captured in the ambiguity of the phrase to 'change someone's mind'. Where Hume talks of changing Caligula's mind, it is clearly a form of surgical operation that is envisaged – hence the talk of changing a piece of his brain. It is the equivalent of dealing with a psychopath by giving him a lobotomy rather than inducing him to see the error of his ways. But another sense of 'changing someone's mind' is rather different. If someone changes my mind in this second sense, then it is both the case that they influence me to change it *and* that I freely choose to do so. It is this sense of 'double agency' that has proved most fruitful for those who have sought to make sense of SDA carried out by a disembodied God.

But here again it is a concept of limited usefulness. The idea of God being able to exercise a degree of personal influence which affects and inspires and even converts me, without compelling me or overriding my will, is certainly attractive. It corresponds to much religious experience, such as Paul's famous comment that it is 'not I, but Christ in me', who performs an action. Many of those who claim to 'experience' God in one way or another refer to being fulfilled or completed from 'beyond' themselves. They often address the paradox that they are most fully themselves when they are most dependent upon the divine other. Such is the 'perfect service' of God.

But this has limited value because, whilst it might help to explain how an early Christian martyr could remain steadfast in the face of persecution, or how an individual Christian might resist temptation, it does not explain, for instance, how a man might be raised from the dead. Indeed, it is not clear that it doesn't collapse into another form of GDA. The Christian summoning the strength to face the lions in the amphitheatre or the wild beasts 'inside' simply draws on their awareness of the God who is always there, the 'universal steer' in both a moral and a physical sense. This God who is creator and sustainer of the world may also be the God of grace without recourse to SDA.

Conclusions

I began this chapter by examining the notion of an 'act of God'. I argued (looking at the issue in Christian terms) that this notion is significant right across the theological spectrum. However, this is not to deny that there are some who see 'acts of God' as a representation of existential truths about the human person.

It is common to read about beliefs in acts of God being made impossible by the 'impenetrable webs' and 'closed systems' of modern science. I intend to look at these 'webs' and 'systems' further in the next chapter, but here I pointed out that the language of action, where human beings are concerned, is one of intentions and reasons which runs parallel with, and does not 'break into', the language of causes. Cannot the same be the case where God is concerned? Cannot God act in the world to still a storm just as I act in raising my arm to switch on a light?

The problem here is that there is no 'instrumental substructure' to God's actions, or what the philosopher of religion Austin Farrer referred to as a 'causal joint'. We are dealing with a God who is a disembodied agent (unless we view the world as God's body, which I have ruled out in this chapter). I have also ruled out confining God's actions to 'internal' ones, which may in any case involve physical changes being made, as in the touch to Caligula's brain demanded by Hume.

The believer in SDA appears to be left with the position outlined by Saunders in the conclusion to his book, namely that it is 'beyond the capabilities of human reason to discuss the causal nexus of SDA' – a position which he cannot accept. Indeed his sophisticated analysis ends up with the bleakest of conclusions concerning the possibility of SDA (Saunders 2002; 214–16). I shall try to suggest something a little more positive, but first it will be useful in the next chapter to turn to some contemporary developments in scientific thinking – developments which in Saunders' view only reinforce his pessimism about SDA.

Notes

1   Buri's article can be found in the second volume of Bartsch (1972) which was originally published in German as *Kerygma und Mythos*. It was entitled 'Entmythologisierung oder Entkerygmatisierung der Theologie', clearly implying that Bultmann had only reached a halfway house, failing to see that his continued attachment to the kerygma as an act of God retained the mythological elements he was supposedly seeking to eliminate through 'demythologisation'.

2   For further discussion see Dilley (1983). See also the discussion in chapter 1 of Wiles (1986).

3   Thomas (1983) reprints the Gilkey article of 1961 and includes Gordon Kaufman's article, 'On the Meaning of "Act of God"'.

4   It is interesting to note that Ian Ramsey developed this idea of 'disclosure situations' in the context of interpreting John Locke's *The Reasonableness of Christianity*. See his introduction to the edition of Locke's work published by Stanford in 1958.

5   See the writings of Hans Frei, especially *The Eclipse of Biblical Narrative* (1974).

6   *Divine Action* is the title of an important collection of essays inspired by the theology of Austin Farrer. See Hebblethwaite and Henderson (1990).

7   For a longer defence of disembodied agency, see Thomas Tracy (1984).

8   This is the famous Part XI to the *Dialogues* where Hume considers the problem of evil. See Wollheim (1963), p. 181.

Chapter 4

Miracles and Modern Science

A large number of scientists who are also theists would certainly disagree strongly with the idea that God plays no 'active role' in the world. However, it is important to understand what this 'active role' is, because it is not at all clear that these scientists feel that their commitment to such a role requires them to support the notion of SDA.

Changes in Scientific Thinking

Let us consider a model of God's relation to the universe that was widely held about fifty years ago – at the time when Bultmann wrote about his world of washing machines and wirelesses. It was a time when many theologians warned about the dangers of a 'God of the gaps' argument, one which Bonhoeffer expressed his concern about when he asked us to understand the God 'who makes us live in this world without using him as a working hypothesis' (1971: 311).

At the risk of oversimplification, the model could be summed up as follows. Before Newton it was believed that some form of divine intervention was required to explain the movement of the planets; after him a self-sufficient mechanical system excluded such intervention. As the astronomer Laplace famously remarked to Napoleon when the dictator asked him if he could see God through his telescope, 'I have no need of that hypothesis.' Eighteenth-century astronomy could make sense of the heavens perfectly well without God. Then in the nineteenth century Darwin closed another set of gaps when the doctrine of evolution drove out that of 'special creation'. An explanation was found for the emergence of new species, including the human species, which once again required no special acts of divine intervention. By the twentieth century, the model goes, the web is 'complete' and a natural world that is a closed continuum of cause and effect has been established. God can perhaps be affirmed as the creator or sustainer of 'the whole show' (Darwin himself believed something like this), but God cannot any longer be summoned as an explanation of the 'difficult bits' in science (planetary movement, new species). Such an approach would only lead to the gradual elimination of God from every last redoubt as science advanced. It would be a disreputable and ultimately fruitless endeavour to try to offer a supernatural explanation every time there were (inevitably temporary) difficulties in achieving a natural explanation. Moreover, by the mid-twentieth century the achievements of science in our ordinary lives were so all-embracing that it really did not make sense to continue with a project of trying to insert God in the few remaining gaps (if any) in the web of scientific explanation.

Scientists at the beginning of the twenty-first century would have what is in many ways a very different picture of God and the universe to this rather complacent picture from the age of 'the white heat of technology'. A contemporary writer on science and religion may well begin by emphasizing that the modern understanding of the world has little to do with that advanced in the classical physics of Isaac Newton three centuries ago (see, for instance, Polkinghorne 1998, Peacocke 2001b and Saunders 2002). In the light of relativity theory, there is no longer a belief in absolute space and time. In the light of attempts to study systems at the sub-atomic level, there is no longer an 'absolute object' in terms of some small piece of matter that is in principle identifiable and constitutes the fundamental building-block of the universe. The contemporary writer would say that there is no longer an 'objective observer', at least in the sense that it is impossible to describe the physical world as if the investigator has no effect on what he or she is describing. Whatever structure exists cannot be seen as independent of the observer trying to understand it. We are both onlookers and actors in the drama of existence. Finally, there is no longer an absolute determinism which believes that the distribution of objects in the world changes in a predictable manner according to the laws of mechanics. Twentieth-century quantum theory, the uncertainty principle and (later in that century as a child of the computer age) chaos theory have undermined such determinism. Instead it is suggested that there are certain systems at the sub-atomic level of which one can in principle never say what new state will follow from any previous state at a particular instant. No longer can it be claimed – even in principle – that the parts of the universe already laid down may decree what all the other parts shall be.[1]

Of course it is perfectly arguable that scientists were aware of all these developments (except perhaps chaos theory) when Bonhoeffer and Bultmann were writing in the mid-twentieth century. Yet it does not seem to have penetrated theological thinking at that time. Bultmann's world of washing machines and wirelesses is still the ordered classical universe of Newton, the perfect machine which must not be tampered with, and which is to be unpacked by the objective observer without recourse to divine intervention.

It is true that by the time Bultmann was writing in the mid-twentieth century, the principles of quantum mechanics and relativity were already known. But it is surely to an older science that he is really appealing, a science confident in its seamless webs and its closed systems. Despite all his 'modern' talk of wirelesses and washing machines, he is looking backwards rather than forwards. One can almost imagine these domestic applications of modern technology finding their place against the pleasant background of the Bultmann family home and functioning with the perfect regularity of planets orbiting in a Newtonian solar system.

It is not difficult to see how the Newtonian physics of the seventeenth century led to the comfortable Deist ideas of the eighteenth. Nature was a self-sufficient mechanical system set up (created) by the 'watchmaker' God who then stood back and interfered no more. From an Olympian perspective outside and detached from God's handiwork, the great divine observer could look down and see that what had been made was good – and by implication could now be left alone. It was absolutely self-sufficient within its parameters of space and time. It was going to last forever – the sort of watch that never breaks, never needs winding up and can endure any hardships imposed by its wearer. The minor cogs and wheels that made up its complex design, minuscule as atoms but in principle there to be seen, would go on working day in, day out in their predictable way, and in principle anyone clever enough to map out the intricate arrangement of this universe could determine its movement at any point in the future. From outside the universe God the Creator observed in a satisfied manner but did not interfere. Tampering with the product was for those whose craftsmanship left something to be desired.

The twenty-first century universe is not a self-sufficient piece of craftsmanship which will last forever. It is a temporary arrangement, however long 'temporary' might mean in this context. It is a universe at an intermediary stage of evolution between being a dispersed cloud of gas and ending up as a ball of crushed matter. There may be arguments over how it all began ('Big Bang' and other theories) and over how it will end (slow refrigeration through constant expansion or dramatic cremation), but the general view is that it is finite and perishable, just like us, the crew of a small and vulnerable spaceship (planet earth) who (viewed from a perspective of millions of years) could easily be wiped out by a well-placed asteroid and will in any case disappear in the final implosion of the universe, when matter is finally squeezed out of existence at an infinite density. This twenty-first century picture will itself change, and of course the description offered here is only one of many images currently on offer. But it does show that there is an alternative to the clockwork self-sufficiency of Newton's world.

Despite Newton's importance in the history of science, it is arguable, as I suggested in the first chapter, that he is now more of a restraint upon our acceptance of the world we actually live in (see Polkinghorne 1998: ch. 3).[2] It is difficult not to feel that even today many people are much more comfortable with Newton's universe than with one of relativity, quarks and black holes. The idea of innately unpredictable elements within sub-atomic systems, as if in this case there was a gap that in principle could never be filled by science, or of quantum mechanics as irreducibly statistical, has proved as hard to accept in our own day as Newton's own concept of action at a distance proved to be in his.

Moreover, it is arguable that contemporary scientists are a little less confident about 'pushing back the frontiers of science' than some of their predecessors were. They would not deny Dietrich Bonhoeffer's apt warning against using God as an explanatory principle to plug gaps in our knowledge which science might in principle close. But the warning could easily create a misleading impression. Bonhoeffer seems to have suggested that the frontiers of knowledge were being pushed further and further back, while God was being pushed back with them, and was therefore continually in retreat. But the idea of frontiers of knowledge being pushed further and further back is not quite right. The truth is surely that science both pushes frontiers back and creates new ones. The science of relativity, quantum mechanics and chaos theory both increases our knowledge and makes us aware of its limitations. Science both discovers answers ('closes gaps') and unearths new mysteries to be solved. It is not as if the scientist is putting more and more pieces of the jigsaw together, with by implication fewer and fewer pieces left available to be claimed for 'divine intervention'. Rather, scientists discover new puzzles to be solved even as they manage to plug the gaps in old ones. Developments such as quantum mechanics provide (in the view of some) new entry points for God to get involved, just as other points of entry are closed off by scientific progress.

The Post-Newtonian Universe and SDA

However, the further question that needs to be asked is how far this post-Newtonian view of the universe changes the picture of GDA and SDA (general divine action and specific divine action). Certainly it is a view that allows contemporary 'scientist-theologians' to argue strongly that creation does not involve 'setting up' some system external to God which then works in a self-sufficient manner of its own accord (roughly speaking the 'clockwork universe' of Newton). Instead we have a universe constantly maintained in being, a tune perpetually on God's lips rather than a pot created, finished and then left to stand by itself. God does not 'set the universe rolling' and then let it go but is constantly present to it, sustaining it and interpenetrating it.

Thus in a recent work Arthur Peacocke is keen to observe what he calls the 'somewhat static terms' in which God's sustaining activity was interpreted in the past and to insist that in view of the 'epic of creation' it has to be 'clothed with much more dynamic imagery'. He is convinced that 'the scientific vision we now possess reinforces and enriches this understanding of God's creating and sustaining interactions with the world'.

But by 'this understanding' he means GDA or God's general providence. He immediately goes on to insist that 'this is not the case when we consider the possibility of particular events, or patterns of events, being other than they would naturally have been because God intended them to be different' (Peacocke 2001b: 135). Peacocke believes that by stressing the fact that creation is a constant activity, and by stressing that the universe is never completely separate from God but is in some sense a part of God's being,[3] he can avoid the danger of Deism without having to concede the existence of special divine actions. Indeed it is a general rule with many of the 'scientist-theologians' that whenever you find God's general providence is being lauded, you know that God's special providence is about to be denied.

Thus Polkinghorne tells us that modern science 'in no way condemns God, at best, to the role of a Deistic Absentee landlord'. Instead it 'allows us to conceive of the Creator's continuing providential activity and costly loving care for creation' (1998: 75). There is no mention here of SDA, only of the 'continuing providential activity' which is effectively what is meant by general divine action. As for the 'costly loving care', that too remains uncashed in terms of special actions.

At first sight this reluctance to concede SDA might seem strange. For there surely are certain aspects of this twenty-first-century scientific vision which open the door to SDA. Don't some of the arguments surrounding the uncertainty principle and chaos theory allow room for SDA? We are told, for instance, that there are certain systems at the sub-atomic level of which one can in principle never say what new state will follow from any previous state at a particular instant. Does that not allow room for SDA? Doesn't the 'uncertainty principle' effectively show that the net is full of holes and some kind of specific divine action can therefore always get through?

Unfortunately, it does not. For one thing, we have to separate unpredictability from indeterminism. There may be times when we want to argue that there are things which we can never predict at the micro-level, whilst still insisting that each event at that level has a specific cause. In such circumstances the 'holes in the web' would lie in our knowledge, not in reality itself.

In the second place, the principle of indeterminism involves the claim that there is, in principle, no order in certain events. The processes are irreducibly statistical. But if it is in principle impossible to itemize particular occurrences and say what caused them, then what sense would it make to say that one was caused by God? Wouldn't this be to deny the very randomness in events which supposedly allows God a way in? In other words, if there is no randomness in events, then God can't be admitted as a cause. But if there *is* randomness in events, God cannot be admitted as a cause either, precisely because specific causes at this level are in principle unknowable (Polkinghorne 1998: 48–75; Saunders 2002: 83–93). As Peacocke puts it, 'God cannot know the precise outcome of any quantum event because God can only know what it is logically possible to know' (1998: 368). To say this is no more to constrain God's power than it constrains God's power to say that 2 and 2 make 4 for God as well as for human beings. It is a part of the logic of creation which is itself the work of God. In other words, we can't have a 'God of the gaps', not because there are no gaps, but because the gaps we do have are in principle uncloseable.

As for the work on chaos theory which emerged in the late twentieth century, this has produced some very interesting arguments but they too have been more concerned with GDA than SDA (see Saunders 2002: ch. 7).[4] The analysis is complicated and concerns the predictability of systems. In the light of the rise of the computer, scientists naturally explore the machine's infinite number-crunching capacities by feeding in endless amounts of data and examining the range of possible outcomes they get back. The result is a complex picture of the way in which everything is connected to everything else.

Saunders cites the so-called 'butterfly effect' as an example. So sensitive are the world's weather systems, it is argued, that the flap of a butterfly's wings in 'one part of the world could indirectly cause a major storm in another. The implication in Saunders' closely argued analysis, however, is not that God by some kind of subtle 'touch upon the tiller' can alter the course of world events in a more benign direction (thereby opening the way for SDA). The point is that processes are so complicated that it is virtually impossible to track them. If discovering the origins of a storm, for instance, requires an analysis of every butterfly's wing in another part of the world, then even a computer (which only represents numbers to a certain precision) might find the task daunting. This simply leaves us with a universe that is unpredictable rather than deterministic. Once again the gaps are in our knowledge, not in the workings of the world.

In other words, the result of chaos theory (perhaps surprisingly, given the obvious power of computers) is to enhance the sense of the physical universe as an immeasurably complex interplay of systems. If it strengthens the case for theism at all, then it is once again in terms of an emphasis upon that complex overall design – in other words in terms of GDA, rather than SDA.

The Anthropic Principle

Can the same be said of the use various scientist theologians make of what they call the 'anthropic principle'? The principle argues that if a wide variety of the physical quantities that characterize our universe had been slightly different ('physical quantities' meaning, for example, the precise pull of gravity or speed of light), then not only would the development of the universe as a whole have been entirely different, but the chances of life on earth would have been zero (Barrow and Tipler 1986; see also Polkinghorne 1991: ch. 6 and 1998: ch. 1). It is an interesting theory and deserves consideration.

What the supporters of the anthropic principle seem to be saying is this. Suppose that for some reason you have to run across a field. It is a pitch black night but you have no choice. You must run and keep on running. Morning comes and you've reached the end of the field. You look back. On looking back, you see that there was only a single narrow path which could have taken you across the field. On either side of it is a deadly swamp in which you would have had no hope of survival, had you run into it. Yet for some reason – without even being aware of the risk of what you were doing – you managed to keep to the path as you ran. It seems to me that the anthropic principle makes this sort of claim about the way human beings have evolved (see Peacock 2001b: 70–72).[5]

Of course the anthropic principle can be challenged. To return to my example of running through the field, someone could easily make the rejoinder that endless numbers of people had already made that run and had fallen into the swamp on either side. But if enough people make the run, then at some point someone will get through (rather as it used to be argued – before computers! – that if enough monkeys banged enough typewriters for long enough then one of them would eventually produce the works of Shakespeare). It could be argued that the anthropic principle misinterprets the fact that we happen to be the monkey who typed Shakespeare to mean that there must be some creative genius at work in our writing. It could be argued that our 'successful' universe simply happens to be the one that 'got through', where countless failed universes didn't.

However, it should be noted that what is being described by the anthropic principle is not simply a lucky 'escape' but evolution to higher levels of being that both retain and go beyond the preceding levels. People are attracted to the principle, not simply because they think we are 'lucky' to have got to where we are, but because each step taken in bringing us here seems to draw out of the preceding stages more than they could hope to generate in their own terms. Such a conviction leads to the notion of God providing a creative pull, drawing out the thread of evolutionary development. The argument has been defended and attacked by supporters and opponents of 'transcendental Thomism' (see TeSelle 1990), but is succinctly expressed in Austin Farrer's *A Science of God?*:

> Where were the laws governing the operations of consciousness before anything was conscious? Don't tell me Dame Nature had them up her sleeve. There is no such sleeve and no such lady ... [As for the idea that] the laws governing the workings of consciousness were implicitly contained in the laws governing the operations of certain sorts of living tissue, I'm not sure that I like 'implicitly contained in' any more than I like 'Nature's sleeve'. It was for saying things like 'implicitly contained in' that the medieval thinkers were cursed by the founders of modern physics. Still, don't let's be hasty; let's give 'implicitly contained in' a run for its money. Only if we do, we shall have to have more of it. The principles of rational thought were implicitly contained in the principles of pre-rational animal behaviour and the principles of animal behaviour were implicitly contained in the reactions of pre-sentient animal bodies and the reactions of such bodies in the chemical reactions of cells and the reactions of cells in the functioning of inanimate substances – and to cut a long story short we come at last to the simplest, most elementary particle of energy from which, we must suppose, all more complex forms or structures have, in due course, been built up. Clever little thing! It contained (implicitly, of course!) all the future developments of nature within it. I wonder how it managed to have enough folds in it to tuck away all those implications; for it was, in itself, such a simple little creature, with scarcely a wrinkle in it.
>
> (1966: 55)

The principle is not just that we have been 'lucky' in our development, avoiding obstacles, but that we have evolved. At least some of the current discontent with Darwinism derives, I think, from a sense that changes take place which cannot be spoken of (in the language Farrer parodies) as 'contained' or 'implicit' in what has gone before.

Yet even if the anthropic principle were to be accepted, this might only strengthen the case for GDA. The anthropic principle is essentially a modern version of the argument from design. Instead of the walker tripping over a watch and saying that this object must be a piece of craftsmanship, as in Paley's famous watchmaker example, here the walker looks back and argues that without some overall divine planning of the route they could never have got to where they are.

Transcendental Thomism

Despite the way in which they change our perspective, none of these contemporary scientific breakthroughs appears to open up a path for SDA. Nor, in the view of many theologians, do they need to. Theologians like Wiles and Peacocke are deeply conscious of the sort of identification of Deist theology with 'non-interventionist' and theist with 'interventionist' which one finds explicitly made, for instance, in David Brown's work *The Divine Trinity*,[6] but it is an identification which they firmly reject.

Whether it be language talking about the world as neither separate from God (Deism) nor identical with it (pantheism) but contained within it (panentheism),[7] or the image of the world as God's body which we looked at in the last chapter, these writers are determined to lay the Deist ghost without requiring SDA as their exorcist. As Wiles puts it:

> The physical processes of the world are the means of God's self-expression, as the unconscious physiological functioning of our bodies is for us. Here too it hardly seems natural to speak of divine agency at work, any more than we would speak of the agency of a human self in continually maintaining the pumping agency of the heart.
>
> (1986: 35)

By such images, those who wish to rule out SDA put the greatest possible emphasis upon God's constant and abiding presence. Instead of the Deist God who is nowhere, their God is somehow everywhere (God is, after all, defined as omnipresent) and yet without any SDA.

In fact they take their arguments even further. They suggest that their God is 'more' present than the God of the believer in miracles, a God who is ordinarily absent if occasionally present. Their God, they say, is with us constantly. They thus firmly reject Brown's attempt to link 'theism' with interventionism; their view is that interventionism is, if anything, more Deist than theist, because it presumes that when not performing miracles God is 'somewhere else'. Their justification of God's non-intervention is thus to argue that a proper understanding of God's presence makes intervention redundant. It is almost as if they are saying that to ask for God to come and help is to make the mistake of thinking that God has ever gone away.

This perspective of Peacocke, Wiles and others is helpful, because it warns against envisaging miracles as if God is looking down, watching, observing from above just like a spectator at a match, or as if God is surveying some kind of activity on the part of God's 'human pets' and then occasionally putting a hand into the cage in order to sort out disturbances that might get out of hand. This is not an acceptable way of looking at God, and it is why in the opening chapter I criticized the notion of a miracle as an act of divine 'intervention'. Christian theology seeks to stress both the immanence and the transcendence of God, both God's otherness and God's presence. Writers such as Wiles and Peacocke certainly recognize this – it is precisely what Peacocke's emphasis upon panentheism is seeking to reflect. Their problem with SDA is that they are unable to accept a notion of special divine action within the framework of immanence and transcendence which they see as central to Christian theism.

But are they right to take this position? One approach which has tried to reach an understanding of SDA that does not deny God's constant presence is that of 'transcendental Thomism'. This school of thought seeks to defend SDA whilst denying that divine causality replaces human or finite causality at any point, even in the case of a miracle. No giant divine hand appears over the Red Sea to part the waters, sweeping away the power of wind and currents as it goes. God does not act to break the causal web. A miracle is not an occasional break-in by God to upset the self-sufficient, causally ordered habitat that human beings are used to.

The transcendental Thomist denies that God inserts the Deity into the causal series by exploiting a gap, as envisaged by those who think of the microworld as somehow containing 'gaps' which God might fill without ousting some finite cause in the process. God neither ousts a finite cause nor adds a divine cause to the finite causes already present. The third possibility, argues the transcendental Thomist, is that God exploits the potentialities of finite causes beyond what they are naturally capable of.

This raises, of course, the general question of the validity of Thomist (and Aristotelian) categories of thought, a huge subject that can hardly be entered into here. But one or two observations on the transcendental Thomist position can be made.

The first is that this image of 'realizing potentialities' is far more easily understood when applied to, for instance, the relation between teacher and pupil, than when applied to the Red Sea. As I pointed out in the last chapter in relation to the notion of God as 'acting within', we can think of realizing potentialities of which we are not naturally capable in terms of the sort of personal inspiration that comes from a good educator. We can then apply that to the relation of the human person to God, who is a constant inspiration, lifting us beyond what we can normally do and even leading to the Pauline comment 'Not I, but Christ in me'. This is comprehensible, as was the poet Robert Browning when he pointed out that a person's reach must exceed their span, or what's a heaven for. Education is always a good image because its literal meaning of *e-duco*, 'leading out', supports the idea of the true educator enabling people to see what they themselves are capable of, rather than stuffing them full of facts, opinions or exam answers, as educators so often do nowadays. But it hardly makes sense to describe the Red Sea as a churning mass struggling to realize its potential to part, or the irreparably damaged brain of Jesus in the tomb as led to realize its potential beyond the grave.

What is noteworthy about, for instance, the book on *Divine Action* inspired by Austin Farrer and referred to extensively here, is that so many of those who explore the notion of SDA and speak about the necessity of a 'causal joint' between divine action and the course of nature end up with examples of personal inspiration by God. The focus becomes 'God's action in our lives'. But God's action in our lives can be interpreted to mean the constant presence of one who, by being ever more than we are, leads us on to realize more than we thought we had in ourselves. We have the inspiring teacher who never goes away. But where miracles are concerned, it is not God's action in our lives that is the problem; it is God's action in changing water into wine or reconvening the assembly of cells in the corpse of Christ.

The second point is that the transcendental Thomist position has a useful counter-argument to Peacocke and others when they argue that God's occasional presence in a miracle implies God's ordinary absence. Transcendental Thomists argue that in the normal course of events both God and natural forces (taking for granted that we know what 'natural forces' are) are active in the world. When a miracle occurs, God continues to be active but the natural forces do not. A miracle represents, therefore, not the sudden intervention of God – God is present all the time, acting in the world – but the sudden absence of the natural forces, normally the 'co-actor' in whatever happens but on these rare occasions not included. A miracle is therefore not something 'extra' but something 'missing'. The emphasis is upon the occasional absence of the 'secondary cause' rather than the occasional presence of the 'primary cause'.[8]

Whilst this manner of seeing a miracle is useful in supporting the idea of God as always present to and in the world, as opposed to occasionally arriving 'from outside' in order to change things, it still raises all the 'causal joint' issues which have proved so difficult all along. Just how do these primary and secondary causes 'normally' operate? What does God (as opposed to nuclear fission) do to make the sun shine? The image of the 'natural' wheel coming off when a miracle occurs, and the wagon continuing to move from God alone, does not help us to understand how these two wheels are ordinarily connected with one another.

Must we therefore conclude, with Saunders, that there is effectively no case for SDA? It is hard not to agree with his pessimistic conclusions about SDA, but there is one aspect of the position taken by a number of the scientists and theologians I have considered in this chapter which I believe is open to question, and which may help to rescue some concept of SDA.

Conclusions: A New Biblical Perspective

Even if the post-Newtonian perspective may not manage of itself to reinstate SDA, the insight of chaos theory into the sheer complexity of our existence, and the attempt of the anthropic principle to describe the 'fortunate' nature of our emergence, do change our perspective on the world. Instead of a timeless mechanism which lasts forever, we are presented with a universe which is not only unfathomably complicated but has at all stages of its development been highly precarious. Peacocke (1979: 256) offers the image of a vulnerable 'spaceship earth', destined eventually to go down with all aboard her, while Polkinghorne lays a similar stress upon the inevitable demise of our physical universe.[9] Such a world as this is arguably much more in tune with the biblical understanding of salvation history than is the 'timeless mechanism' image. Instead of a changeless universe which lasts forever, we have a world with a beginning and an end. Just as our own lives are brief and vulnerable, so is the life of the universe as a whole. The theist who believes that God makes (rather than 'made', given that creation is an ongoing process and not something which happened only 'in the beginning') a cosmos out of chaos in order to realize a specific purpose will feel more aligned with a universe which combines breathtaking and wonderful complexity with vulnerability, for this is precisely (at the risk of oversimplifying such a wide range of texts) the 'biblical view'. The earth and all that is in it is infinitely rich in substance and yet it will not live forever any more than we will. The physical universe is fantastic but finite; it is here for a purpose, like ourselves. In this sense the Deist view of the universe has surely passed away.

In another respect, however, the contemporary scientist-theologians seem rather wider of the biblical mark. It is noticeable how much of what they write about God's eternal 'presence' ignores the fact (here I am speaking from a Christian perspective) that Creation is followed by a Fall. For Christians, there is a sense in which God *has* gone away from humanity (or, it might be said, a sense in which humanity has gone away from God).

The doctrine of Creation is careful to distinguish itself from Neoplatonist ideas of 'divine emanation', as if the universe was merely a case of God overflowing into the world. Among other difficulties with their approach, the Neoplatonists were seen as failing to acknowledge the distinctness of the world from God. The Christian tradition of creation 'ex nihilo' (out of nothing) was not simply a way of pointing to God's complete freedom in creation, unconstrained by any pre-existent matter which might impose its conditions on the divine designer, but also a way of rejecting the idea that Creation is 'out of God', an extension or overflow of heaven onto earth. It was a means of pointing to the separation between the physical universe and its Maker. Saying that God did not make the world out of pre-existent material protected God's freedom; saying that God did not make the world out of God protected God's separate being. Both aspects of the doctrine are important.

It is interesting that a theologian like Wiles seems more comfortable with the notion of Creation as the transformation of chaos into cosmos, in other words as an ordering activity, than with the traditional doctrine of creation out of nothing.[10] Perhaps because of their genuine appreciation of the wonders of the physical universe, writers like Peacocke make very little reference to the Fall and the implicit notion it contains of separation between humanity and God (the symbolic expulsion and banishment from Eden). Instead we have the sort of language found when Peacocke tells us that 'God creates all-that-is within Godself' (2001: 139). Such language, it seems to me, is in danger of absurdity, filling up the world with a non-existent God. It is surely arguable both that God eternally sustains the world in being and that God is not spread around everywhere like some kind of invisible ether. The scientist-theologians may well have as much difficulty explaining the sense in which God is here 'all the time' as the believer in SDA has in explaining how God acts occasionally.

I have fully endorsed the notion that 'occasional presence' implies 'ordinary absence' and that for this reason to describe a miracle as 'intervention' is inappropriate. The reason for this is that it is in danger of suggesting that God is only involved with the world when God performs miracles. This would imply that for the rest of the time God remains apart from and indifferent to the universe.

God is not only involved with the world when performing miracles. However, this does not rule out a separation brought about by the malaise in the human condition outlined (in mythological terms) in the story of the Fall.

Before taking this further it would be useful to consider the issue that makes the doctrine of the Fall central to Christianity, that of theodicy, and whether miracles can be justified in a world so plagued by violence and injustice as our own.

Notes

1   I am attempting to summarize the description given by Peacocke (1979: 52–5): 'The twilight of the absolute gods of space, time, object and determinism.'
2   Polkinghorne remarks that 'the world is stranger than Newton had enabled us to think' (1998: 52).
3   Peacocke himself arrives at a 'panentheist' position which is criticized later in this chapter.
4   Note that Polkinghorne disagrees with Saunders and believes that chaos theory does allow entry for a form of SDA. See Polkinghorne (1998), ch. 3.
5   Polkinghorne (1998: 7) prefers the image of a fish that is just the right size for being caught.
6   Brown (1985: x).

> whether one adopts an interventionist or non-interventionist view of God (in Chapter 1 respectively labelled deism and theism) can only be determined by philosophical and theological considerations.

7   Peacocke makes the panentheist case in many of his writings. See, for example, 'In him we live and move and have our being' (2001b: 135–44).
8   The philosopher of religion Alvin Plantinga (1986) takes this view.
9   Polkinghorne writes 'science tells us most surely and clearly that the end of present physical process lies in futility, the bang of cosmic collapse or the whimper of cosmic decay. Carbon-based life will have its day and then it will disappear for ever' (1998: 90).
10   See the chapter in Wiles (1986) entitled 'God the Creator'. Wiles seems to enthuse about the idea of creation as 'the giving of form to formless matter' (p. 15), pointing out that this definition has more scriptural warrant than creation out of nothing. Yet, as he concedes on the next page, 'Creation is creation out of nothing or it is nothing.'

Chapter 5

Miracles and the Problem of Evil

If the idea that a modern 'scientific' understanding of the world rules out belief in miracles has been overstated, the existence of a widespread reluctance to accept miracles on grounds of moral principle has arguably been understated. There is a presumption that 'ordinary people' reject a miracle such as that of (shall we say) changing water into wine because it goes against all the tenets of modern science. But their reasons may well have more to do with a moral revulsion against a God who 'tinkers' with the world, leaving so much suffering unalleviated while performing 'tricks' here and there. For this reason I believe that a chapter on the relation between miracles and the problem of evil is justified.

Moreover, in the previous chapter I argued that the 'scientist-theologians' undervalued the doctrine of the Fall. This doctrine may help to throw some light upon the problem of SDA and how to make sense of special divine actions in the world.

There are many ways of interpreting the Genesis material relating to the Fall of humanity, but most agree that emphasis is being placed upon a distance established between creature and Creator. That distance may, to use Professor Hick's distinction (1966), be an 'Augustinian' distance established as a consequence of human sin, or it may be an 'Irenaean' distance established in order to let humanity mature, expulsion from Eden being akin to overgrown stay-at-home adolescents sent out by parents to fend for themselves.[1] But either interpretation of the Fall involves banishment, expulsion from Eden and by implication a loss of the divine presence. The human person becomes separated from God.

Once such a separation is established, however, the question arises as to how exactly it is overcome (from the side of God) through the various divine initiatives that form the backbone of 'salvation history' – revelation, inspiration, miracle. What, if anything, does God do in order to make life easier for God's fallen creatures, whether or not their fall is a well-deserved punishment or an appropriate learning context?

The Helping Hand

One obvious model for specific divine actions crossing the divide between God and the world is that of the hand reaching into the 'cage' and rearranging or ameliorating conditions there. When thinking, for instance, of how God might be moved by compassion to work a miracle, we might think of those natural history programmes in which a camera crew filming a lost tiger cub agonize

53

over whether to 'let nature take its course' or intervene and return the creature to its mother.

Like the interfering camera crew, let us suppose, God sits up in heaven observing the course of human development, whose beauty is marred by violence. God knows that 'nature must take its course', in human affairs as in those of the animal kingdom, but occasionally God cannot tolerate the cruelty. At that point the hand reaches into the cage. The sea is parted in order to free the Israelites just as the cub is scooped up and driven to its mother. Though it operates at the level of instinct rather then reason, we may presume that the cub finds a ride in a landrover more puzzling than a trip by paw through the jungle. But the natural order is soon restored and human interference comes to an end. In a similar manner we may puzzle over the manner in which a dry passage can be found through the Red Sea, but our reason is no more able to cope with an act of God than the instincts of a cat are able to cope with the act of a sympathetic film crew.

One thing made clear by this analogy is that the motivation for interference is not quite that of the watchmaker tampering with a faulty mechanism. In this case nature is taking its 'proper' course – we could say that unlike the watch that has stopped working it is still 'working properly' even when the cub gets lost – but part of the implications of nature being itself is that violent and cruel actions will take place and indeed do take place on a daily basis. The mechanical error in the watch is a defect to be put right; the cruelty of nature is part of the design. Hence interference in the natural world can only be a token gesture. Indeed too much interference, for instance a wholesale effort to eliminate violence from the natural world altogether, would effectively stop it working. We would say that the 'balance of nature' had been upset. Too many rescued tiger cubs would destroy the system. Where the violence of the natural world is concerned, the theist has to argue that it is a necessary part of the overall design, even though there may be a strong desire to interfere when we encounter that violence (such as the bird with the broken wing, the cat with one eye and all the other casualties of nature that we may be moved to deal with – though of course these creatures may well also be casualties of an encounter with us, as the daily death toll of animals on our roads shows). It is impossible to use human intervention in order to make the system pain-free, because without pain there wouldn't be a system. Rescuing animals in pain is a mute protest against a natural order in which they are designed to suffer.

Does something similar animate our understanding of human violence and cruelty, though in this case action is expected (or demanded) from God rather than ourselves? I have argued that the equivalent of the camera crew filming the lost cub is the divine 'observer' looking down upon the Israelites trapped on the banks of the Red Sea. Once again we may argue that divine action can only be occasional, since (in this case human) nature must be allowed to take its course. Human beings must have the freedom to go astray. But at the same time, with humans as with animals, only a small proportion of the suffering can be alleviated. The 'helping hand' image, in this respect, is too tame. It is not as if God helps us when things 'get difficult'; that would require intervention on a scale which no one admits to. People are suffering and committing injustice, inflicting or feeling pain, all the time.

However, whilst in the case of animals it is difficult to see how nature could take its course without violence, in the case of human beings it might be argued that societies will eventually arise which promote and ensure peaceful coexistence. The helping hand of the film crew could therefore be said to 'go against nature', whilst a helping hand from God could be seen as a form of encouragement to realize a better way of life. Unlike animals, which cannot survive without inflicting pain and suffering, we can achieve a 'higher' form of existence, though it is questionable whether we have got very far in doing so. But at least this means that the divine 'helping hand', though it cannot possibly relieve more than a tiny fraction of the world's suffering, might be a way of presenting, reminding or encouraging us to realize that 'better end'.

SDA and the Limits to God's Knowledge of Us

It might be argued that there is an additional problem in the case of God's intervention, arising from the fact that God, unlike the camera crew, does not 'happen to observe' acts of cruelty which inspire intervention but presumably knows exactly what is going on in all places and at all times.

But do we really need to argue that God predetermines or even foresees all that is to come? It is possible to take a 'radical' view of the self-imposed limits to divine omnipotence and omniscience whilst maintaining a belief in SDA. Thus it could be said that God not only does not compel human beings to respond as God would like them to do, but God does not even know what that response will be. It is sometimes argued that such a limitation upon God's knowledge is incompatible with divine omniscience. Against this we can argue that it is not a limitation upon God's powers to say that God does not know the future, but part of the logic of what God has created. This point is made by Brian Hebblethwaite:

> God's omniscience, like his omnipotence, is self-limited by the nature of what he has made. In each case the limitation is logical, given the actual nature of God's creation.
>
> (1979: 440–41)

In other words, once God is committed to creating a world, God must be committed to accepting limitations upon what even God can know. Denying God's knowledge of the future is not a way of limiting God but of understanding what God has done – or is doing – in creating the universe. Though Hebblethwaite recognizes in more recent writing that 'on this view God's self-limitation in the creation of a temporal world goes further than many have supposed' (2000: 69), he nevertheless defends the position and in a mock dialogue between a 'believer' and an 'unbeliever' puts the following comment into the mouth of the believer:

All I can say is that much traditional theology has not taken human freedom seriously enough. That goes for Augustine, Thomas Aquinas, Luther and Calvin. I would argue that to give creatures the power of free response to each other and to himself is indeed an act of self-limitation on the part of God.[2]

(2000: 65–6)

It seems to me that God cannot know the future if the future is yet to be determined. Hall's position (2003: 62) that God does not 'determine' human choices but nevertheless knows what they will be is not sustainable. For only having determined them would enable God to know (as opposed to predict with various degrees of confidence) what they will be. Just as it is impossible to create free creatures who always choose the good (a frequent suggestion made by those who protest at the free-will defence of the existence of evil in the world), so it is impossible to choose free creatures knowing what they will do in advance. Indeed it is precisely the latter consideration which allows one to affirm the former.[3]

It should be emphasized that this stress upon divine self-limitation in relation to the created order need not exclude SDAs. It is, for example, because of his view that SDA is not excluded (for instance in relation to the resurrection of Jesus) that Hebblethwaite differs from others who have adopted a similar position in relation to God's self-limitation in Creation (for instance Gordon Kaufman 1968).

A number of analogies have been used to convey this relation of voluntarily self-limiting Creator to free human creature. One explored as long ago as 1941 by the novelist Dorothy Sayers was that of the writer with his or her characters in a novel. It is clear that characters are spoken of as 'taking on a life of their own', and indeed that the better the character the more this will be so. The writer may then talk of the book 'writing itself', or of how when the author thinks up situations and plots he or she may want to say 'no, that character wouldn't do such a thing'. But it is difficult not to agree with Wiles that this analogy falls short of offering the real independence that human beings supposedly have – for instance the sort of independence that enables the 'character' to refuse any dealings with the 'author' (Wiles 1986: 37). On this analogy, moreover, God knows exactly what the outcome will be and whether God's story will have a 'happy ending', whereas I have argued that it is part of the logic of creation that God should not know.

A better analogy suggested by Wiles is that of the improvised drama. God is conceived of as a director working with actors who improvise their own lines and may develop the storyline and outcomes in a way that the director didn't intend. God can then be thought of as the agent of the drama 'as a whole', while the individual speeches are written by the players. In this example, the absence of divine foreknowledge is preserved. Once the play is set in motion, the players determine the script and may come up with something that the director never intended.

Even here, however, it is doubtful whether the creature really has the independence demanded by the logic of God's decision in creating. The film director Ken Loach, to take one example, who inspires characters through an improvised approach to writing dialogue, nevertheless has a clear idea of where the films will go and what they will say. The characters do have the freshness and vitality that comes from the absence of a pre-determined script; nevertheless it is unthinkable that the group of actors brought together to work on *Raining Stones*, for instance, might have ended up producing a film in which the loan shark on the council estate was honoured as an entrepreneurial hero or the father saving up for his daughter's communion dress lambasted as a wastrel. Even in an improvised work there is arguably a degree of control that God does not demand of creation.

It is interesting to consider how far either of these analogies excludes SDA. The first one, that of characters to a novelist, is more likely to exclude SDA, since everything is so closely determined by the author/creator that no further intervention is necessary. The second analogy, in which the characters have more freedom, is the one where the case for SDA is clearer. We can see that on occasion the director will step in and say 'No, I'm not having that line.' Of course in a perfectly improvised production that might be unnecessary, not least because the actors will have been selected with some understanding of their general attitudes and dispositions in advance. Nevertheless we can see that the director would be unlikely to baulk at such intervention if it became necessary. There is, in the ways of God described in the Hebrew Bible – intemperate, demanding, passionate, destructive and then repenting of earlier fury – much that is reminiscent of the best theatre and film directors.

A third analogy, which gives humanity a similar degree of autonomy to that of the improvised script, is that of the chess game. God is the perfect chess player who can anticipate all the moves that humanity may make, but that does not amount to God knowing what moves will actually be made or how long the game will take. The analogy to God as a chess player (as Wiles ruefully observes) does not merely fail to rule out SDA, it specifically rules it in. There must be special divine actions in order to account for God's moves in the game.

'How and where does God make his moves in the game of chess?', asks Wiles (1986: 66). Fair enough – this is the question that we have been struggling with all along. But the point to be made here is that we can allow for an interpretation of God's self-limitation which rules out either God's making the future happen, or God's knowing what will happen in that future, without ruling out SDA. Indeed we can argue that the more we push the case for divine self-limitation in relation to human freedom, the more we will want to argue for the necessity of SDA.[4]

The Selectivity of SDA

Nevertheless, even if God does not predetermine or foresee the whole course of events, theists still face the problem of why special divine actions come at one point and not another. The rescue beside the Red Sea is not repeated during the long years suffering in the concentration camps. Wiles makes the point succinctly when he comments that:

it would seem strange that no miraculous intervention prevented Auschwitz or Hiroshima, while the purposes apparently forwarded by some of the miracles acclaimed in traditional Christian faith seem trivial by comparison.[5]

(1986: 66)

Whatever its achievements, it is likely that the twentieth century will be remembered above all for the Holocaust. This is something humanity has to learn from; it is also something traumatizing. Comments such as 'after Auschwitz there can be no poetry' express this sense of trauma. Apart from the necessary political or economic lessons that need to be taken to heart (and to head), there is a profound religious question that, at least so far as believers are concerned, needs to be answered: why did God permit this to happen?

It is plausible to suppose that those who talked in 1940 about the 'miracle' of a nine-day calm at Dunkirk later asked themselves why there was no miracle as the trains to the death camps took their ordered course and an earthly hell was established and maintained until the very end of the war.[6] Biographers record that Hitler, following a few unsuccessful attempts on his life (including the notorious plot of July 1944, when an attaché case packed with explosives was planted under the conference table at his headquarters at Rastenburg by a German army officer, Graf von Stauffenberg) persuaded himself that he was protected by divine providence (certainly many of his followers believed this). He was undeniably 'lucky'. Is it possible to believe that God kept the wind at bay while the small boats evacuated thousands from France, when the chance position of a heavy desk enabled the worst dictator in history to survive being a few feet from an explosion with little more than a ringing in his ears?

Two centuries ago the paradigm evil event was the Lisbon earthquake of November 1755. Apart from destroying the city itself, the earthquake brought fires and a flood of the River Tagus in its wake, killing tens of thousands of inhabitants. People struggled to make sense of a natural disaster in which those who were faithfully praying in the cathedral in the centre of the city lost their lives, while those who were enjoying themselves in the brothels located in the suburbs survived.

But despite hard questions concerning who managed to be caught up in the disaster and who managed to escape it, the paradigm of suffering here was one of 'natural' rather than 'moral' evil, where the pain and suffering caused was the result of a natural event (an earthquake). This is not to say that 'natural' and 'moral' evil can ever be completely separated. One might argue, for instance, that the deaths caused by an earthquake are at least partly to do with the failure of governments to invest in stronger structures, or, most recently, to provide advance warning of a tsunami. In this sense some 'moral evil' is involved even in a natural disaster, whose consequences are made worse than they otherwise might be because of human neglect. Nevertheless the Lisbon earthquake, the paradigm for earlier writers who considered the question of whether God's goodness was compatible with human suffering, was primarily an accident of fate, a sudden and unanticipated event which, like the tsunami of 2004, happened to deprive thousands of innocent victims of their lives.

The paradigm evil event for us in the twenty-first century is different. To Jews and Christians alike the Exodus story of a miraculous liberation from oppression in Egypt is a foundation document of their faith. But in the last century there was no liberation from an oppression which, probably unlike that of Pharaoh, sought initially to work the slaves to death and then to eliminate them altogether. Certainly, insofar as we can do more than guess about the historical circumstances then prevailing, we can suppose that Pharaoh was concerned about the fact that the Israelite population was growing faster than that of the Egyptians. We can also agree that he worked them hard and, when they complained, even harder, denying them the straw to make bricks. But was he carrying out or even planning genocide? Was even the most famous 'intervention' of all in Jewish and Christian tradition, the parting of the Red Sea, an 'intervention' at the wrong time and in the wrong place?

The Holocaust was an act of inhumanity carried out by large numbers of people on a systematic basis over a considerable period of time. In this case, unlike that of the Lisbon earthquake, the suffering was brought about by human agents, who were not only victims but perpetrators. The Holocaust was a 'well-organized' affair, in which thousands of people at all levels of society and from a wide range of European countries worked hard in order to make the murder of millions a practically feasible outcome. As the wheels ground on, as ordinary people fretted day after day over railway timetables and the requisitioning of rolling stock, they wore themselves out in the Sisyphean task of fighting a war and at the same time managing a continental programme of racial extinction. If the two aims clashed, then on the whole they preferred to proceed with their programme of extinction. Meanwhile there was no interference from above. In a curious way both God and humanity seem to have been trapped in a policy from which there was no escape. The human beings, with a few exceptions, fulfilled all the administrative and logistic requirements of mass extermination; while the hand of God remained stayed as the long process of annihilation took its course.

I pointed out in Chapter 1 that where natural disasters like an earthquake are concerned, it is common for there to be talk of 'miracles', though these are miracles in the sense of 'special acts of providence' (the child trapped in the air pocket who survives several days before being rescued) in which God acts through rather than apart from the laws of nature. Nevertheless it is clear that God is believed to act. When people talk about 'miracles' in the context of the Holocaust, they tend to leave God out of it. As Dr Michael Berenbaum, Professor of Theology at the University of Judaism in Los Angeles, has pointed out, Auschwitz was not a place for miracles. The victims far outnumbered the survivors. If the language of 'miracles' can be used at all in such a context, it refers to acts of kindness or self-sacrifice in the camps that showed how human goodness and dignity remained as a glimmer of light in the midst of so much cruelty. The miraculous is seen in terms of what human beings did, not what God did. For God did nothing. The poet's charge remains – 'Did heaven look on, and would not take their part?'

Faced with a traumatic recent past of this kind – a past which, for all its European setting, undoubtedly has worldwide resonance – it is understandable that people might prefer a God who never acts at all to a God whose actions are bound to raise questions about the priorities of the Deity. Such people would argue that a God who didn't act in a special way over the Holocaust must either never act or must be condemned as immoral. The goodness of God might just be rescuable if there was an absolute divine refusal ever to act – for instance in order to let humans determine their own destiny. But if God does sometimes act, then why was nothing done during the slow unfolding of this brutal attempt to exterminate a people? It is as if the failure to interfere during the long and hateful process of the Holocaust, a collective enterprise involving thousands of people working to realize a wicked end, casts a pall of triviality over the claims to miraculous healings or feedings made by Christians past and present.[7] Faced with what God didn't do in that context, what possible interest could there be in what God did do elsewhere? Only if God never acted could there be a justification for God not acting in this process of extermination. The argument is a variant of Stendahl's idea that God's only excuse is not existing; in this case God's only excuse is not 'intervening' (I use the inverted commas because of my concerns about 'intervention' implying occasional presence but ordinary absence). Thus it might be argued that Auschwitz has put paid to miracles as much as to poetry.

Yet the view that there are special acts of God persists. In an interesting collection of essays Stephen Davis defends the idea of God 'intervening' miraculously on earth. Such 'interventions' must be rare, he believes, but they happen. 'Hick considers the idea perilous, but I do indeed think that God decides to intervene on some occasions and not others', he writes (2001: 102). The peril from a moral point of view is, as we have seen, clear. If God sometimes 'intervenes', what criteria are deployed to determine when God 'intervenes' and when God chooses not to?

God the Parent

Hebblethwaite makes an interesting point in *Evil, Suffering and Religion* (2000: 68–70) when he considers whether, if we really thought no creation at all was better than the risk of innocent suffering, we would be unable to justify having children. As the character in Hebblethwaite's dialogue points out, we *do* take the risk of having children, even though we know that they might suffer or even die. Do we not therefore by our own actions implicitly condone God's actions in creating us?

The comparison to children is an interesting one and in many ways a natural one. As I point out later in my discussion of kenosis, we are all said to be children of God, who is our 'father' or even (depending on how you want to translate the Aramaic word 'abba') our dad. God is also – to recall other images in the Bible – the shepherd who looks after every single sheep (Luke 15:3–6), the housewife who turns a house upside down searching for a lost coin (Luke 15:8–10) and the mother eagle who nurses us as her young (Deuteronomy 32:11). The biblical texts are full of imagery suggesting God's parental relationship towards humanity. In one famous passage, from Matthew's version of the Sermon on the Mount, Jesus tells the people to put away 'anxious thoughts' about food, drink and clothes. Life is more than this, he insists. Look at the birds of the air. 'They do not sow and reap and store in barns, yet your Heavenly Father feeds them. You are worth more than the birds' (Matthew 6:25–8). In Luke's gospel Jesus assures his hearers 'Are not sparrows five for twopence? And yet not one of them is overlooked by God. More than that, even the hairs of your head have all been counted. Have no fear; you are worth more than any number of sparrows' (Luke 12:6–7).

It is all too easy to read this passage as if the birds are the family pets and human beings the family members, all of them taken care of in God's extended household of loving care. Moreover Christians all know that their single most important prayer is the Lord's Prayer addressed to God as their father, the 'provider' whom they are expected to ask for their daily bread.

The notion of prayer is instructive here. For surely at least some prayers, for instance those which are petitionary, must elicit a response. Maurice Wiles makes the point in *Reason to Believe*, where he talks of miracles as 'an expression of God's personal love and care for his children' (1999: 41). For this 'relationship' between the divine father and his children must 'surely find expression in divine response to human prayers as well as in human prayer to God'. And if those divine responses are genuine responses, Wiles asks, 'must they not often involve direct divine intervention which alters what would otherwise have happened?' (1999: 41).

Wiles does not think that this is a sustainable argument. For one thing, the inherent rarity of miracles, necessary if they are not to overwhelm the regularity of the natural order that Wiles believes is essential to scientific progress, cannot be maintained if they are to be attached to such a basic and recurring aspect of Christian life as prayer. But he correctly perceives how difficult it is to sustain the idea that we are all children of a loving divine parent without such a belief. Children are constantly asking for things, and on many if not most occasions parents think it right to give. In the end Wiles rejects such repeated acts of divine 'intervention', arguing in this section of his book that 'God is not the magician who adjusts the particularities of life at our request, but God is one whose loving presence has the power to transform our experience of every eventuality of life.'

Such vague notions of a 'loving presence' will not, in my view, do. Wiles has seen the nature of the problem more clearly than he has seen the solution. There are enormous difficulties in seeing God as a loving parent of any kind. It is not hard to see what they are.

Without denying the complexity of child-rearing and the abundance of theories about it, there is no doubt that human parents combine allowing their children a measure of freedom with frequent and necessary acts of interference. No parent allows a toddler to discover the danger of eating anything it can lay its hands on, but they might later allow a greedy child to eat himself or herself sick. There eventually comes a point where the child is entering adulthood and acts of interference cease. Until then there is a judicious mix of allowing children to find out for themselves what is undesirable and denying them the chance to do so. In the case of God, however, there is a question about both whether these acts of 'intervention' take place at all and, if they do, why they take place on the occasions they do.

Indeed many people would argue that this sort of analogy simply won't do on any reading of either the natural or the human world and the endless tragedies that mark their course. God neither looks after the birds nor after human beings with the sort of protective care which human beings show towards their offspring. To suppose that God does is the worst form of sentimental presumption. If we really suppose that God acts towards us as a father does towards his children, then it is difficult to see how, given the level and extent of human suffering during the last century alone, God could measure up even to the worst examples of fatherly neglect and abandonment (see Puccetti 1967 for further discussion).

The Limits to our Knowledge of God

Seeing the difficulty involved in explaining how God behaves towards us like a loving parent, we might wish to argue instead that we cannot explain God's behaviour towards us at all. We could say instead that we have to accept our creaturely ignorance. Like Job, we can repent of our presumption in trying to assess the ways of God (see chapters 39–42). After all, we tend to accept the majesty and incomprehensibility of God where the 'natural' qualities of the Deity are concerned, so why not with the moral categories? Why not say that we can no more get a handle on God's goodness than God's infinity? Can we not, as in Kierkegaard's interpretation (2001) of the parable of Abraham and Isaac, be prepared to say that God's will must be followed even when it flies in the face of all our moral instincts?

But can this wriggling out of the problem through humility in the face of God's majesty be acceptable? Can we be so ignorant of God's love or goodness that we have no clear idea as to whether they are more accurate descriptions of God's nature than hatred or evil? Can we, just because God's transcendent and infinite being exceeds our understanding, be uncertain as to whether we are dealing with a loving father or a cosmic sadist? It is precisely these questions which make the doctrine of the Incarnation so important to Christianity, for it is so much easier to say that Jesus was a 'good' man (in a sense that we can recognize) than to say that God is good. Though Jesus of Nazareth is said to have replied to someone who addressed him as 'Good master' with the words 'Why do you call me good? One only is good, God alone' (Mark 10:17–18), we might feel that it is far harder to see why God is good than why Jesus was. A theology which insists that we must derive our understanding of God from the nature of Christ at least has the merit of establishing the moral qualities of the Deity, which might otherwise be unrecognizable. It does, however, encounter other difficulties that all such 'orthodox' Christologies encounter – some of which I consider in Chapter 10.

I would argue that a form of agnosticism is the only way of dealing with the problem of evil. We cannot claim to understand, when observing the world, how

God behaves like a loving parent – God patently does not. I am assuming here that we cannot go down the path of blaming the Devil, that useful counterpart to 'the good God' who can take the blame for all that is bad in the world. We have to say that God made the world, sanctions and tolerates much of its suffering and treats us in a way that we'd never apply to our own children. In the general process of reaching for metaphors, we can call God 'father' or even 'dad'; but there is a danger in doing so. Words like 'father' and 'love' and 'goodness' seem accessible and comprehensible when compared to a word like 'infinite'; yet unless there is an infinite quality to God's love and fatherhood, in other words unless these terms apply to God in a quite different sense to that in which they apply to ourselves, then they only mislead us. If God was a father in human terms, his children would need to be taken into care.

Precisely because of the dangers involved in affirming a 'solution' to the problem of evil, John Roth remarks, in his contribution to *Encountering Evil*, that 'increasingly I understand my position to be one that protests against theodicy itself' (2001: 4). His reaction to Auschwitz may be compared to Alyosha's reaction when confronted by Ivan's list of human atrocities in Dostoevsky's *The Brothers Karamazov*. Alyosha, it is important to remember, declares that he would *not* consent to create a world if one tiny creature (a child) had to be tortured to death in the process. Alyosha's faith is based upon trust in a God who understands things that we don't. It is not based upon a claim to be able to perceive exactly why the world is being created and sustained in the way it is.[8]

In the view of Roth, any response to evil that claims to understand how it could be part of a 'greater good' is unacceptable. As he puts it, 'to suggest that there could be no adequate display of human virtue – or no sufficient glory in heaven – without such testing odds [as incarceration in death camps] … well, that proposition mocks the victims far more than it honours them' (Roth 2001: 10). The only way to honour the child torn to pieces by hounds for the pleasure of his persecutors is to deny any understanding of how a world which allowed such suffering could be permitted. So far as the form of 'protesting theodicy' which he commends is concerned, 'no good that it can envision, on earth or beyond, is worth the freedom – enfeebled and empowered – that wastes so much life' (Roth 2001: 10–11). A similar outlook can be discerned in Ulrich Simon's *A Theology of Auschwitz*, where he declares that 'Auschwitz discloses that the human condition is incomprehensible and insoluble in merely human terms' (1979: 27).

On the other hand, we find Roth in *Encountering Evil* challenging David Ray Griffin's contribution to the book. Griffin questions the traditional Christian understanding of creation as of 'ex nihilo' (out of nothing). Instead he introduces the notion of a permanent constraint upon God's creative activity exercised by the nature of the material with which God has to deal. Indeed it was precisely this that encouraged the doctrine to emerge in the first place; even a master craftsman is constrained by what can be done with the stuff he is dealing with. A creator forming a world 'out of nothing', however, is subject to no such limitations (of course there were other impulses behind the formulation of the doctrine too, such as the notion that matter must have a beginning). Roth challenges Griffin's argument, however, by suggesting that his God is 'too small' – 'This god inspires too little awe, little sense of holiness' (Davis 2001: 128). Roth prefers a God who is responsible for the evil of the world and can be the object of protest to a God who can slide away under the cover of limited power. Something of a similar sentiment can be discerned in a maverick work by R.C. Zaehner, *Our Savage God* (1974).

Roth refuses the two obvious means by which God might be 'exonerated' in terms of the existence of evil. Both of them limit God's power – either in terms of God's adversary the Devil 'gumming up the works', or in terms of the difficulty God faces in creating a world, the constraints upon the divine hand imposed by the material God has to deal with. This will not do, for Roth. He would rather sweep away all 'excuses' and make his protest before the God he is prepared to challenge, the God he can only continue to love and worship if he is able also to shake his fists at the Deity who permitted Auschwitz.

Theodicy and SDA

I want to conclude by suggesting three things about a theodicy that may help to find a place for special acts of God.

First, the Christian doctrine of the 'Fall' is not an explanation of why there is evil in the world. Exonerating God by blaming Satan only raises the question of how Satan could have been permitted by God (the old conundrum of a God at once all-good and all-powerful). Blaming the first pair for our suffering fails too; what sense would it make to say that God was justified in punishing us for the sins of people whose decisions we could never have influenced? These are arguments which have been pursued along a well-worn track, and they do not represent a helpful manner of understanding the Fall. The doctrine is important for other reasons; it introduces a note of realism into our understanding of human nature, which can both reach the heights and plummet the depths, and it stresses, through the idea of banishment, that distance is established between God and the human person. This distance caps our understanding of God and limits God's presence.

Second, I have suggested that the Fall, and the distance it sets between ourselves and God, puts limits both upon God's knowledge of us and upon our knowledge of God. Where God's knowledge of us is concerned, I have suggested that it is a part of the logic of creation (which the Fall arguably helps to express) that a God who wills not to determine the outcome of God's act in creating cannot foreknow that outcome. I have tried to suggest three models of God's relation to the human creature, and it is noticeable that of the three models offered, those that accentuate human freedom to respond to and reject God are precisely the models that allow room for divine intervention.

Where the limits placed by the Fall upon our knowledge of God are concerned, I have taken the view that there is suffering whose place in God's 'overall design' we cannot understand. I have argued that this is a much more appropriate response to the problem of evil than various attempts to find a 'scheme of things' in which God is teaching us endurance through pain or how to face the 'challenges' of life. We cannot explain the 'problem of evil' in terms of the 'tough love' of a parent. To try to second-guess the divine intention and ask why an intervention comes 'here' and not 'there' is impossible.

Third, the argument that a God who would change water into wine whilst leaving millions to die in Auschwitz is so totally unjustifiable that it is better to ban miracles altogether presupposes that a God who never does anything is any more justifiable. I do not see that a permanently neglectful God is any less of a cosmic sadist than an idly tinkering God. The idea that Auschwitz means an end to miracles won't work. A God without SDA is no better than a God with SDA. A God who never acts is as much to be condemned as a God who acts at the wrong time.

At the end of the last chapter I suggested that the scientist-theologians tend to underplay the significance of the Fall. There is a sense in which the scientist-theologians, so used to discerning breathtaking patterns of ongoing creative accomplishment in the physical universe, dislike the broken, patternless forms that appear once we try to take account of evil in the world and all our notions of 'design' (God the father caring for us, God the teacher educating us, God the mother rearing us) break down. But break down they do. The doctrine of the Fall prepares us for that.

My conclusion is that before we insist that God cannot possibly 'intervene' anywhere when so much suffering has been left untouched, we should consider exactly what a miracle is meant to be. I am not referring here to the problems about making sense of special divine actions, though I am aware of the fact that they still represent an unsolved problem. I am referring to that element which some commentators have stressed as the most important and even defining characteristic of a miracle, namely its religious significance. A miracle is not like a birthday present, giving you 'something you need'. It is an act of power, a demonstration of God's awful love and an invitation to be embraced by it. I have already suggested through the comparison between 'interventions' in nature and in human history that in the case of the latter God can 'intervene' in order to teach us something, to point to a better way of living, an approach that does not make sense in the context of relieving animal suffering. But this means that divine 'intervention' may not necessarily come at the point where our suffering is greatest. The idea that God performing a miracle is akin to a United Nations intervention force going in to end a brutal dictatorship is as ineffective as any other 'explanation' as to why God acts in the world.

Roth is the harshest of all critics of a theodicy. He ends up with an 'anti-theodicy', protesting against God. But at least his God is not too small. He refuses to put his faith in the tame little deities that supposedly keep us in their loving care. By having a God 'big' enough to protest against, Roth makes room for miracles as actions which are not there to justify God, to 'prove' that, after all, God is on the side of good against evil, but rather to make God's power manifest in the world.

This raises the question of why miracles take place, and in order to discuss that I intend, in the second part of this book, to examine the role of miracles within the Christian tradition. In the first three chapters I shall examine the miracles of Jesus and then the miracles of earlier and later periods in the history of Christianity. In the two subsequent chapters I will examine the central Christian miracle of resurrection. The final part of the book will then return to the issue of 'acts of God' in the context of examining miracles in other religious traditions and in the modern world.

Notes

1   The two schools identified by Hick are associated, as the names suggest, with Augustine of Hippo and Irenaeus.
2   It seems reasonable, in the context of reading the whole chapter, to identify Hebblethwaite's view with that of the 'believer' in the dialogue. See also the interesting collection of articles edited by Pinnock (1994), particularly that of Richard Rice, 'Biblical Support for a New Perspective'.
3   Hall supports this criticism of those who believe in the possibility of a pain-free world in which everyone 'as a matter of fact' only chooses the good. But I would argue that the fact God cannot create a world in which all automatically choose the good illustrates that God cannot create a world in which God knows in advance what people will choose.
4   As the example of Hebblethwaite shows, it is possible to adopt a radical position on the need to recognize how far God has chosen to limit divine power and knowledge in order to respect human freedom, whilst maintaining a 'conservative' view of specific divine actions. Another interesting example of this combination would be the Catholic philosopher Peter Geach (1969 and 1977), though his acceptance of SDA goes much further than Hebblethwaite's.
5   Note too Nicholas Saunders' apt summary of Maurice Wiles' outlook:

> Throughout Wiles' work we see a theologian grappling to come to terms with the evil in the world and one of the results this has had is a straight denial of SDA.
>
> (2002: 24)

6   C.S. Lewis discusses this notion of God 'predetermining the weather at Dunkirk' in his work *Miracles* ([1947] 2002), originally written in 1947 shortly after the end of the war. It is natural enough that this idea would have appealed to people still rejoicing at their victory after a long struggle. Yet to read Lewis suggesting that in predetermining such weather God 'must be supposed … to have taken into account the effect it would have not only on the destiny of two nations but (what is incomparably more important) on all the individuals involved on both sides' does raise the question starkly about God's failure to 'predetermine', for instance, Hitler's position in relation to the bomb which nearly took his life in 1944. See the discussion in the Appendix to *Miracles*, pp. 283–5.
7   Even David Brown remarks that one is led to doubt the historicity of Jesus' miraculous transformation of water into wine because 'it flies in the face of the type of God revealed elsewhere, where miracles exhibit some deep pastoral concern' (1985: 65).

However, the problem is not just that some miracles do not seem to reflect such 'deep concern'; it is that (assuming there are indeed some miracles) the absence of miracles at times of great need and suffering may also point to a lack of 'deep pastoral concern'.

8   See the useful discussion of Dostoevsky's book in Hebblethwaite (2000), p.68.

PART II
MIRACLES IN HISTORICAL PERSPECTIVE

Chapter 6

The Miracles of Jesus

At the end of the last chapter I argued that miracles are not to be seen as actions to relieve the worst of the world's suffering in areas where human need is (judged by us to be) greatest. They are not the equivalent of a UN intervention force. Rather, they are linked to a specific religious purpose and cannot be separated from that. I propose now to look at the Christian tradition in some detail in order to illustrate this point.

Undertaking any kind of analysis in the huge realm of biblical studies can seem a nightmare for anyone who is aware of the amount of writing in the area and (in this case) his ignorance of so much of it. Nevertheless an attempt to interpret the miracle stories associated with Jesus of Nazareth is unavoidable in any work claiming to be focused on the Christian tradition. Such an enterprise can hardly escape the charge of naivety, but it can at least try to achieve clarity and a consistent position.

The Justification of a Selective Approach

It seems to me that a selective approach in interpreting the miracles of Jesus is unavoidable. By 'a selective approach' I mean one which argues that some of the miracle stories about Jesus describe special acts of God and some of them do not. There is a further question as to whether the biblical authors *intended* these miracles to be understood as special acts of God. I would suggest that in some cases they did not. Though it would be a mistake to think that the biblical authors were simply writing 'legends' or 'literary fictions', it would also be wrong to think that they were simply recounting facts in a courtroom.[1] Indeed the problem with a lot of 'conservative' biblical scholarship is that it refuses to practise exegesis in the manner of the biblical writers themselves. If the original authors did not intend to refer to a special act of God when writing a miracle story, then a 'fundamentalist' exegete who insists that they did is not being faithful to the text.[2]

It will be noted that I do not say that some of the miracle stories are to be understood 'literally' when I say that they describe special acts of God. This is because, somewhat paradoxically, some of the most 'conservative' or 'fundamentalist' writers on the miracle stories of Jesus end up denying their character as miracles. They point out that some reputable scientist has shown that sandbanks on the sea of Galilee were a common phenomenon, thus 'explaining' Jesus walking on the water, or that sudden squalls often erupted and disappeared there at a moment's notice, thereby 'explaining' the stilling of the storm. These 'fundamentalist' exegetes have as their primary concern what they see as the infallibility of the biblical text. If in order to preserve the text they have to jettison the miracle, then this is a price worth paying. The miracles simply become instances of strange geological and meteorological phenomena which are presumably exploited by Jesus in order to trick or impress his audience.[3] Hence understanding a miracle story 'literally' does not necessarily involve believing that it describes a miracle.

A selective approach which believes that some of the miracle stories describe special acts of God and some do not must offer one or more criteria for distinguishing between the two. In the pages that follow I shall consider some of these criteria.

It might be said that there is one way of avoiding a selective approach and that is to understand *all* the miracle stories in the New Testament or Greek Bible as referring to special acts of God. I have already suggested that such an understanding conforms more to the assumptions of the exegete than to the intentions of the biblical writer, but there is another reason for questioning it. It seems to me that even *this* approach is selective. It is selecting those miracles of Jesus which are affirmed in the New Testament, in other words in the particular selection of texts which the church first recognized as constituting an authoritative canon in the fourth century CE.

Thus it is doubtful whether someone who wanted to take every miracle story about Jesus as referring to a special act of God would not hesitate at the miracles, for instance, associated with Jesus in the *Infancy Gospel of Thomas*, where as a precocious 5-year-old he is angered by a child who bangs into his shoulder, tells him 'You shall go no further on your way' and the child drops down dead.[4] The dead child's parents complain to Joseph, telling him that unless he can teach his child 'to bless and not to curse' he will have to take his family away from the village, because Jesus 'is killing our children'. Joseph tries to admonish his son, but to no effect. Instead all those who spoke against the child are blinded. 'Every word he speaks, whether good or evil, happens and is a miracle' comment those who see what is happening. Joseph, however, reacts by pulling his son's ear, after which he is perhaps fortunate to receive only a verbal reprimand.

The boy is then taken over by one Zaccheus, who sees that he is 'a smart child'. Zaccheus tries to teach him but finds that the boy is already so advanced that he cannot understand his speech. He asks Joseph to take him back, 'for I cannot bear the severity of his glance'. 'This child is not earthborn', he comments. Reading this text, we may well agree, but the Jesus of this narrative appears more like the child Damian in *The Omen* than the Son of God.

Though the formation of the Christian canon was a long and complex process involving a range of considerations, it is difficult to believe that the exclusion of the *Infancy Gospel of Thomas* didn't have something to do with a desire not to select these particular miracle stories for the canon, perhaps because they were regarded as morally offensive. In any case even a determined believer in an 'authentic miracle' associated with every single miracle story in the Bible has to recognize that the Bible itself is the product of a selection process.

Selection According to what is 'Morally Offensive'

The notion of what is 'morally offensive' is an important criterion which some use in order to judge whether a miracle story is 'authentic', by which I shall understand them to mean that it describes a special act of God. Take one of the best-known of Jesus' miracles, the turning of water into wine at the wedding in Cana-in-Galilee. This miracle is contained in only one gospel, that of John, and it clearly generates some discomfort among commentators, perhaps because it is not a response to sickness or suffering. Though it was taken up by some in later centuries as a model to be imitated (after his death Thomas Becket was credited with having changed water into wine three times at the Pope's table), it has struck many as almost flippant. Those who struggle with the occasions when a special act of God has been apparently absent (for instance during the slow grind of attempted mass extermination of the Jews and others during the Second World War) do not like to affirm that on an occasion like this the hand of God was not stayed.

We therefore see a possible principle of selectivity coming into focus, namely the idea that a miracle story can refer to a special act of God if it is not offensive to a sense of human decency. Consider, for instance, an old but still widely quoted work, Alan Richardson's *The Miracle Stories of the Gospels* (1941). When he turns to this particular miracle he remarks that 'the difficulty of believing that St. John intended us to take it literally is … its somewhat unreasonable character'. Richardson tells us to 'face the fact' that 'to create such a quantity of good wine when men have drunk freely is hardly an act of common sense'. He therefore embraces an interpretation in which the passage illustrates that Judaism 'must be purified and transformed in order to find its fulfilment in Christ', and links the miracle to sayings in the synoptic gospels about not putting new wine into old wineskins (1941: 121–2).

The interesting thing about Richardson's approach is the preparedness to judge whether or not a miracle story refers to a special act of God in terms of whether it appeals to our 'common sense'. He thinks that the miracle at Cana-in-Galilee does not so appeal, and thus is ready to embrace an interpretation which does not understand the miracle as referring to a special act of God. Such an approach is of course controversial. Some would see it as a clear attempt to thrust forward fallible human moral reasoning as a judge of what is theologically 'acceptable'.[5]

I have already questioned the idea that miracles occur simply where human need is greatest. For that reason I would be suspicious of arguments which seek to assess the credibility of miracles on the basis of 'how much good' they do. Nevertheless, Richardson does provide a criterion for distinguishing between the various miracle stories.

Selecting According to the Author's Intention

Another criterion is far more complicated, and it is unavoidable that a great deal of very sophisticated biblical criticism must be simplified in making it. It is illustrated clearly enough by Richard Swinburne in *The Resurrection of God Incarnate* where he comments:

> It is not always clear when he [the author of John's gospel] is seeking to recount history and when he is telling a story with no historical basis solely to make a theological point.
>
> (2003: 81)

I have deliberately used the words of a philosopher of religion, who is likely to express himself in ways that the biblical critic may find naive. Yet it seems to me that Swinburne's point is useful. I have already suggested that it would be a gross misunderstanding of the literary traditions of the first century to suppose that the biblical writers felt compelled to write in the kind of literal manner that certain Protestant fundamentalists wish them to. There is also the danger of a patronizing assumption that as 'literal-minded primitives' the authors of the Greek Bible believed that everything they were writing was a straightforward exercise in 'giving the facts'.[6]

Swinburne sees no reason to suppose this. As an example he considers the man sitting beside the pool at Bethesda. Many invalids – blind, lame and otherwise disabled – lay among the colonnades beside this pool waiting for the annual event of the water being disturbed by the coming of an angel (the angel reference is only in some versions), after which the first person into the pool was healed. We are led to imagine a bizarre scrimmage among the disabled in order to be first into the water, in which those who were lame presumably lost out. The man Jesus encounters had been waiting his turn for 38 years.

This story is only found in John's gospel, so it is not case of multiple attestation. It is also, Swinburne suggests, highly symbolic, and can only rightly be understood in these terms. Thus the 38 years which the man has spent by the pool parallel the 38 years which the people of Israel spent in the wilderness before Joshua led them through the River Jordan to the promised land. Swinburne (2003: 74) is prepared to believe that John wrote this story as a literary fiction in order to remind his readers of the parallel between the Jews finding the promised land through the Jordan and the followers of Jesus finding salvation through baptism. No miraculous healing of a paralysed man need have taken place, nor need the author of the gospel have intended his readers to interpret him in that manner.

Swinburne offers a similar interpretation of what is perhaps the most famous healing miracle of all, the raising of Lazarus. Once again he reads the text in terms of a carefully crafted symbolism, through which the story of Lazarus is intended to throw light on Jesus' resurrection. To give an example which Swinburne doesn't develop here, Lazarus comes out of the tomb bound in graveclothes. This symbolizes the fact that he is merely resuscitated and will die again. He is brought back to this life. When Jesus leaves the empty tomb, on the other hand, the graveclothes are neatly folded in the corner. This symbolizes the fact that unlike Lazarus he has not come back to have more life on earth and then die again. He has been 'glorified'. His body is a glorified body which will never die again, unlike that of Lazarus. The 'binding' with graveclothes in the one case, and the fact that they are left behind in the other, illustrates a theological point about the difference between Lazarus *redivivus* and Jesus risen from the grave.

Swinburne is perfectly entitled to say that some of the miracle stories in the fourth gospel are 'fictions making theological points'. He is also entitled to remind us that even though these stories may have been consciously framed as fictions (and John himself refers to the miracles as 'signs', 'semeia', as if their significance lies in something else that they point to rather than what they are in themselves), they might nevertheless illustrate how John came to understand the life of Jesus. Furthermore, even as what Swinburne terms 'fictions' or 'parables', they help us to understand more about the character and beliefs of Jesus as a historical figure.

Swinburne admits that such an approach is another form of selectivity. He also admits that it does not always provide a clear way of telling whether the miracle story is to be understood as referring to a special act of God. There are times when it does. Swinburne clearly states that there are times when 'the literal sense has priority' (2003: 79), and by 'literal sense' I understand him to mean 'referring to a special act of God'. Otherwise it would be difficult to see, for instance, the force of Swinburne's quoting Josephus' comment upon Jesus as a 'doer of startling deeds' (2003: 85) Professor Swinburne is clear that 'The Gospels abound with stories of miracles (in some sense) – so many that it would be totally implausible to suppose that they have no historical basis' (2003: 85). He is therefore prepared to say that there are some miracle stories which are to be interpreted as referring to special acts of God, some which are literary fictions and some where it is unclear which camp to place them in. Such an approach might be seen as 'complicated' or 'messy' by some, but I see no reason to suppose that it is intrinsically implausible.

Swinburne's selectivity is based on something different from what I have called the 'sense of decency' that causes Professor Richardson to draw back from the idea of Jesus miraculously producing more wine for people who have already had enough. It involves considerations such as whether there are parallel accounts in other gospels and/or whether it is clear that the details are constructed for a theological purpose. It is arguable the the broad range of biblical scholars operate using criteria such as those of Swinburne, obviously in a more sophisticated manner than he or I could do, but nevertheless broadly in agreement that there are ways of determining which accounts of miracles are to be understood as referring to special acts of God and which are not.

Denying Any Special Acts of God – Morton Smith

There is one interesting approach to the miracles of Jesus which denies altogether that any miracle story can be referring to a special act of God. It is adopted by Morton Smith in his controversial *Jesus the Magician* (1998). Because this book reaches a conclusion that is clearly incompatible with orthodox Christian belief, it has received short shrift from many Christian scholars. However, it deserves serious attention. I do not agree with Morton Smith's conclusions and I find some of his arguments bizarre, but I also think that there are many reasons for giving his work careful consideration.

Morton Smith pictures Jesus of Nazareth as a healer who is a trained magician, one who has 'qualified' in Egypt (he sees this as the reason for the story of the holy family's flight into Egypt in Matthew 2:19–21) and returns to his native land, possibly tattooed with magical charms. Hence Paul's reference to 'bearing the marks of Jesus branded on my body' in Galatians 6:17, which Smith (1998: 62) suggests are the same magical markings as Jesus carried on his own body.[7]

To continue with Morton Smith's account. Jesus has by now been through the strict regime of self-torture required of any shaman at the beginning of his career (Jesus' days in the wilderness before his 'ministry' begins) and has received a spirit as his constant companion, someone whom he can order about in order to effect cures without elaborate rites (Jesus' baptism by the holy spirit). He then sets about gathering followers. In the process he not only rejects his own family but encourages others to do the same. In Mark 3:31–4, when there is a crowd around him, he is told that his mother and brothers could not get through the mêlée to reach him. He merely indicates his disciples and says 'These are my mother and my brothers.' Such actions make him understandably unpopular in his home town, leading to the reflection that 'a prophet is without honour in his own country'.

The spellbinding force of Jesus' charisma works its effect on those he encounters. Fishermen 'drop their nets' (that is, abandon their livelihoods) in order to follow him and be 'fishers of men'. One man even leaves his father unburied in order to join the group. Jesus then initiates the disciples into 'the mystery of the kingdom', which they learn as insiders whilst to all others the truth can only be made known in parables (Mark 4:33–4). Jesus' ministry (or the life of a travelling magician and vagrant performer who earns his daily bread from his 'act') then begins with a number of healings and exorcisms (where according to standard magical practice he makes devils utter his name). As his fame spreads far and wide the magician-god unites his followers to himself by giving them his body and blood to be eaten and drunk (the rite of the eucharist). In the end he is killed, but his devoted and entranced followers are by then psychologically primed for seeing him 'rise from the dead' and for continuing his work.

Having produced his interpretation of Jesus' career, Smith then compares him to other wonder-workers of the period. Was there some difference in kind between the magician Jesus and other magicians? Morton Smith thinks not. Some commentators have looked for differences in the way Jesus heals – for instance, it is argued that he does not accompany his exorcisms with 'magical formulas' or religious incantations. But Smith counters that there are many parallels between Jesus' techniques and those of other 'magicians'. The use of touch, particularly the idea of conveying healing through being touched, the use of saliva in healing (for instance the healing of the deaf man in Mark 7:33–5), the use of words in a special language at the moment of healing (for example the Aramaic word

'Ephphatha' in the case of the deaf man, or the Aramaic phrase 'talitha cum' spoken to Jairus' daughter in Mark 5:41) were all well-known techniques employed by magicians. Reviewing descriptions of Jesus from sources outside the New Testament, Smith points to the *Dialogue with Trypho*, in which the second-century writer Justin puts into the mouth of Trypho the claim that Christianity was 'a godless and libertine heresy' which had 'arisen from a certain Jesus, a Galilean magician'. Presumably, argues Smith, the Christian Justin was faithfully putting into the mouth of Trypho a common perception about Jesus of Nazareth.

Smith also examines the claim that Jesus is different to other wonder-workers less because of his methods of healing than because the miracles are never all that he does. He is also significant as a teacher – in the New Testament, as we have seen, the teaching of Jesus and the miraculous deeds are very often bracketed together. Exorcists were not usually talented teachers, and it is the combination of the two which, it is claimed, sets Jesus apart from other healers of his time. Luke's gospel in particular stresses that the crowds who in Mark flock to Jesus for healing come 'to hear him and to be healed of their diseases' (Mark 3:8–11, cf. Luke 6:17). Yet Smith also denies that Jesus is unique in being both miracle-worker and teacher and gives examples of others, like Apollonius of Tyana, who combined the two roles.

Morton Smith's analysis rules out the possibility of understanding Jesus' miracles as 'special acts of God'. Therefore Jesus' success as a healer must have come from his power as a magician or at least as some kind of charismatic individual. Smith thinks that this is a perfectly plausible conclusion. How convincing is such an argument?

It is important to recognize that Jesus lived in a world without hospitals, without modern medicine and without anything like universal provision of whatever 'medicine' was available. In such an environment any itinerant healer would attract interest and, if moderately successful, a following (I examine this in Chapter 8 in connection with the early modern period, which has been brilliantly analysed by Keith Thomas in his *Religion and the Decline of Magic* (1973)).

How would he have approached the work of healing? Almost certainly Jesus, like his contemporaries, thought of illnesses in terms of 'possession' by evil spirits. This would even be so where the illness was physical. In Luke 13:11 a woman who has curvature of the spine is described as having 'a spirit' and Jesus describes her as having been 'bound for eighteen long years' by Satan (Luke 13:16). In many passages of the New Testament Jesus appears to be 'angered' when he finds people sick, as if he is encountering a hostile power. This is probably the right translation of the word 'enebrimesato' in John 11:33 (though the RSV says he is 'greatly disturbed'), during the story of the raising of Lazarus. In the Lucan story of Jesus healing Simon's mother-in-law he 'rebukes' the fever (Luke 4:39 – and some commentators prefer to translate 'epitaman' as 'subjugate'), and even in Mark 1:41, where Jesus is usually described as being 'moved by compassion' when healing a leper, some ancient manuscripts have the word 'angered'. Jesus would have believed, like others in his day, that not only mental but also physical diseases could be seen in terms of being taken over by evil powers, and that he was therefore confronting them even when curing a fever or leprosy. 'Healings' were the outcome of a contest between good and evil powers.[8]

Though such a view of illness is often interpreted today as evidence of 'credulity', such an accusation would be unfair. Before modern medicine could explain disease in terms of viruses and bacteria, the idea that it represented a takeover of the body by 'foreign powers' was as plausible an explanation as any other. Nor is the idea that Jesus shared such an assessment problematic for most theologians. They would agree that he shared the intellectual outlook of his day.

Given this assessment of the presumptions about disease in his day, which we may presume Jesus shared, how did his healings work? For Morton Smith it is not difficult to accept that as a charismatic figure Jesus might have effected the sort of cures that contemporary medicine acknowledges in terms of the power of 'mind over matter'. Success of this sort would also tie in with the demand that those who are cured should have faith or believe ('pistis', 'pisteuein'). In most (but not all) of his cures Jesus demands faith from the person who is cured. In the Matthaean version of the Syro-Phoenician woman who cajoles Jesus into curing her daughter, Jesus makes clear that it is the woman's faith that overcomes his resistance (Matthew 15:28). In many other passages 'faith' is the key ingredient in recovery. Even the woman with a haemorrhage who touches him in a crowd and is immediately healed is told that it is her 'faith' which has cured her (Mark 5:34). And to return to the story of the Pool of Bethesda which was described at the beginning of this chapter, it is noteworthy that Jesus' first question to the sick man is 'Do you want to be made well?' (John 5:6) – in other words the patient *wanting* to recover is an essential ingredient in being able to effect a cure.

On the other hand, in places where Jesus can do few 'mighty works' (for instance his own neighbourhood) it is the lack of belief that he identifies as the cause (Mark 6:5–6). Morton Smith makes much of this failure to perform when Jesus returns to his home town, and sees these passages as a further indication of the faith healer's dependence on faith in order to be able to achieve results. Thus where a more orthodox interpretation might think of faith as something rewarded by God with a special act of healing, Morton Smith sees it more as a necessary condition of the healer's having any power to heal.

Critics of Morton Smith concede that this approach might explain at least some of the healing miracles in the gospels, though it is difficult to say exactly what diseases Jesus treated. In many cases there is a lack of clarity about what exactly the sufferer had (does 'lepros', for instance, necessarily mean what we mean today by 'leprosy'?) and there is often uncertainty about whether the illness was physical or mental or both. But what about all the other miracles which are part of the 'repertoire' of Jesus' miracle-working career? How are we to understand the nature miracles, for instance, like stilling the storm or walking on water? Even where healing miracles are concerned, can Jesus' charismatic power as a healer account for his bringing dead people like Lazarus or Jairus' daughter back to life? And what about the resurrection of Jesus himself?

Clearly anyone who takes Morton Smith's position, arguing that Jesus' reputation as a miracle-worker was based upon his powers as a magician, will judge which miracles are 'authentic' on that basis. Thus we find Smith in *Jesus the Magician* arguing that reports of multiplying food or walking on water are 'obvious inventions' (p. 196), that resurrections from death, like Jairus' daughter, must have been cases of 'hysterical coma' (p. 156) if they occurred at all, that seeing Jesus transfigured was 'a magical seance' which ends abruptly when a disciple talks and 'the spell is broken by an inauspicious act' (p. 161) and that his rising from the dead was a case of hallucination ('Jesus' resurrection, ascension and miscellaneous post-resurrection activities belong to the psychopathic histories of his disciples' – p. 183). But advancing a criterion on the basis of which to justify a selective approach which claims that some miracle stories are 'authentic' and others are not is, as we have seen, a necessary part of biblical exegesis. Morton Smith acts in a manner that is in principle no different from that of any other biblical commentator.

Morton Smith also claims to see in the later development of Christianity an attempt to suppress its 'magical' roots. He writes:

> the reader of the gospels must keep in mind that the gospels were written in a hostile world to present the Christian case. Consequently, elements in them that could be used to support the charge of magic are probably only the tips of the iceberg of suppressed traditions, while elements that counter the charge must be viewed with suspicion as probably exaggerated, if not wholly invented, for apologetic purposes.
>
> (1998: 123)

Naturally such an approach has to be treated with suspicion. To reduce the argument to a *reductio ad absurdum* – if the gospels are full of 'magical' activity, they prove that Jesus was a magician; if they are devoid of 'magical' activity, it proves that Jesus was a magician but they were trying to hide the fact. But once again it is not uncommon to find more orthodox scholars claiming to unearth older traditions about Jesus which they believe represent an 'original' account that has later been marginalized as inappropriate to the needs of the early church (for instance on the question of how Jesus was tried and condemned, whether he claimed to be the Messiah or what were the nature of his relations with the Pharisees). It is not in itself an unreasonable thing to do, once it is admitted that in the development of Christian tradition there has been embellishment and even the suppression of material.

The Significance of Morton Smith's Approach

Morton Smith's book is idiosyncratic, and I think that a number of readers will find it odd that it has been accorded so much space here, particularly in view of the fact that I disagree with its conclusions. The reason, paradoxically, is that in two important ways I find the book refreshingly 'conservative'. For one thing it is committed to the idea that something of the 'Jesus of history' can be recovered from the documents available. It does not leave us stranded with the 'Christ of faith' behind whom there is apparently no way back to the original Jesus. This means that the church is not given carte blanche to proclaim the Christ it has created/received as the only Christ.

The second (to me) welcome aspect to Smith's approach is his conviction that the impact of Jesus cannot simply be explained in terms of his teaching. It must be seen in the light of his 'miraculous' healings too. Though Morton Smith denies that there is any real miracle in the sense of a special act of God (Jesus' healings, in his view, are psychosomatically induced), I believe that he builds up a more convincing portrait of Jesus of Nazareth than many other commentators, precisely because of his willingness to accept that Jesus' 'miracles' were central to his ministry.

He does not marginalize the miracles as a product of later 'mythologizing'; on the contrary, for Morton Smith it is the miracles that are revealed all the more clearly as central to Jesus' activity when demythologization has taken place. Compare the position of Bultmann in his famous essay 'New Testament and Mythology' (1972). It is Bultmann's conviction that 'the miracles of the new Testament have ceased to be miraculous', that it is impossible to defend their historicity and that 'it is impossible to use electric light and the wireless and to avail ourselves of modern medical and surgical discoveries, and at the same time to believe in The New Testament world of spirits and miracles' (1972: 5). In such circumstances, all Bultmann can do with the miracles is find a way of getting rid of them. They are shunted aside as part of the New Testament mythology which comes from 'Jewish apocalyptic and the Jewish redemption myths', and we end up with a 'kerygma' or essential preached message of Jesus that is little more than a generalized existentialism.

Morton Smith, on the other hand, does not shunt the miracle stories aside. Paradoxically, it is precisely his conviction that the miracles were *not* instances of 'supernatural intervention' that allows him confidently to place them at the centre of Jesus' ministry, where others in their embarrassment at the notion of such 'intervention' have sought to conceal or underplay them. It seems to me that in the two presumptions of his work, namely that it is essential to attempt to reconstruct, as best we can, the life and ministry of Jesus, and that when we do we find that the miracles were an essential part of that ministry, Morton Smith is absolutely right.

Miracles and the Social Teaching of Jesus

My own difficulty with Morton Smith is twofold, and I shall examine both aspects in the next two sections. In the first place I believe he underplays, not the fact that Jesus' teaching and miracles are interrelated, but the specific nature of Jesus' teaching, which is more connected with a transformation of society than he recognizes. I shall concentrate upon this objection in the present section.

Occasionally Smith makes a nod in the direction of what might be called Jesus' social teaching. *Jesus the Magician* mentions Lucian's comments on the 'credulous communism' of the Christians, for instance, (p. 72), and he accepts that they had an ideal of having all things in common (p. 86), but he clearly does not regard any of this as of fundamental importance. He is prepared to sum up Jesus' life as pictured by those who did not become his disciples as that of someone who 'formed a small circle of intimate disciples whom he taught to despise the Jewish law and practise magic' (p. 88). That Jesus might have been perceived as having a dangerously subversive social message is largely ignored; for precisely this reason, the charges of sorcery and magic are largely taken at face value by Morton Smith, rather than being seen as evidence of diversion from a more challenging message.

We can see this by examining an example of what I would consider to be Morton Smith at his most bizarre, the idea that in Galatians 6:17, when Paul is speaking of how he 'bears the marks of Jesus branded on my body', he is referring to a magical charm. Surely such a peculiar interpretation owes much to the failure to perceive how far the early followers of Jesus were likely to have suffered physical persecution for what were, after all, dangerous beliefs. Paul was himself dragged out of the city of Lystra, stoned and left for dead (Acts 14:19). He might well have thought of himself as sharing the scars of one who was scourged, beaten and slowly tortured to death. Too much of Morton Smith's analysis leaves out of consideration the social and political dimension to the tensions experienced by the early Christian community.

Ironically a very different approach can be considered which bears similarities with Morton Smith's approach in its rejection of the idea that miracles represent special acts of God, whilst offering a completely different criterion in terms of which to assess the healings and other miracle stories. This different approach is that of liberation theology. Whereas Morton Smith's Jesus the 'magician' cures the individual through his psychosomatic power, the liberationists' Jesus the 'revolutionary' cures society by 'raising its consciousness'.[9] The liberationists claim that Jesus announces a coming reversal of roles in society, where the poor are exalted and the rich brought low. The first will be last and the last will be first. Christ reaches out to the outcasts of society, the 'tax collectors and sinners'. Those who are 'possessed by unclean spirits', from this perspective, are those rejected by society, and Jesus, the 'friend of the poor and sinners', rejects their exclusion and welcomes them into the fold. His 'cures' are therefore a form of social acceptance. When in his parables Jesus talks of welcoming the lost (or prodigal) son or hunting for the lost coin (which a woman turns her house upside down in order to recover) or the lost sheep, he is talking of healing the divisions in society and restoring the health of the whole community. The liberation theologians link the cures to a general healing of society where Morton Smith links them to a specific healing of individuals.

To the liberation theologians, Jesus' resurrection is explained not through the idea that his disciples hallucinate his return from the dead (as Morton Smith avows), but through the idea that they commit themselves to the social revolution he proclaimed at the cost of his life. In either case, however, whether it be the hallucinations of Morton Smith's followers of the magician or the 'Che lives' convictions of Jesus' disciples according to a liberationist analysis, specific acts of God are ruled out.

However, there are problems with the liberationist approach too. It seems to me that a liberationist approach is in danger of denying the very practical realism which is at the heart of its approach to Scripture. Jesus, this approach emphasizes, tackles (to use modern jargon) issues of social inequality and exclusion. He does not simply speak in general terms of 'love' and 'reconciliation', but in practical terms of helping the poor and outcast. But precisely for this reason it is difficult to read the miracle stories as metaphors for overcoming prejudice or exclusion. If the healing of a leper means leaving him with his disease but ensuring that he is accepted by society, or if casting out demons means healing the rifts and tears in the social body, then a practical problem of being confronted by physical and mental illness is subsumed within a general point about building social harmony. Arguably this represents just the sort of departure from concrete need to abstract generalization that liberation theology wants to avoid.

Of course there is a clear linkage between the healing of individuals and the healing of the rifts in society. Healing someone on the sabbath is bound to be political as well as personal. But subsuming one within the other in order to avoid what liberation theologians might call 'the diversions of supernaturalism' would be strange, given the liberationists' own commitment to concrete need in particular cases. Practical measures to bring back to life a dead child may require a miracle, just as practical measures to end poverty may require a revolution (which, though it might itself be called a 'miracle', is within the realms of human possibility). The trouble with liberation theology is that when faced with a choice between believing in miracles and giving up its commitment to the practical, it is tempted to opt for the latter, not least because it sees belief in miracles as striking at the heart of other aspects of some liberation theology, such as the rejection of 'supernaturalism'.

What I am suggesting is that liberation theology does not adopt a practical approach to the miracle stories. The sick become people in need of acceptance rather than health, though the poor are always in need of more than understanding – they need practical things like a roof over their heads. In reality the poor may need shelter, but the blind also need to see, a leper needs to be able to use his limbs again and a young girl with irreversible brain damage needs a recreated body. Good news to the poor and acts of healing are often associated in the New Testament (for example Luke 7:21–2, where the disciples of John ask whether Jesus is the Messiah) but they cannot be equated with one another.

If this seems like a rejection of all that the theology of liberation has contributed to exegesis, it is not intended to be. Some exegesis practised by liberation theologians is crucial to understanding Jesus in his historical context, and like Morton Smith it is not afraid to attempt a historical reconstruction of Jesus' life and ministry. Some of its radical conclusions may be correct. The argument, for instance, that Jesus rejects the Roman economic system, based as it was on slavery and conquest, is a plausible one. The point that Jesus himself possesses no money (he asks for a coin in his famous challenge to the Pharisees concerning whose head is on a coin in Mark 12:15ff.), that the disciples are sent out without money (Mark 6:8), that food for the crowds is to be given, not bought (Mark

6:35–7), the moneychangers' tables are overturned (Mark 11:15) and the Messiah is betrayed for money (Mark 14:11) adds up to a demand that his followers distance themselves from the monetary system. It is arguable that in many areas of exegesis the sharply practical and historical focus of the theology of liberation interprets the biblical narrative more convincingly than other forms of interpretation.[10] But highlighting the sense in which Jesus rejects the 'Roman system' does not in itself rule out miraculous cures. The argument here is that the theology of liberation can present a gospel with a radical social message without sacrificing the 'metaphysical structures' which some, but not all, liberation theologians see as undermining that message.

Jesus' Reluctance to Work Miracles

A second significant failing of Morton Smith is his failure to recognize the significance of Jesus' refusal or reluctance to perform miracles on certain occasions, or else he misinterprets that reluctance. As a result he builds up a distorted picture of Jesus as a magician.

Jesus the Magician argues that material such as the temptation narratives in Matthew and Luke, where Jesus explicitly rejects the temptation to cast himself from the top of the temple and have his fall broken by angels, is later material designed to 'discredit the picture of "Jesus the magician"' (1998: 140). It is perhaps unavoidable that exegetes will describe passages that do not conform to their interpretative framework as 'later' material designed to discredit the 'correct' picture, but it seems to me that these passages are absolutely fundamental to Jesus' self-understanding.

Then there are the passages in which Jesus tells those whom he heals to tell nothing about what has happened to them. This, we are told by Morton Smith, is because sharing the experience may 'break the spell' in one who has been healed by means of psychosomatic manipulation and cause the sort of relapse that occurs when a demon returns with seven friends after having been expelled (Matthew 12:43ff.). The idea that proclaiming yourself healed could have the same effect as eating toffee with a newly crowned tooth might strike us as one of Morton Smith's bizarre moments. After all, the same restraining order is placed upon witnesses – for instance those who witness the raising of Jairus' daughter from the dead (Mark 5:43) and those who bring him a deaf mute to be healed (Mark 7:36). Finally, there are passages, such as Jesus' refusal to satisfy the Pharisees' demand for a sign, which receive no clear explanation from Morton Smith, but which I would like to suggest are central to understanding the basic 'kerygma' of the gospel.

Miracles and the Renunciation of Power

Let me at this point outline my own view concerning the miracle stories in order to defend this critique of Morton Smith. In doing so, however, I would like to stress again the aspect of Morton Smith which I so much appreciate. He recognizes that the miracle stories are of crucial significance to the gospel writers. They do not portray a teacher who occasionally performed miracles. The teaching and the miracles were both inextricably linked to the authority which Jesus claimed for himself as one sent from God.

Thus the (probably) oldest gospel, that of Mark, opens with Jesus being baptised by John, going into the wilderness and then arriving in Galilee preaching that the Kingdom of God was at hand. He collects disciples, enters the synagogue and teaches 'as one having authority', unlike the scribes. Immediately afterwards he cures a man with an 'unclean spirit' and everyone there is amazed at the fact that 'with authority he commands even the unclean spirits, and they obey him'. His authority is thereby linked both to his teaching and to the cures he effects. From this point his fame spreads throughout the region. By evening he has cured Simon's mother-in-law of a fever and 'the whole city' is at the door seeking cures from 'diseases' and 'demons'. The following morning he gets up long before dawn to find a quiet place in which to pray. But he is not left alone for long. 'Everyone is looking for you.' He explains that they have to move on to other places. He is soon preaching and 'casting out demons' in 'all the synagogues' of Galilee. Then he heals a leper and commands him to 'see that you say nothing to anyone'. He is simply to go to the high priest, show that he is clean and do what is necessary in order to be readmitted to society. But the leper disobeys. He tells everyone what has happened and before long Jesus can no more put in an appearance in towns. He stays outside in deserted places, but the crowds still flock to him 'from every direction'.[11]

This first chapter of Mark sets the tone for the whole gospel. Jesus of Nazareth moves from one place to another on a lightning tour. His ministry lasts barely three years. From the very beginning he is hounded by people seeking cures or teaching. In the very first chapter there is already a sense of the pressure exerted by his popularity. He rises early in order to pray alone; he refuses to stay in one place; he tries to tone down the effect of his miracles; he has to keep out of the towns. The pressure continues throughout the gospel. Unsurprisingly, he concentrates on priming the disciples who will continue his work after he has gone. He explains to them the teaching which others hear only in the form of parables (Mark 4:33–4), and he also passes on at least some of his powers as a miracle worker, giving them 'power over unclean spirits' (Mark 6:7).

Jesus withdraws to the desert and even to the sea (Mark 3:7), but the crowds never leave him alone. His disciples prepare a small boat so that he can avoid being crushed by the multitude, not least because of those seeking to touch him in order to be healed (Mark 3:9–10). The 'feeding of the five thousand' appears in the context of 'multitudes' seeing Jesus leaving for 'a deserted place' with his disciples and 'running there on foot from all the cities'. Eventually Jesus sends the multitude and the disciples away, retiring to pray. The following morning he appears to them walking on water, one of the few so-called 'nature miracles' in the gospels. Another miraculous feeding takes place three chapters later, once again with emphasis upon the crowds pushing in on Jesus.

The miracles continue while the gospel moves towards its climax and conflict grows with the authorities. Understanding the source of that conflict is itself a very large issue. We are told that the scribes and chief priests started to consider how to destroy him 'because all the people were astonished at his teaching' (Mark 11:18). But the miracles were also a source of controversy from early on, when we read that scribes coming down from Jerusalem claimed that 'by the ruler of demons he casts out demons' (Mark 3:22). Moreover the very existence of a large following for Jesus, which proved oppressive enough at times even for him, would also have presented a problem for the authorities of his day. Was this movement a potential threat to the established order? Could a rebellion break out? These fears would have been stoked by his teaching and his miracles alike. For both raised the same question about the legitimacy of traditional forms of power. In arguing with the Pharisees and scribes about eating bread with unwashed hands (Mark 7), Jesus contrasts the commandment of God with the tradition of men – the washing of pitchers and cups and so on (Mark 7:8–9). In the same way, Jesus behaves as a miracle worker as if the power to declare people healed was his (or God's working through him) rather than being strictly vested in the priesthood. His acts of healing, as much as his teaching, challenge the religious authority of the Temple and threaten the established order – sometimes directly, as when he heals a man with a withered hand on the sabbath (Mark 3:1–6). Both teaching and miracles effectively throw into question the essential mediating role of the religious hierarchy, whether as a source of doctrine, ritual or wonder-working.[12]

What I have tried to show in this brief survey of the first gospel is that to extract the miracles from the rest of the text as a superfluous piece of (supposedly later) mythological musing would be highly questionable. The miracles are part of what appears to attract Jesus' followers and to alienate his opponents. They are also inseparable from the rest of his ministry, specifically his teaching. To quote a famous saying found in Matthew and Luke (Matthew 12:28; Luke 11:20), 'If I by the finger of God cast out demons, then is the Kingdom of God come upon you.' But this is the point which I have been trying to stress in the context of ruling out miracles simply as a response to extreme need. They have a religious significance. Jesus works miracles because in him the Kingdom of God has arrived. As I pointed out in the first chapter, the New Testament stresses the religious significance of miracles as much as their dramatic effect – the wonder is also a sign. The placing of Jesus in Jewish tradition as its fulfilment is specifically connected to his miracles. When John the Baptist sends his followers to ask whether Jesus is 'the one who is to come' (the Messiah), the answer is that 'the blind receive their sight, the lame walk, the lepers are cleansed, the deaf hear, the dead are raised and the poor have the good news brought to them'. In other words the fulfilment of ancient hopes about the Messiah (see, for instance, Isaiah 29:18–19) lies in the miracles which are taking place all around them.

Now in the light of Morton Smith's approach, how can we integrate these passages into some general understanding of Jesus' ministry? As conflict with the religious authorities brews, and the Pharisees come seeking 'a sign from heaven', this is refused (Mark 8:11) because Jesus is not going to perform a miracle as a show of force to cow his opponents. This, I believe, is a fundamental principle of the gospel story, from the moment in the wilderness before his ministry begins, when Jesus is tempted by Satan to throw himself from the pinnacle of the temple in order to have the angels break his fall (Luke 4:9–10, Matthew 4:5–6), to the final self-renunciation of the cross at its end, where Jesus once again recalls the power of 'twelve legions of angels' to prevent his arrest (Matthew 26:53). Against Morton Smith's interpretation, I would argue that the authors of the gospels are aware that the renunciation of power is at the heart of their story. Their account is of someone who voluntarily submits to an excruciating death which he had the power to avoid. They know that for all the miracles they describe, their central character refuses to perform a miracle to save himself. Indeed he is himself taunted with this fact while he hangs on the cross. 'He saved others; he cannot save himself. Let the Messiah, the King of Israel, come down from the cross now, so that we may see and believe' (Mark 15:31–2).

The very core of what Paul calls Jesus' 'kenosis' (literally 'self-emptying', a voluntary surrender of power, see Philippians 2:5–11) lies in that refusal to come down from the cross and 'prove his credentials'. Instead the Christian must renounce power, take up his or her cross and 'die to live'. It would be inconceivable in this context to present miracles as a show of force by which to compel acceptance.

The Reluctant Miracle-Worker and the Reluctant Messiah

The gospel accounts of Jesus' miracles present them less as a deliberate policy of self-aggrandisement and more as an almost incidental part of his ministry, towards which he is moved by compassion or even persuasion. A woman touches him in a throng and involuntarily power 'goes out of him' (Mark 5:30–34). A Syro-Phoenician woman overcomes his initial reluctance and cajoles him into helping her daughter (Mark 7:25–9). In Luke's gospel the servant of the high priest, who has his ear cut off during the arrest of Jesus, receives it back again – 'Permit even this' (Luke 22:51). The miracles arise in the course of his ministry as a natural outcome of his dealings with men and women. They have no ulterior motive beyond providing a way of handling the specific situation he finds himself in. They are of enormous significance, for they proclaim the coming of the Messiah and his Kingdom, ('If I by the finger of God ...'), but they do not force anyone into that Kingdom and they are not 'staged' in order to convince people that it has arrived.

The miracles of Jesus can be compared to what Wilhelm Wrede ([1901] 1971) coined the 'Messianic secret'. Wrede calls attention to the apparent unwillingness of Jesus to proclaim himself publicly as the Messiah during the course of his ministry. He commands the demons who recognize him and call him 'the Holy One of God' or 'the Son of God' to be silent (Mark 1:24–5, 3:11–12) When he raises the question with the disciples, 'Who do men say that I am?', and Peter answers 'You are the Christ', Jesus 'strictly warns them to tell no one about him' (Mark 8:27–30). Such reticence may be explained by the fact that an early declaration that Jesus was the Messiah could have created more confusion than understanding. After all, it creates immediate confusion among the disciples themselves, the inner cabinet of Jesus' adherents. When he tells them that the Messiah must suffer, be rejected and be killed he is rebuked by Peter, to whom Jesus replies 'Get behind me, Satan. For you are not mindful of the thing of God, but the things of men' (Mark 8:31–3). Yet it is understandably hard for the disciples, who have witnessed miracles of healing and other displays of divine authority like the stilling of the storm or walking on water, to believe that one with such power can submit to the powerlessness of suffering and the cross. Only when it becomes clear after his arrest that this is the route Jesus is to take does he consider it possible openly to proclaim that he is the Messiah (Mark 14:61–2). He may have felt by then that his Messiahship could no longer be misunderstood, although much of the later history of the church might be said to show that it could be.

Jesus' reticence about his miraculous powers can be linked to his reticence about admitting that he was the Messiah. Both could lead to misunderstanding. The miracles would be seen as a divine show of force in which the man from Nazareth sweeps all before him. It has already been argued that the placing of Jesus in Jewish tradition as its fulfilment is specifically connected to his miracles. Earlier I pointed to the fact that when John the Baptist sends his followers to ask whether Jesus is 'the one who is to come' (the Messiah), the answer is that 'the blind receive their sight, the lame walk, the lepers are cleansed, the deaf hear, the dead are raised and the poor have the good news brought to them'. The fulfilment of ancient hopes about the Messiah lies in the miracles which are taking place all around them. But therein lay a potential source of misunderstanding. The miracles, it might be thought, demonstrated that Jesus as Messiah would trounce his enemies and rule in power.

There were traditions of a suffering Messiah whose power lay in self-sacrifice – there was even a tradition of a Messianic secret cited by Matthew 12:19 ('he will not wrangle nor cry out, nor will anyone hear his voice in the streets', citing Isaiah 42:2) – but these would not necessarily have been the first to be called to mind. The idea of a suffering, dying Messiah may have become the core of Christian belief, but in its time it was still – though scholars differ concerning to what extent – a surprising, if not a scandalous claim. The identification of Jesus as Messiah had to be released at the point where its meaning could not be misinterpreted. In this context the miracles were as much a potential source of misunderstanding as a proof of his authority.

I would therefore argue that far from wanting to use miracles to call attention to himself, as Morton Smith would have us believe, Jesus knows that they are a sign of the Kingdom which could easily lead to misunderstanding. In practical terms, he yields to the demands of those who need them and tries to prevent them adding to his difficulties. Few figures in history seem to have combined possessing such a mass following with being so thoroughly misunderstood. The crowds turn against him and taunt him, the disciples flee the scene, the one who first recognizes that he is the Christ denies him, he dies on the cross abandoned by them and even, in his own mind, by God himself – 'why have you forsaken me?' (Mark 15:34). It is hardly surprising that such a person might have been concerned about being misinterpreted. Those who ran after the source of power dispersed at the demands made by its voluntary renunciation. With such a message, miracles were dangerous things to place at the centre of his ministry.

They were also dangerous for another, very practical, reason. And here Morton Smith (1998: 53) is absolutely correct to emphasize the place of Jesus' miracles and the accusation that he was a magician (linked to the charge of false prophecy and possibly implied by the description of Jesus as a 'doer of evil' in John 18:28ff).[13] People who claimed to perform miracles would not only attract a following; they would also attract hostility. This is made clear at the start of Mark's gospel where Jesus is not only accused of himself possessing a demon or of 'casting out demons by the Prince of Demons' (Mark 3:22), but is said to be 'out of his mind' (Mark 3:21) and in need of being taken under the wing of his family, whom he apparently rejects (Mark 3:31–5). In his own neighbourhood, as we have already noted, he was rejected as an upstart whose claim to perform 'mighty works' were a way in which he rose above his station as a poor provincial carpenter's son (Mark 6:1–6). Charges of madness or demon possession occur in other passages of the New Testament too. Naturally these charges are linked to his controversial teaching as much as to his cures, but the association of healing powers with forces that are malevolent rather than good illustrates that miracle-working could invite criticism and suspicion as well as devotion. Moreover this is one of the aspects of Jesus' ministry that is undervalued by those who believe that first-century people were 'primitives' incapable of the sceptical turn of mind that supposedly comes easily two millennia on.

Jesus' miracles bring him potential problems as well as fame (and a degree of notoriety). Through miracles his message could be misunderstood. He is not there to perform tricks or even to cure illness, but to bring good news to the poor and call for repentance. This message must not be lost through fastening upon his miracles and failing to see their proper significance as a sign that the Kingdom of God has arrived.

We can return to the story of the healing of the man with an infirmity at the pool of Bethesda (John 5:1–17) in order to illustrate this. I have already pointed out that Jesus asks the lame man if he wants to be made well. The man explains that he has no one to put him into the pool and is told to take up his bed and walk, an action that both shows he is cured and breaks the sabbath law. Later Jesus finds him in the Temple and says 'See, you have been made well. Sin no more, lest a worse thing come upon you' (John 5:14). Jesus is not on earth to work miracles but to proclaim the gospel, to overcome sin rather than disease. This can easily be forgotten by those who are astonished by his cures – they are reminded that these cures are for those who have 'faith', that is, they are not to detract from the central message of the gospel. Far from 'winding people up' to a psychological condition where they were able to be cured, as Morton Smith suggests, Jesus tries to set the cures in perspective and to prevent the miracles becoming a distraction. In many ways he was reluctant to carry them out.

Conclusions

A selective approach to reading the miracle stories of the New Testament is unavoidable. I began by trying to illustrate how various writers try to select which of the stories refer to special acts of God and which do not. I then looked in some detail at Morton Smith, who argues that none of the stories refers to a special act of God. He sees Jesus as a charismatic figure who gets people to believe that they are capable of anything (if they have 'faith' interpreted as confidence in his abilities).

Morton Smith is, I believe, correct in seeing that any attempt to extract the miracles as a superfluous or distorting addition to the gospel message is inappropriate. He is also right in seeing that Jesus' miracles create suspicion and hostility – perhaps even a form of jealousy in his own neighbourhood – as well as enthusiastic support. It is wrong to think of all first-century Galileans as being credulous people willing to latch onto any wonder-worker. But I believe that he misunderstands the way in which Jesus plays down his miraculous cures and never conceives of them as a show of force to deceive or impress his opponents. If anything, Jesus fears a wrong interpretation of his miracles, just as he fears a wrong interpretation of his Messiahship.

In conclusion, the gospels do not present miracles as if they were theatrical displays. They are even matter-of-fact about them. When Jairus' daughter is healed, Jesus tells them to keep quiet about it and give her something to eat (Mark 5:43). Rather than a great display of power or a proof of his Messiahship, the miracles announce the coming of the Kingdom of God even as they open the way to misconstruction of what that Kingdom is. They often appear in the gospels as a burden, bringing overwhelming crowds into the presence of Jesus, and as a distraction, threatening to undermine the core of his message about the powerlessness of the Messiah who (as his opponents don't fail to remind him) though he heals others cannot heal himself. In places it is their very awkwardness that could be taken to suggest their authenticity. Confronted by human suffering, Jesus is moved to anger and pity (note the reaction to Lazarus' death, 'Jesus wept', John 11:35), but not to ignore it.

Inevitably the question arises as to whether the miracles 'actually happened', in the sense of whether there were special acts of God of the kind described in the first chapter, and my argument has been that some were, although I would be happy to go along with the sort of criteria which Swinburne explores in considering which miracle stories are to be interpreted in this light.

The argument that these miracles are only made possible by the faith of those who benefit from them is one which I have chosen to question in this chapter. Miracles are not a reward for good behaviour; any more than they represent God intervening where suffering is worst. They are a sign of the Kingdom. They are not a proof of the truth of the gospel, despite the efforts of some Enlightenment thinkers to proclaim them as such, an approach which Hume effectively undermines (see Chapter 2). Indeed, those who have the ability of a doubting Thomas to observe miracles directly (by seeing the print of the nails in the risen Christ's hand or the wound in his side; John 20:27) have nothing to gain by it. 'Thomas because you have seen me, you have believed. Blessed are those who have not seen and yet have believed' (John 20:29).

The miracles could get in the way of Jesus' mission and distort his message – but this needn't mean that they were not part of his original ministry. The argument here is that they were an inseparable part of it, but that Jesus had to be careful about how they were interpreted.

Though Jesus the Messiah undoubtedly suffered a fate which many of his enemies saw as fitting for 'Jesus the Magician', the 'magic' was not a vehicle for his messianic claims. Though Morton Smith may be right to say that in practice one person's magic may be another person's religion, there is in principle an important distinction between the two. Magic, given the right actions and formulas, always compels. Religion is always about a grace freely given and freely accepted. In a magical world, with one bound the hero is free. In the Christian world he submits to a painful death, unrescued and (at least according to the last psalm on his lips; Mark 15:34) forsaken.

Notes

1   I have tried to explore some of these issues in the chapter on 'The Foundation and Form of Liberation Exegesis', in Rowland and Corner (1990), pp. 35–84. The present book is clearly critical of much liberation theology, but I think that the defence of its exegetical principles in that earlier work still stands.

2   See the passage on 'Liberation Theology and Fidelity to the Text', Rowland and Corner (1990), pp. 65–9.

3   This paradox is highlighted in James Barr's classic work *Fundamentalism* (1977).

4   This quotation and those following are all taken from *The Infancy Gospel of Thomas* (Ehrman 1999: 255–9).

5   Kierkegaard believed that the story of Abraham being commanded to sacrifice his son was intended to highlight the human presumption of setting up our sense of what is right or wrong as a criterion in terms of which to judge God's revelation. Broadly speaking the neo-orthodox school associated with Karl Barth took this position in the late twentieth century, pointing out that while in the area of God's 'natural' qualities we seem prepared to admit that the infinite Deity is beyond our understanding, God's 'moral qualities' seem to be open to all manner of human scrutiny. Why are we so humble in the one area and so confident of our right to judge in the other? I have difficulties with the neo-orthodox position, but it does make an interesting point. For further discussion, see the debate in Chapter 5 over the problem of evil, and in particular Roth's rejection of Griffin's God as 'too small' (p. 65).

6   It is common to encounter protests from conservative scholars against 'allegorical' rather than 'literal' readings of scripture. But what else is Paul doing, for instance, in 1 Corinthians 10:1–4, when he links the exodus of the Israelites from Egypt with Christian baptism? And when Jesus talks in parables, for instance in explaining the meaning of the Parable of the Sower in Mark 4, is this not a case of 'allegorical' exegesis? The problem with the conservative approach to scripture is that it cannot be both 'biblical' and (at least with respect to every part of the text) literal. I try to argue this point in detail in Rowland and Corner (1990), ch. 2.

7   I have not listed all the references in the subsequent summary of Morton Smith's book.

8   For a useful discussion, see Remus (1997).

9   Liberation theology took and takes different forms in different parts of the world, but I hope that my description is a fair summary of themes held in common. For a good discussion of the theoretical strategy employed by the movement, see Segundo (1976).

10   These points about Jesus and money are made by Rowland (1988: 24–5). Note the interesting interpretation of Jesus' confrontation with the Pharisees and the famous 'Render to Caesar …' saying (Mark 12:14–17).

11   This is a summary of the first chapter of Mark. Naturally, reading it as a single narrative makes presumptions. What if some bits were much older than others? What if all the references to miracles were later interpolations and originally Jesus did nothing but teach? It has to be admitted that the approach here treats the texts more as a literary or editorial whole (in the manner of 'literary' or 'redaction' criticism) than as separate geological layers thrown together by the passing of time (which I associate more with 'form criticism' and more recently structuralist and postmodernist critiques). There is, of course, a huge debate about forms of interpretation. Supporters of form criticism point out that it is their 'scissors-and-paste' approach which enabled scholars to recognize how the various gospels were put together from various separate sayings and traditions. Structuralists and postmodernists highlight wider influences in terms of social, cultural and psychological structures on the way the gospels are formed. The redaction and literary critics feel that more weight has to be given to an overall editorial intent on the part of the evangelists themselves, and reject any 'death of the author', whether from the perspective of form critics and structuralists in the last century or postmodernists in this.

12   The question of how miracle-workers were viewed by the authorities in their day is an interesting one which crops up at several points in the course of this book. Some miracle workers, like Moses or the Apostles, seem to have been leaders of their communities; others, like Jesus and Elijah, seem to have been prophets whose relationship to their own communities was tense and full of conflict. Such conflicts reappear in the later history of Christianity and arguably continue to this day.

13   Whether this charge against Jesus can be highlighted to the extent Smith does, with the more traditional charge of 'blasphemer' underplayed (for example p. 50 – 'claiming to be the Messiah does not constitute blasphemy' etc.), is open to question.

Chapter 7

Miracles after Jesus

The purpose of the next two chapters is to examine Christian beliefs about miracles after the resurrection and ascension of Christ. Needless to say Christianity, like other major world religions, has progressed in different directions since the death of its founder, and it is not possible to trace its course along each one. What this chapter can do is show how the question of miracles influenced the development of the Christian churches and played a role – sometimes a central one – in the differences that emerged between them. At the same time, a historical survey can help to throw some light upon the philosophical questions involved in understanding miracles.

Miracles and Authority: St Paul

One thing which becomes clear in the course of Christian development is the link between miracles and authority. We are made very much aware of it from the very beginning, in the writings both of and about St Paul. Paul's Damascus Road experience, where he encounters Christ, is something which he interprets as much more than a vision. It is to be seen as on a par with the appearances of Christ to his disciples after the resurrection – for instance the appearances on the road to Emmaus. The event on the Damascus Road is mentioned three times in the Acts of the Apostles and it is quite clearly at the heart of Paul's claim to be able to admonish and direct various Christian communities. He asks in 1 Corinthians 9:1 'Am I not free? Am I not an apostle? Have I not seen Jesus our Lord?', thereby specifically linking his encounter with Christ to his authority as an apostle. In 1 Corinthians 15:5–8 he lists the appearances of the risen Jesus after his resurrection, adding himself to the list in terms of an appearance 'to one untimely born'. What these words mean is unclear, but they may have meant one who, unlike the others to whom Jesus appeared, had never lived with or followed him during his lifetime (see Wright 2003: 326–9). It is not difficult to imagine how easily someone like Paul might be regarded as an upstart and his authority challenged as one who came so late to the Christian cause, indeed as one who used to persecute it, and who now claims to be one of its leaders. He never sat down with Christ and heard his teaching. He was not one of the disciples chosen to follow him. Yet now he claims a leadership role in the early church. The tensions this created are clear in several letters, particularly 2 Corinthians where Paul is driven to 'boast' of what are probably his own revelations and visions of Christ, in order to justify his right to admonish and direct (2 Corinthians 12:1–4).

The nature of Jesus' appearance to Paul has generated much controversy, some of which I consider in a separate section on the resurrection. The purpose here is simply to isolate one aspect, namely the link between a miracle (the encounter with the risen Jesus) and authority (the right of an ex-persecutor of Christians to a leading role in the community he used to oppress and whose founder he never personally knew). We shall see this aspect of miracles, namely the legitimizing role which they play in giving authority to those who witness or perform them, recur again and again in Christian history.

Such an understanding of the role of miracles does not show the miracles to be 'false'. It is possible to say that the risen Christ chose to legitimize Paul's ministry by appearing to him, just as it is possible to say that Paul imagined an encounter with Christ in order to persuade himself that he had a right to authority in a community he had so recently tried to destroy. This is not an understanding of miracles designed to rebut the notion that miracles 'happened' but to highlight the role they played in the Christian community and (at times) in the power struggles going on within it. There is, moreover, nothing surprising about this understanding. Jesus' own miracles, as we have already seen, were variously seen as underscoring his own authority and as challenging the authority of others.

Miracles Performed by Apostles

We are now in a position to look in closer detail at the miracles associated with Christianity after Christ. After the ascension of Jesus 'special acts of God' are described as continuing through acts of the apostles (recorded in the New Testament book of that name). From Peter's first address after Pentecost we read of 'many signs and wonders' being done through the apostles (Acts 2:43). The word 'through' is important, since the miracles are carried out in Jesus' name and it is made clear that the power to heal is his. Indeed the occasion of miracles is used by the apostles as a way of introducing Christ, the one who performs them through his servants. After the healing of a lame man in Acts 3:1–10, Peter asks the crowds why they are looking so intently at the apostles 'as though by our own power or godliness we had made this man walk' (Acts 3:12). He then rehearses the story of Jesus' arrest, crucifixion and resurrection and reminds his audience that it is the faith which comes from Christ that has 'made this man strong' (Acts 3:16).

In terms of content, many of the miracles carried out by the apostles are similar to those performed by Jesus. The sick and those possessed by 'unclean spirits' are healed (Acts 5:16), and the unclean spirits recognize Paul in the way they recognized Jesus in the gospels (Acts 19:15). Sometimes miracles occur without the apostles being present – an apron or handkerchief of Paul's is enough (Acts 19:12 – cf. the woman who is cured of a haemorrhage when she touches the clothes of Jesus; Mark 5:25–34) and in Peter's case his shadow is sufficient (Acts 5:15). The dead are raised too – Peter brings Tabitha back to life (Acts 9:36–43) and Paul does the same for Eutychus, who drops off to sleep while the apostle is speaking and falls to his death from a third-storey window (Acts 20:7–12).

Dreams and visions play an important role in Acts. Peter has a vision of the heavens opening and a great sheet descending from the sky which contains all kinds of animals (Acts 10:11). The vision convinces him that a gospel which is for Gentiles as well as Jews cannot make circumcision and ritual cleansing a condition of belief. As with Paul's encounter with Christ, so here also it is easy to imagine that Peter's vision would be a powerful legitimizing tool for a 'change in policy'. The same could be said where visions play a role in directing the movements of the apostles. For instance, in Acts 16:9 a vision appears to Paul in the night. He sees a man pleading with him to go to Macedonia, and duly changes course.

There are no nature miracles to compete with Jesus walking on water or stilling the storm. Instead Paul foresees a tempest which he does not prevent (Acts 27:10ff.), and continues to give advice to the sailors based on the promptings of an angel (Acts 27:23–4). During the voyage he is bitten by a viper but suffers no harm (Acts 28:3–6).

Sometimes the apostles receive assistance in their mission which goes beyond advice about directions and extends to practical protection. Thus an angel of the Lord appears in the night to open prison doors and release them from captivity (Acts 5:19 – cf. Acts 12:7–11 where an angel breaks the chains binding Peter and leads him out of prison). At other times reliance is more on native wit than supernatural assistance. Paul, like Jesus himself during his own interrogation, is adept at exploiting differences among his opponents (Acts 23:6–9). He also stresses his Roman citizenship in order to avoid ill-treatment (Acts 22:24–9) and secure a hearing before Caesar. But there are moments where such ill-treatment simply has to be endured. In Acts 14:19 Paul is dragged out of the city of Lystra, stoned and left for dead, but his friends find him and he revives (Acts 14:20).

How do the miracles attributed to the apostles compare overall with those attributed to Jesus? When asking a question like this, it has always to be remembered that what is now termed the New Testament was the product of a centuries-long selection process, something which I have already discussed in the context of mentioning the *Infancy Gospel of Thomas* and its apparently disturbing account of the punitive miracles of the infant Jesus. It can be debated whether this selection process could best be described as a case of the obviously superior texts standing the test of time, or whether it was more a case of weeding out texts that did not conform to the changing standards of orthodoxy.

Be that as it may, it was not until Athanasius' Easter letter of 367 that we find a list of 26 texts corresponding to those of the New Testament which we have today, and even after the fourth century there were many parts of the Christian world which preferred a different set of texts (it is important to avoid the anachronism of thinking in terms of the Bible or the New Testament as a 'book' in the modern sense; a better image might be a collection of scrolls stored like bottles in a wine rack; such an arrangement makes it easier to imagine a variety of 'taste' which is only slowly moulded into the form of a 'fixed canon').[1] At the very least this slow, centuries-long emergence of the canon requires us to be aware of the important role played by texts which today lie firmly marginalized outside the canon, but which at the time may have played a significant part in shaping the ideas of the early Christian community.

One difference sometimes cited between the miracles of Jesus and those of the apostles is that the miraculous acts of the latter occasionally cause harm to people – such events are sometimes labelled 'punitive miracles'. This is not the case with those attributed to Jesus in the canonical texts, though of course where other forms of life are concerned there is the withering of the fig tree, not to mention the sad fate of the Gadarene swine. In Acts 5, on the other hand, both Ananias and Sapphira die when reprimanded by Peter for failing to share all of their possessions with others (though the text doesn't show him asking for their deaths). In his trial of strength with Elymas in Acts 13, Paul deliberately makes the sorcerer blind for a time. A 'miracle', in the ministry of the apostles, refers to a special act of God which sometimes brings harm to the opponents of Christianity. There are moments when a miracle is an occasion for demonstrating the superior power Christian forces can muster to overwhelm their opponents.

Such 'punitive miracles' arguably represent a different perspective from that which we find in the gospels themselves. Indeed, since it is part of my own definition that a miracle should have a beneficial effect, I am not clear that a 'punitive miracle' is a miracle at all. More important, perhaps, is the question of understanding the purpose of miracles. In the chapter on Jesus' miracles I tried to argue that the heart of the Christian gospel, as presented by the four evangelists, lies in Jesus' voluntary acceptance of weakness, suffering and ultimately death. He will not succeed by force, though force is available to him. When the disciples cut off the ear of the high priest's servant, Jesus rebukes them, reminding them that he could always pray to the Father and receive twelve legions of angels in support (Matthew 26:53 – and in Luke's version Jesus restores the ear, Luke 22:51). It is the essence of his ministry that love does not compel, that the Messiah does not come to establish his Kingdom by force of arms but in humility, riding a donkey. In this sense, I concluded, miracles might easily become a vehicle for misinterpreting Jesus as one who intends to establish the Kingdom by compulsion.

Yet in Acts (and I am not denying the likelihood that Luke and Acts are by the same person), the twelve legions of angels are readily at hand, supervising the mission of the apostles and releasing them from captivity when they end up in prison. There are still, as we have seen, times when the apostles have to confront their persecutors with all the powers of endurance and cunning at their disposal. At other times, however, they are delivered from their oppressors through supernatural assistance. To what extent, then, has the focus for miracles ceased to be acts of compassion in the face of practical need and become a question of demonstrating superior strength in the face of sustained opposition to a 'sect' that its opponents claim is 'spoken against everywhere' (Acts 28:22)? To what extent, in other words, does the understanding of miracles as evidence of superior divine power now become the dominant one?

Miracles and Power Contests

The Acts of the Apostles presents a contest between a new sect struggling to survive and its opponents. The author tends to call these opponents 'the Jews'. In reality this was very much a contest *within* Judaism, between those who believed that the Messiah had come and those who rejected such a notion. It was precisely because of this that the issue of circumcision and ritual cleansing assumed such importance for the new Jewish sect of Christians. In this contest between the different interpreters of Jewish tradition, there was a natural tendency to claim that God was on one side or the other. The Acts of the Apostles contains a number of 'set-piece' encounters between the new sect and those who are hostile to it, which are in effect contests between different miracle-workers. Thus in Acts 13:8 we encounter Elymas 'the sorcerer', who is 'seeking to turn the proconsul away from the faith' (Acts 13:9). Paul condemns him for 'perverting the straight ways of the Lord' (v. 10) and makes Elymas blind. Elymas starts looking for someone to lead him by the hand, as a result of which the proconsul believes (v. 12 – though his astonishment is linked to the teaching rather than the miracle, it is clearly occasioned by the blinding). Another example can be found in Acts 19:13–16, where 'itinerant Jewish exorcists' invoke the names of Jesus and Paul in order to drive out evil spirits. The evil spirits fail to recognize the exorcists who are attacked by the man possessed by devils and are left 'naked and wounded' (v. 16). Once again, there seems to be a contest between the apostles and other Jewish exorcists, although on this occasion it is the evil spirits who 'decide' the contest.

These 'contests' are more marked in the apocryphal New Testament than in the texts which were eventually deemed canonical. Part of the Apocryphal New Testament describes a contest between Simon and Jude on the one hand, and two Persian magicians on the other, which is reminiscent of the encounter between Aaron and Pharaoh's magicians in Exodus 7:8–13, not least in the use of serpents. On this occasion the Persian magicians call in a host of snakes but the apostles make them bite the magicians themselves. The King wants the losers in the contest killed, but the apostles exercise 'clemency' by having the serpents suck their own poison back out of the magicians, a process which causes them three days of agony after which they recover (see James 1924: 331–2).

This understanding of miracles in terms of a contest between rival powers recalls the role of miracles in parts of the Hebrew Bible (Old Testament). It is clear from Acts that many of the early Christians liked to see themselves as a persecuted community dependent upon the superior power of God to confound its enemies, much as Moses and Aaron depended upon that power to achieve deliverance from bondage to Pharaoh in Egypt. Those described as 'the Jews' in the Acts of the Apostles play the role of the Egyptians in the Exodus narrative. A particular Jewish sect thereby plucks itself out of its historical context and presents itself as the new 'remnant' or chosen people, while the rest of the Jews are transposed into oppressors, as alien to the new sect as Pharaoh was to the Israelite slaves in Egypt.

The miraculous powers of 'the Jews' in the Acts of the Apostles, like those of Pharaoh confronted by Moses, prove to be inferior to those of their opponents and the Jews are confounded by the superior power of (in this case) the Christian God. Just as the miraculous 'vision' on the Road to Damascus legitimized the authority of Paul within the early Christian community, so the punitive miracles in these set-piece encounters between 'Christians' and 'Jews' legitimized the power of the Christian God as deliverer from oppression and means of triumph over the new sect's enemies.

Miracles in the Post-biblical Period

In the post-biblical period the situation changed. The contest between the new sect and its opponents, both within and outside the Jewish faith, was effectively won by the Christians over the next two centuries. In the early fourth century of the common era, after the conversion to Christianity of the Emperor Constantine, the Christian 'sect' became the official faith of the Roman Empire and (in the view of some) the oppressed became the oppressors instead. At this point miracles were no longer required for the survival of the followers of Jesus, at least on the territory of the former Roman Empire. Does this mean that they stopped? After all, the battle was now won and the victors could lay down their arms.

If miracles were primarily to be seen as irresistible weapons wielded in the fight against unbelief, their existence might indeed have no longer been claimed. However, they had other purposes too, and for this reason many believed that they did not die out with the 'triumph' of Christianity. The fact that they were widespread within 'Christendom' during the medieval period shows this to be the case. Miracles during this later period can be associated with a whole range of motivations – doctrinal, political, socio-cultural and economic. I shall try to bring this out by examining a familiar medieval focus of miraculous activity – the shrine of a saint.

Miracles, Shrines and Relics

There was an important theological insight behind the attachment to relics and the stress upon places where saints were buried. When the Christian martyrs sacrificed their lives in the amphitheatre, other Christians would try to collect what was left of their mangled corpses, often at great risk to their own lives. Such behaviour made the point that Christians did not abominate a corpse. They did not regard the body as a worthless shell, to be discarded at death by an immortal soul that had at last been released from bodily captivity. They did not abominate the body of Christ himself, which they took and buried after his crucifixion. Moreover, they had faith in a Messiah who had been raised *in* the body, not *from* the body. Hence their belief in the empty tomb; had the soul simply 'escaped' the body and gone off on its own, it would not have troubled Christians to believe that the body of Christ stayed where it was inside the grave. Instead it was the body of Jesus which they proclaimed as risen and glorified. This is something which is discussed at some length in Chapter 9.

Belief in shrines and relics therefore served to emphasize that the life of Christ and of those who followed him were lives of human beings and not those of gods or angels veiled in an outwardly human form. The use of relics made its own indirect contribution to upholding doctrinal orthodoxy. Those who believed that new life could be made available at the tomb of a saint knew that their faith was built upon the experience of one who died an excruciating death as a human being, was laid in a tomb himself and was finally raised up to a new and different life of glory (see Brown 1981: ch. 4).

Besides the theological associations, however, there was a socio-political dimension to shrines and their unifying power in a disparate empire. Through the use of relics shrines were able to go 'on tour', making it possible for someone to receive miraculous assistance without having to visit the saint's final resting place. It was unsurprising that at a time when travel was dangerous and difficult, not everyone would be able to go to the shrine of a saint. Most peasants would have been unable to take the necessary time off work. Even so, many tried to do so, and they could always bring back something to help those who couldn't make the journey – for instance dust or oil from the saint's tomb. Such substances were themselves instruments of healing, allowing saints to perform miracles in places they had never visited. Gregory of Tours, for instance, liked to carry around dust from the tomb of St Martin of Tours which he'd then mix with potions in order to produce healings.[2]

Hence though not everyone could go to the shrine, it was at least possible that something associated with the shrine could go to them. It was natural enough that an African shrine would come to contain 'a piece of the wood of the cross, from the land of promise, where Christ was born', since the journey from, say, Morocco to Palestine was hardly a simple one. Perhaps Jerusalem might have become a Christian version of the Moslems' Mecca, to be visited once in their lives by every true follower of Christ, but instead the sacred shrines or their contents were farmed out throughout the Christian world. Relics were transported to outposts of the Holy Roman Empire where they were received on the model of an imperial visit, the saint's arrival deliberately intended to evoke the 'adventus' of the Emperor.

Another factor which has to be taken account of in every period, including that of the modern day, is the economic and financial side of miracles. We can see this in the biblical period when, for instance, we read in the Acts of the Apostles that those who practised magic are converted and bring their books to be burned. We are told that the value of the books destroyed was 'fifty thousand pieces of silver'. Sorcery paid, which only intensified the bitter feelings towards a Christian sect that appeared to be undermining a source of living as well as traditional values.

The economic dimension is obvious in the case of Simon Magus in Acts 8:9ff. Simon Magus is a character who apparently astonished the people of Samaria with his 'sorcery'. He is converted and baptised, but then is rebuked for offering money to receive the power to pass on the Holy Spirit through the laying on of hands (hence the corrupt practice of 'simony', paying for ecclesiastical office, in the later Christian churches). The text further reinforces the point that 'sorcery' was a good way of earning money and worth paying for.[3] A further example can be found in Acts 19:23–9, where the Asian silversmiths complain about the threat posed by Paul to their business as makers of silver shrines for Diana.

Hence it is to be expected that in the medieval period the significance of shrines and relics was in part one of economics. Pilgrimages brought in the medieval equivalent of tourist income, while the presence of a shrine boosted the status of a particular region – an insight which is not lost on the modern day either, where a communist mayor is prepared to support a local miracle in order to boost the local economy in a poor suburb of Rome.[4] It is hardly surprising that when St Martin of Tours was dying, delegations from both Poitiers and Tours arrived at the deathbed, eager to stake their respective claims. In the end it was the Tours delegation which triumphed by spiriting the saint's body through a window of his cell and setting up an enormous funeral procession to accompany the corpse to its final resting place. It was also unsurprising that relics might be exchanged, fought over or stolen, or that false claims would be made about possessing them. In 580 a 'relic-monger' visited Tours and was imprisoned while his 'relics' were examined. They turned out to be moles' teeth and herbal roots. Such investigations could be taken as evidence of a limit to credulity; they also, however, represented an economic concern to avoid debasing the currency. The value of relics depended upon there not being too many of them and they needed the ecclesiastical equivalent of an OPEC cartel to limit output.

Miracles and Protest

There is an altogether different interpretation of the shrines and their significance which identifies them less with forms of social and economic control than with forms of protest. The writings of Peter Brown, in particular, have sought to bring this out. Whilst it is not within my competence to assess the complicated historical arguments involved, we can at least see how the question of miracles became intimately tied up with the question of power in the church.

That the Christianization of the Roman Empire was a problem at the time is shown by the fact that the 'triumph' of the church in the fourth century was not universally welcomed. It helped to provoke the movement of the 'desert fathers' into solitude. They were imitating Christ's own period in the wilderness and reacting to the fact that they could no longer reproduce in their own lives the suffering of martyrdom which their founder had to endure and which the earliest Christians could reproduce by sharing Christ's Passion. If the martyrs had the Colosseum, the monks would have the desert. If the martyrs had the forces of Rome to contend with in the amphitheatre, the monks would have the forces of Satan to contend with in the wilderness, the place where Jesus himself was tempted by the Devil. For a few of them it might be possible to argue that the lack of opportunity for martyrdom was a by-product of the church's welcome triumph over paganism. But for many that triumph was less clear-cut. To some it was a case of taking their protest against the worldliness of the newly triumphant church as far from the corrupt structures of the new order as they possibly could.

Where the extent and nature of the dissident voices in the desert is concerned, it is difficult to obtain clear information and there is always the danger of oversimplification.[5] Our knowledge of the desert father Antony, for instance, is determined to a considerable degree by the life written by Athanasius, the Bishop of Alexandria. Athanasius does not present any considerable tensions between the monk on the one hand and the bishops in charge of their sees on the other. Indeed Antony is presented as complaining, for instance, about the stream of visitors to his mountain retreat seeking cures and as encouraging them to turn to the 'usual channels' provided by the church instead. But we may wonder whether in reality things were quite so easy.

The cult of the saints may have originally been part of a similar protest against society to that of the retreat to the desert. The procession of pilgrims to the tomb of a saint outside the city walls constituted a form of critical withdrawal, matching that of the 'desert fathers' into the wilderness. By locating the cult of the saints in cemeteries outside the city walls, and by building what were often great pilgrimage sites in cemeteries, these areas could amount to a 'city beyond the city'. St Jerome commented that in worshipping the saints 'the city has changed address'. Prudentius described the crowd streaming out to the shrine of St Hippolytus in the countryside as the 'true Rome'. Moreover the community that formed outside was able to challenge society within the city walls. Pilgrimages to shrines saw two groups whose position in society was restricted and difficult – women and the poor – brought together with those from whom they were ordinarily kept apart. Men and women, patricians and plebeians, joined together in the procession. Whilst it would be anachronistic to see a pilgrimage to the shrine of a saint as a kind of socialist-feminist rally, it would not be unreasonable to see it as a conscious withdrawal from one form of society and the recognition of another which, in Prudentius' words, 'banishes distinctions of birth' (see Brown 1981: ch. 2).

Where the withdrawal to the shrines beyond the city walls is concerned, it is interesting to note Peter Brown's remark that this was something that the bishops of western Europe had to adopt and orchestrate in order to establish their own power. By such means anything potentially subversive in the withdrawal could be taken over and neutralized by the medieval church. Brown writes:

> it was through a studiously articulated relationship with great shrines that lay at some distance from the city – St. Peter's, on the Vatican Hill outside Rome, Saint Martin's, a little beyond the walls of Tours – that the bishops of the former cities of the Roman Empire rose to prominence in early mediaeval Europe.
>
> (1981: 8)

It may, therefore, not be altogether wide of the mark to suggest that in the early medieval period a process of 'normalization' took place. An act of piety that had previously been a form of social protest, or at least a way of maintaining a certain distance from the norms of life within the city walls, lost that ingredient when the shrines were brought inside the medieval establishment. Whether a similar move was made with the desert it is difficult to say. In any case it is possible to aver that belief in the miracles surrounding saints and their shrines might have been more a way of maintaining forms of social and political criticism in this early period than later historians, keen to attack the 'blind superstition' of the age of antiquity, have been able to recognize.

Miracles and the Conversion of 'Barbarians'

I argued in an earlier section that if miracles were primarily to be seen as irresistible weapons wielded in the fight against unbelief, they might have ceased with the conversion of Constantine and the 'official' triumph of Christianity. The victors had their victory and could now lay down their arms. However, the political situation was not as simple as that. The empire that had 'triumphed' faced continuing challenges, and these soon posed a threat to its existence. In order to consolidate its triumph, Christianity had not only to Christianize the empire, but also to convert the 'barbarians', as the history books used to describe the various tribes who put increasing pressure on Rome, until eventually they stood at the gates of the capital and finally sacked it.

A common perspective on the medieval church is the notion that in converting pagans to their beliefs, Christians effectively adopted many of the ideas and principles of those they converted. There are those who see the momentous events of the early fourth century, when the Roman Emperor saw his vision of the Christian Cross during the campaign against Maxentius, less in terms of Constantine's conversion to Christianity than in terms of Christianity's conversion to Constantine. As early as the eighteenth century Edward Gibbon's classic of the Enlightenment, *Decline and Fall of the Roman Empire* (1909), described the way in which the Constantinian establishment adopted the constitutional structures of pagan Rome, the Pope no more than a spiritual Emperor and his cardinals the proconsuls of the new order. In the same way there are those who see in the efforts of Christianity to co-opt the 'barbarians' laying waste to the Roman Empire a deliberate adoption of 'pagan beliefs' in order to make the religion palatable. As Benedicta Ward puts it: 'The barbarian invasions caused a new need for teaching and preaching and wonders were very often the best contact with pagans' (1990: 133). She points out that Augustine starts to apply his mind 'to the analysis of the miraculous' not during his monastic life but when he has become Bishop of Hippo and the relics of St Stephen arrive in town in 416. The result is 'the first collection of miracles at a shrine', as recorded in Augustine's *City of God*. Miracles, records Ward, are presented by Augustine as 'a witness to the power of Christ's resurrection, issuing in cures of power to convert unbelievers and to reassure Christians'. Once again the role of miracle as a demonstration of superior divine power comes into play. This time it is not the Jews facing Pharaoh in the Exodus narrative, or the nascent Christian sect against 'the Jews', as in the Acts of the Apostles, but the established

Christian church facing a crisis engendered by the decline of the very empire which it had eventually won over to its cause.

This is not to say that the emphasis upon miracles was simply a process of kow-towing to the 'superstitious prejudices' of 'barbarians' in order to slip them into the Christian fold. A very different emphasis is put upon the process by Valerie Flint (1991), who is concerned to justify the intellectual and spiritual credentials of the worldview which Christianity supplanted. Flint criticizes language about 'barbarians at the gates' as the Roman Empire imploded. She argues that where the adoption of pagan forms of belief and practice by Christianity in late antiquity is concerned, we are dealing with a sophisticated cultural and religious compromise and not some kind of deliberate process of intellectual stooping to conquer.

Flint concedes that that there was a 'Christianization' of pagan practices and beliefs. Gregory the Great specifically enjoined Bishop Augustine, when he set off to Saxon England, that 'the idol temples of that race should by no means be destroyed, but only the idols in them. Take holy water and sprinkle it on these shrines, build altars and place relics in them' (Flint 1991: 76). The approach was one of adaptation rather than destruction.

The question Flint considers is whether this approach compromised the Christianity it was serving. She points out that the presumption behind the idea of 'capitulation' is the view that pagan modes of thinking were inherently irrational or immoral. What she suggests instead is that there existed a lively and energetic non-Christian world, with an established habit of devotion and spiritual aspiration, which it would have been wrong (and not just inconvenient) to destroy. It would be better to preserve it while avoiding elements that were gross or cruel.

Hence, she explains, pagan incantations recited over those who were ill became in the medieval world Christian paternosters and creeds; the casting of lots turned into the practice of placing sacred books on the altar, opening them at random and interpreting the passages found; the cross of Christ was said to have a miraculous power, not only through its association with the rod of Moses but also with a magic wand (an inscription on the Rutwell cross showed Jesus healing the blind man with a wand rather than with his fingers). These examples show how the 'Christian magicians' took over paganism. They certainly, Flint admits, had to temper the practices which had so alienated observers like Pliny – 'a severed viper's head attached in a linen cloth, or the heart taken from the creature while still alive; the snout and ear tips of a mouse, the mouse itself being allowed to go free; the right eye gouged out of a living lizard; a fly in a bit of goat's skin, with its head cut off', etc. (Flint 1991: 14) (we can presume that Pliny exaggerated). But she insists that there was nothing inimical to Christianity in replacing these pagan practices with a Christian form of 'magic' through practices like the wearing of relics in little caskets round the neck.

Flint finds a potent symbol of successful assimilation in the magi, the 'wise men' who are described in Matthew's gospel following a star in order to pay homage to the infant Jesus. Their rehabilitation is complete when their supposed bodies are moved from Milan to Cologne in 1164, by which time the presentation of the gifts of gold, frankincense and myrrh to the Christ child has become linked to the bread and wine presented as gifts to the Christ who is present at the altar during mass. By now Christian 'magic' has been effectively constructed on the basis of its pagan antecedent and the priestly 'magicians' are firmly in control. Valerie Flint provides an interesting point of connection with many of the arguments used in Morton Smith's *Jesus the Magician*, which I examined in the last chapter.

Assimilation and Power

The whole question of pagan and Christian 'magic', however, is rather more than a matter of techniques of conversion. It is precisely this question of control that points up the limitations of Flint's 'positive' thesis concerning the Christian appropriation of paganism. There may well be a sense in which pagan reverence for stones, trees or springs represented a form of spiritual devotion (many modern pagans would claim that it did and would blame an absence of care for the environment on the fact that not enough people shared in such devotion). There may also be a judgemental and dismissive attitude towards the past on the part of contemporary writers with an ill thought out notion of intellectual and moral progress. But the emergence of the early medieval church wasn't just about systems of thought learning to live with one another; it was about a power struggle. The earliest Christians were in a position of weakness when they challenged the authorities; the Christians of the early medieval period were in a position of power where they could simply redefine the beliefs of their day in their own terms. Nothing cemented the power of the medieval church more effectively than its becoming established as a reservoir of magic, a repository of supernatural power managed by those (the clergy) whose own authority was guaranteed by their role in dispensing this supernatural power to the laity.

Relics, whose early connection with forms of protest I have already discussed, eventually served this purpose of ecclesiastical control well. From the point of view of the church authorities, miracles were much more useful, and certainly less threatening to their own power, when performed by dead saints rather than by live ones (see Moore 1997). Miracles performed 'in vita' – that is to say while the miracle-worker was still alive – could add up to a holy man mobilizing the community in unpredictable ways. Miracles performed 'post mortem', that is to say after the miracle-worker had died, were sanctioned and controlled by the church which now had the saint (in the form of his or her relics entrusted to its care) firmly under control.

A live miracle-worker, Moore points out, received his authority from popular acclamation. If he was to perform a healing, then a crowd of people sought him out and led him to the patient. He might touch or kiss or breathe over the sick man or woman. This was a special function which by the ninth century was reserved for those who 'possessed religious authority' – so for any 'unauthorized' person to attempt such a thing might evoke the sort of hostility another miracle-worker encountered when he tried to heal on the sabbath.

Having pronounced a blessing and the sign of the cross, the saint would then go on his way. The people around the patient would themselves decide whether a cure had taken place and, if so, proclaim it to the world. The power of determining a miracle therefore lay in their hands. Later recognition of the saint's powers through canonization and an 'official biography' (hagiography) represented the post factum acceptance by the authorities of something carried through by the community as a whole.

Miracles 'post mortem', on the other hand, could be controlled by the custodians of the shrines and even used to back up the system of dues, labour service and holy day observance associated with them. Hence Robert Moore's suggestion (1997) that the gathering of holy power to the shrines and the formalization of canonization are familiar aspects of the general shaking down of authority, both secular and ecclesiastical, in the second half of the twelfth century. From this time forth it is only posthumous miracles that are essential for canonization. The rationalization was that the saint was in heaven and could now intercede on behalf of his supplicants. The more obvious point is that deciding on a posthumous miracle could be safely entrusted to the authorities, while miracles performed in life were entrusted to the dangerous forces of popular acclamation. Moore shows how the religious authorities sought to close down 'in vita' miracles and replace them with the 'post mortem' variety that both generated income and could be controlled by the representatives of the living church.

In rationalizing this move, the medieval church took advantage of the idea that miracles can be worked by the devil as well as by God. As we know from the gospel accounts of Jesus' miracles, it was a common criticism that 'he casts out demons by the Prince of Demons'. The church could suggest that miracles 'in vita' are always ambiguous, whilst those which occur after death must be genuine, since in heaven there can presumably be no dubious characters interceding with God to promote the cause of a new saint. It was in these terms that Pope Gregory IX was able to decree in 1232 that miracles 'in vita' were not a ground for canonization. It was for that very reason that the miracles 'in vita' of that highly controversial figure Thomas Becket only slowly began to emerge some time after his death. Only in retrospect, when it was safe to think in terms of his sainthood, could one happily recall his many miracles from boyhood on, including the fact that he turned water into wine three times at the Pope's own table. Ecclesiastical control continues to enable the canonization process to be closely managed in the modern day concerning controversial figures such as Padre Pio and even Mother Teresa, ensuring that their promotion is fast-tracked or held back as appropriate. I touch on this in Chapter 12.

Such observations remind us that claims about miracles do not necessarily reflect the intellectual credulity of the 'vulgar and uneducated'. These claims may instead be a means by which this 'uneducated' part of society asserts its own authority in relation to those holding power. When John of Salerno shows some apparent embarrassment at the 'excesses' of the miracle-workers of his day, it is tempting to applaud his more 'rational' approach. 'Let those who like to do so', comments John, 'praise exorcists, raisers of the dead and all other people famous for miracles. I will praise patience as the first virtue of Odo' (John of Salerno 1958: 16). It is natural to warm to the apparent preference for reason over superstition, for moral virtue over wonder-working performances. But beneath the appeal to reason and virtue, lay a fear of the social dislocation and even (at its most extreme) the revolutionary fervour that might lie behind an explosion of popular enthusiasm about the miracle-working powers of a holy man or woman. What the Enlightenment sceptics tended to forget was that opposition to miracles might proceed from something other than intellectual sophistication, and likewise that the eager embrace of miracles might proceed from something other than intellectual credulity.[6] If, therefore, we read that around a millennium after Christ, John of Salerno and Odo of Cluny are both reticent about the power of miracles (Odo insists that he has put his faith in witnesses to the life of Gerard of Aurillac who have not laid great emphasis on the miracles which mean so much to the 'vulgus'), we need to recognize that this was not simply or even mainly a matter of not being drawn into the superstitions of the age. It was a matter of power. Those who taught and performed miracles 'with authority' were as troubling to the architects of the Carolingian *renovatio* in the eleventh century as they were to the temple authorities in first-century Jerusalem.

Conclusions

In the course of this chapter I have tried to show the variety of roles that miracles played in the period after Jesus. I began with a discussion of the importance for Paul of his miraculous encounter with the risen Christ, something that enabled him to assert his authority over other followers of Jesus. I then looked at miracles in the Acts of the Apostles, where we encounter a familiar biblical theme of miracles as a demonstration of power, helping a particular Jewish sect, the Christians, to victory over its enemies, as they had once helped the Jews to victory over their Egyptian oppressors.

I then examined miracles in the post-biblical period, focusing on the traditions surrounding shrines and relics, I showed how miracles could help to unify the disparate Christian communities around the Empire. They could also bring financial profit, as they do today. They had a theological role too, reinforcing other aspects of Christian belief, such as that in bodily resurrection.

But the political dimension is the one which has inevitably received the most attention. During the apostolic period, miracles showed that God was on the side of the Christians against their opponents. After the triumph of Christianity, miracles could help both in shoring up the power of the Christian 'establishment' and in strengthening the beliefs of those who were opposed to it. We see here a pattern which can be discerned in the biblical texts: there are miracles which establish the authority of a national leader, such as Moses and Joshua, against foreign enemies, but there are also miracles which establish the power of those who protest against their own 'national establishment', claiming that their leaders have gone astray. Elijah and Jesus may be put into this category.

I have therefore tried to assess the way in which miracles associated with shrines and relics may have formed a focus for protest against the successful 'religious-political' establishment of the day. Then I looked at the way in which, during the later medieval period, shrines and relics served to shore up ecclesiastical control against the danger of itinerant miracle-workers who might start a following and challenge the leadership of their day. The shrines and relics become something closer to the temple institution in its relation to the wandering charismatic, Jesus of Nazareth.

I considered the argument that paganism had far more sophisticated cultural and religious traditions than it is often given credit for. Despite much that is true in this claim, I feel it considers the relationship between Christians and pagans too much in terms of harmonizing systems of thought and too little in terms of the struggle for power which, in one way or another, has always played a central role in human history. If we notice a change between the time of Jesus and that of his successors, it is in the way that miracles become a sign of where power lies and a means by which that power is exercised and maintained.

It was the Protestant Reformation which broke the connection between belief in miracles and the power structures of the medieval church. It thereby brought about the change in perception which helped to usher in 'the modern age'. In the next chapter I shall discuss the Reformation and then try to examine the way in which miracles have been interpreted in the half millennium since that time.

Notes

1 Issues surrounding the formation of the canon are well outlined by James Barr (1983) in his Sprunt lectures given at the University of Oxford.

2 The significance of cults of the saints in a part of Christendom is discussed by Raymond van Dam (1993).

3 In one of the apocryphal Acts of Peter, however, this story of Simon Magus becomes part of a set-piece encounter between the two of them in the presence of Nero (Peter emerges the victor when Simon Magus shows that he can fly and Peter's prayers show that he can be made to fall to his death).

4 See Chapter 12, particularly the discussion of La Madonina at Civitavecchia.

5 For example, Peter Brown (1978: ch. 4) emphasizes the importance of a crisis of tensions in Egyptian village life in encouraging a retreat to the desert. Such observations ought to make us aware of the problems of generalizing about why the 'desert fathers' emerged in the fourth century, rather than rush to identify them as a protest movement or as performing a simple act of piety.

6 A similar argument can be observed in the New Testament era by those who, like Christopher Rowland (2003), seek to reclaim the central significance of the Book of Revelation.

Chapter 8

Miracles after the Reformation

The Miracle-Worker and the Magician

The Protestant Reformers saw priests as 'magicians'. This distinction between 'magicians' and 'miracle-workers', or between 'magic' and 'religion', runs throughout my survey of the history of Christian thinking about miracles. I have analysed Morton Smith's account of Jesus as a 'magician'. I have pointed to the 'contests' between the early Christians and 'magicians' outlined in the Acts of the Apostles. In dealing with the development of the early Christian Church, I have tried to give weight to the ideas of those like Valerie Flint, in her carefully titled *The Rise of Magic in Early Mediaeval Europe*, who point to the dangers of an easy distinction between 'pagan' magic and 'Christian' prayer or religion during this period.

Certainly there is a distinction often drawn at the philosophical level between 'magician' and 'miracle-worker'. The magician compels, the miracle-worker asks for help and knows that it is God alone who decides. The magician who utters the right formula, or casts the right spell, has the sort of confidence in the outcome of their actions that an electrician has in switching on a light. It is a kind of scientific confidence, an assurance that things will work according to rule. The miracle-worker, on the other hand, has no idea of 'how things work', no insight into a 'supernatural realm' which has its own manner of operating that can be tapped into. The miracle-worker simply asks God to do something which no human being can either do or understand. The miracle-worker exercises no control over what happens. They have no formulae which can summon the genie and make it work. The miracle-worker is a mere supplicant, where the magician is a skilled manipulator of supernatural forces.

However, this distinction, as many of the writers we have considered point out, easily breaks down when we try to apply it to particular groups. For example we find Moses, who according to Acts 7:22 'became learned in all the wisdom of the Egyptians' (which was assumed to be the 'magical arts' – we have already seen how Morton Smith seeks to link the Holy Family's exile in Egypt during the reign of Herod to an opportunity for Jesus to acquire similar skills) being portrayed as a sorcerer in some medieval mystery play. During the Reformation, Calvin tried to tackle the view that the patriarch was a mere 'wizard', at about the time when the English playwright Christopher Marlowe was earning official disapproval for describing him as a 'mere juggler' (Thomas 1973: 323). Conversely, just as respected figures like the patriarchs were tarred with the brush of magic, so the magicians the church of the Middle Ages sought to set itself apart from – the 'cunning men', 'wise women', 'wizards' and other characters analysed in medieval and early modern England in Keith Thomas' magisterial work – adopted many of the traditional prayers of the church and added them to their spells and charms. They did not consciously change from a stance of 'making it happen' to one of asking God to effect what they could not themselves manage but, as Thomas points out, 'for the magicians themselves the summoning of celestial beings was a religious rite, in which prayer played an essential part, and where piety and purity of life were deemed essential' (1973: 319–20).

This difficulty in applying the distinction between 'magic' and 'religion' to particular individuals and groups must be borne in mind when we consider the 'Reformation onslaught' on priests as professional magicians set apart by celibacy and ritual consecration. To their Protestant critics they saw themselves as necessary channels for conveying supernatural power to the world. They were the ones who could make the magic work. They administered sacraments which were believed to be efficacious *ex opere operato*, that is to say simply by being administered. Though some preconditions applied to this doctrine, for instance that the administrant must 'have the intention' of doing what Christ and the church want to do (Lohse 1966: 152)[1], it is easy to see why it appeared much closer to the traditional definition of magic, where the right formulae compel divine action, than to religion where prayer and supplication ask for help but cannot presume to receive it.

As a consequence the mass was condemned by the Reformers as an act of magic, the priest conjuring up Christ as Aladdin might conjure the genie by rubbing his lamp. Thomas Hobbes, writing his *Leviathan* during the 'English Revolution' or Civil War, declared that in their beliefs concerning the power of the priest to transform the bread and wine into the body and blood of Christ, Catholics had turned 'consecration' (of the elements) into 'conjuration' or 'enchantment' . They had confused a religious act with a magical act, a religious prayer with a magical spell. Words and prayers, Hobbes emphasized, had no power in themselves unless God chose to heed them.[2]

By the mid-seventeenth century this was a familiar charge against Catholics, though it was one that was voiced long before the Reformation, even in England whose Reformation is often viewed as a political act imposed from above. Many of the pre-Reformation debates about the eucharist, for instance that concerning whether communion should be in one or both kinds (the laity receiving both bread and wine), were indirectly born of a growing sense that the clergy had managed to set itself up as the sacred guardian of a magical rite. From this point of view the church had effectively taken control of miracles by dictating precisely who was to perform them, and by making the central miracle (the mass) a ritual act which could only be performed by those who had been officially instituted to perform the task.

Hussites in Bohemia and Lollards in England exchanged views on the subject in the early fifteenth century. By now the props for each priestly performance had themselves been invested with supernatural powers. The Fourth Lateran Council of 1215 had ruled that the elements of the eucharist and holy oil should be kept under lock and key. The council declared it to be dogma that once consecrated by the priest, the bread and wine became in substance the body and blood of Christ, and the new feast of Corpus Christi began the ritual of elevating the host for veneration by the people. Two centuries later it was common practice for Lollards in England to 'mumble' (the name 'Lollard' means mumbler) that the sign of the cross was a piece of religious abracadabra, whose practical use was merely that it helped ward off flies in the summer. Three centuries later, with the English Reformation now advancing rapidly, the first Edwardian prayer book of 1549 still thought it necessary to instruct that the wafer must be placed directly into the mouth of each communicant so that it wouldn't be stolen and used as a magic charm – perhaps to cure the blind or ward off caterpillars if sprinkled on the garden (Thomas 1973: 38–9).

The Protestant Reformers easily built up an image of medieval Europe as the 'dark ages' in which spells and charms masqueraded as religion, scholastic learning included divination and the pope was a mere sorcerer or conjurer, or even 'the witch of the world'. When recusant priests came to Elizabethan England to win it back for Catholicism, they were dismissed as 'conjurers'.

This is not to say that the medieval church, or even the architects of the Fourth Lateran Council, deliberately sought to construct a 'system of magic'. Magic is always a collection of miscellaneous recipes rather than a comprehensive theological system, and even the abstruse variations of eucharistic theory were always closely linked to an overall body of doctrine. The idea of the bread as Christ's body and the wine as his blood in the 'miracle of the mass' emerged not as the outcome of some obscure theologizing with Aristotelian ideas of substance and accidents (though this had its value), but in the context of affirming what was perceived as the general truth that Jesus' body had been glorified and that his followers might share in that glory. In practical terms it was a way of stressing the humanity of Christ, not a means of magicking it away. To 'eat God' was to take upon oneself the suffering flesh of the cross. It was a way of connecting with the God who had suffered and died in the flesh, and whose body had been glorified through resurrection, not abandoned by his escaping soul. In this way it is reminiscent of the theological point surrounding shrines and relics mentioned in the last chapter, namely that Christ's body participated in the new life of resurrection. That Christ might be present in bread and wine was a repetition of the mystery that God might be present in the body of a human being. This practical significance has always to be remembered when the theological presumptions are criticized.

A similar aura of magic was seen to surround the practice of confession. The Reformers could easily interpret the command from the confessional to repeat so many 'paternosters' and 'ave marias' as an injunction to perform a magical rite. Part of the reason why so much effort was made to change the language of Christian worship to the vernacular was in order to emphasize that the words themselves were not like ritual chants. When uttered in a language most people did not understand, various prayers could easily be mistaken for the 'abracadabra' of conjuration. Translated into the vernacular they would be seen for what they were, a means of communication rather than a spell to provoke a divine response.

Practices such as praying for the dead, which had given rise to the chantries established for such purposes, were viewed by the Reformers in a similar way, as the product of a purely quantitative view of prayer and its purely mechanical efficacy. Though such an interpretation was undoubtedly a convenient justification, for instance, for the dissolution of the English chantries and a huge transfer of land to the crown under Henry VIII, it is possible to see a coherent theological position. The catchphrase of the Protestant reformers was 'justification by faith', but faith was not to be seen as an inner work, a psychological equivalent of charitable deeds. Justification by faith meant justification by God. It meant that it was the free will of God whom to save and whom to condemn. No form of manipulation by human beings could control that divine decision.

Ironically, again where England is concerned, there was a parallel system to that of the institutional church controlling the means of miraculous dispensation, and that was the institution of monarchy, whose own miraculous powers were dispensed through the royal touch. Cure by royal touch was initiated by Edward the Confessor in the eleventh century and maintained until the eighteenth century. After the Reformation in England, Elizabeth I cited her healings as evidence that the papal bull of 1570 excommunicating her had failed. Queen Anne, whose healing hand supposedly improved the condition of the infant Samuel Johnson, was the last to practise it, although the healing power of the Jacobite dynasty was maintained throughout the early eighteenth century as it sought to regain the throne lost in the Glorious Revolution of 1688.

Such a 'parallel system' for distributing miracles is not surprising. Kings, after all, were believed to rule by divine right, and like the church were an institution ordained by God. In England such theories broke down in the seventeenth century. It began with James I inheriting the English throne in 1603, and asserting his authority against a Parliament that seemed so much more unruly than the Scottish estates he had been used to. It ended with Parliament effectively ejecting James II and his infant successor from office in 1688. Locke's *Two Treatises on Government*, written at the end of the seventeenth century, had a very different conception of kingship than that of James I in his *Trew Law of Free Monarchies*, written in 1598. The miraculous royal touch was undermined in a similar manner to the miracle of the mass. Kings lost their miraculous powers when they were seen to be chosen by human beings rather than instituted by God. Priests lost theirs when there was a similar move to make those with religious authority a product of human choice rather than divine appointment. Miracles had set a particular group apart as specially favoured, indeed specifically authorized, by God. Once they lost this status their special powers went with them.

But if the Protestant Reformers sought to take the magical element out of religion and eliminate the idea that the rites of the church had mechanical efficacy, then what were they going to put in its place? If human beings were going to be cut loose from what Keith Thomas called 'the imposing apparatus of ceremonial' (1973: 87), and their priests, no longer set apart as celibate magicians who can work 'the miracle of the mass', were going to be cut down to size as ministers of the word, then what was going to give human beings assurance in an uncertain world where plague might strike at any moment, where a candle could overturn and set light to your house (with no insurance to cope with the after-effects), where the harvest might fail and your family starve, or where a malevolent neighbour might seek to do you harm?

Alternatives to 'Priestly Magic'

Here Protestants fought one another in order to provide the answer. For some of them it was God's omnipotence that filled the vacuum. The doctrine of predestination put everything that happened firmly into the hands of God. Apparently random fires, famines and floods were special acts of divine providence. Apparent misfortune was divine punishment; apparent good fortune was divine reward. Thomas (1973: 97) mentions that when 30 Westcountry towns were flooded in 1607 a pamphlet was produced emphasizing that God could have drowned the whole of mankind, as happened at the time of Noah. Better to be struck down by a God who controls all things than to be subject to the fickle finger of fate.

Naturally Protestants and Catholics got into the habit of blaming each other for misfortunes. Puritans could happily blame an outbreak of plague on the toleration of Catholics if it wasn't enough to blame the opening of a theatre. Catholics could see the Great Fire of London in 1666 as divine judgement on Britain's embrace of Protestantism, citing the fact that a Catholic chapel in The Strand had 'miraculously' escaped the blaze. Such pronouncements have not gone away, as we will see in Chapter 12 on miracles in the modern world, where even a leading article in *The Times* (1984) is happy to connect a lightning strike on York minster with divine disapproval of a controversial bishop of Durham.

When in 1680 a coroner's jury in Berkshire, reporting on the tragic death of a father and son killed by lightning while in the fields ploughing, declared that the deaths had been caused by 'the immediate providence of almighty God', this remark reflected a determination to believe in the micromanagement of human life by an all-powerful Deity. In the modern day we see Oral Roberts and other part-heirs to the Puritan tradition behaving in exactly the same way (again, see Chapter 12). Puritan laymen in the seventeenth century liked to keep diaries recording the mercies bestowed on them by providence. They might also compile case-histories of the disasters which overtook sabbath-breakers and other sinners. Their motivation is not hard to see. There is a natural desire to believe that (what they interpret as) wrongdoing is punished, but beyond that there is a desire to impose order on the randomness of human fortunes – and misfortunes – and to invoke God's sovereignty against the moral chaos that might otherwise arise from the breakdown of 'priestly magic'.

Furthermore, if the Anglican church were to reject the sign of the cross and holy water, then what could it offer as a defence against evil spirits? Did this not amount to throwing away your weapons in the war against malevolent forces? Some see the dismantling of the church's apparatus of resistance against diabolical terrors as the source of a flaring up of persecution of witches in the sixteenth and seventeenth centuries. The medieval church had preserved exorcism as part of the rite of baptism and had kept the office of exorcist as a minor order since the third century. Now the Anglican Ordinal of 1550 was removing the office. Was not such an act of unilateral disarmament in the face of the devil and his armies of demons and human agents bound to lead to an upsurge in uncontrolled 'maleficium'? Could anyone be surprised if it was argued that witchcraft was on the increase? When Bishop Jewel, faithful to the ideas of the new Anglican communion, declared that the power to command evil spirits to go out of someone was no longer a gift of the church (it had been reserved for the early church only), and recommended instead that the clergy could only ask God to show mercy and could not themselves command the spirit to go, it seemed to some as if the church was declaring itself helpless in the face of the enemy.

Naturally it was the Puritans who were having none of such 'wimpishness'. Inspired by a passage of Mark's gospel, where the disciples fail to exorcise evil spirits and Jesus tells them that 'this sort' can only be cast out by 'fasting and prayer' (Mark 9:29), many Puritan exorcists developed a system of rigorous abstention from food and drink together with long hours of prayer. They ended up supposing that such a regime had precisely the same mechanical efficacy in 'making God act' as Catholic ritual did. Puritan piety, like the Catholic mass, was efficacious *ex opere operato*. The Puritan John Darrell proudly claimed that he could cast out devils unlike the priests of the 'roman church', because he believed that he had the right spells to make the magic work – spells based on inner piety rather than outward ritual.

Theologically this was always the danger of Protestantism, namely that it would return to precisely the doctrine of 'justification by works' that it claimed to oppose, except that the works would be 'inner works' of the sort one might associate with piety and prayer. Prostrate and helpless before almighty God, the Protestant turns his or her very helplessness and worthlessness into an infallible means of forcing God to haul them up into heaven.

The Protestant sects which flourished in seventeenth-century England, particularly during the Civil War period, struggled to maintain miracles without the priestly caste that was supposed to control their distribution. But as I have indicated, they had their own forms of 'control', disguised as mere 'signs' of their election by God. They were awash with prophesying and faith-healing. The ranter Thomas Webbe declared that he would pay no heed to the clergy unless they could perform miracles. Ironically, this was precisely the jibe that Catholics often threw at their Protestant opponents, namely that the latter simply couldn't 'work the magic'. Those in need of an exorcist, for instance, might well abandon their Protestant beliefs and go elsewhere for, as the saying went, 'none can lay a spirit but a papist priest'. Yet 150 miracles were attributed to George Fox, the founder of the Quakers, who left behind a 'Book of Miracles' at his death. In 1657 the Quaker Susannah Pearson tried and failed to raise a fellow Quaker who had committed suicide.

Indeed it is possible to emerge from this debate with an unfashionable respect for the Anglican Church, whose 'via media' is often seen as a mere product of political compromise, but which can here be viewed as a way of denouncing two different forms of 'manipulation', Puritan and Papist. For over a century the Church of England had to tread a difficult path in which it seemed as if a true defence against devils had to be left to Puritans on the one side and Papists on the other. Aware of the potential challenge to its authority, the Anglican Church introduced a canon in 1604 declaring that no minister might cast out devils without the permission of his bishop. In practice such measures were of limited effect. People turned to their local religious leaders for help in times of trouble, and the clergy knew that if they didn't provide satisfaction there were always the informal networks of 'wizards' and 'charmers', not to mention the Church of Rome with its 'superior magic'. It is hard not to feel sympathy for Joseph Hall, Bishop of Exeter, who in 1605 was taunted by a Catholic divine with his church's failure to produce a single miracle (Thomas 1983: 587), nor to avoid feeling that it was the Anglican Bishop whose tradition was more consistent with a founder who refused the Pharisees their demand for a 'sign'.

Yet it was the simple emphasis upon faith and hope, not as a means of compelling God to intervene but as a simple expression of human trust, that finally managed to win through. By then the Anglican *via media*, itself of course only a partial representative of this point of view, had become effectively unassailable as the established church. Catholicism had been excluded from power through the forced abdication of James II in the Glorious Revolution of 1688. The various 'Protestant sects' had changed too, some of them drifting off to the new world, others losing power through the Restoration of 1660 and changing their nature into advocates of a piety that was more a moral example than a way of conjuring up magic. The famous pilgrim of John Bunyan's hymn, of whom it is said that 'Hobgoblin, nor foul fiend/ shall daunt his spirit, he knows he at the end/ shall life inherit', must face 'the devil' with a stoical trust in the almighty, not with a store of magical countermeasures as good as anything a Papist could rustle up. By 1701 the Quakers had stopped requiring every Friends Meeting to make an annual return of judgements that had come upon their persecutors over the previous twelve months. Indeed, by the eighteenth century the belief in 'special providences' had ceased to be the generally held opinion of mainstream Anglicanism or most educated laypeople. Instead something else was preparing to replace both the belief in priestly mediation of the sacred to men and women and the belief in daily acts of special divine providence. That was the secular power of the Enlightenment.

The Enlightenment and Human Self-sufficiency

I have stressed the way in which religious organizations appropriate power to themselves by claiming to be the exclusive mediators of divine favour and protection. Such a technique is only liable to succeed while that divine favour and protection is perceived to be essential for human survival. Insofar as the belief in miracles was a response to a sense of being at the mercy of events that were out of human control – the fear of fire, floods, famine and plague as I mentioned earlier

– then it was not likely to survive the development of an environment more amenable to human management.

There is evidence that the century between 1650 and 1750 saw such an environment develop in England and Wales. The year 1665 saw the last major plague epidemic in the country. Insurance of life and property developed in the late seventeenth century, ensuring that a fire need not spell complete disaster. The hand-squirt (end of the sixteenth century) and the first fire engines (in the seventeenth century) would have improved the chances of controlling a fire. Agricultural advances made periods of famine shorter and less severe, though there were still huge deficiencies in diet. But the key point was not individual 'technical' advances – they would have been happening all the time. The key point was the moment when human beings sensed their own powers of direction over their environment and realized that they could give up belief in its being directly managed by God without feeling that they were left helpless and at the mercy of events that they couldn't hope to control. That moment does seem to have come during the century in question and to have expressed itself in a number of ways, from the power of parliament to control a King to the power of an ordinary village family to control the forces that might threaten their livestock and home.

It came partly through a revolution in communications. In Shakespearean England there would have been no mechanism through which a stolen horse or a runaway apprentice could be found. Consulting the local 'wizard' or 'wise man' about a theft was a result of having no other option. There was no police force to complain to. At least invoking the powers of a 'wise man' created the idea that something could be done. In the same way a powerful prophecy might appeal to someone who felt politically disfranchised and unable to influence the process by which a succession of monarchs exercised more or less absolute power over the realm.

By the eighteenth century that had changed. Of course it was only the well-off who could sit discussing politics in Queen Anne coffee houses, or for that matter vote in elections. But the idea of a system of government instituted and maintained by human will was established, and consummated by the act of a political establishment in inviting over from Hanover in 1714 a man with very little English, a distant claim to the throne and in fact nothing to commend him except the Protestant ideology that the oligarchy of gentlemen constituting the British Parliament at that time chose to favour.

Then again, consider the flood of printed news-sheets, the rise of letter writing (the penny post was established in London in 1680) and the increase in literacy and mobility that accompanied such progress. Out of such developments the person who suffers from theft has at least the possibility of contacting a newspaper office or recouping some of their losses through insurance. A wider world is coming into being where experiences can be shared and (at least sometimes) action taken on a broader scale to deal with personal tragedies and injustices.

It was the Enlightenment that began to think of society managing its laws and institutions, its economic and social arrangements, without relying upon any divine power, however mediated. States derived not from God's institution of a monarchy, but from the free decision of their people to evolve from a state of nature into a state of society (Hobbes). It might not be appropriate to say that the seventeenth and eighteenth centuries envisaged a form of social harmony without God (after all, even Victorian England still taxed itself with the fear of unbridled crime following a decline of belief in eternal punishment for wrongdoing). Nevertheless, there were the beginnings of a realization that without God a stable social and political system might be possible. At the same time progress in making ordinary life less hazardous – in terms of fire, famine and plague in particular – helped to overcome that fear of uncontrollable accidents which was the constant motivation behind the seeking out of all those who could help to prevent such things occurring, whether they were ministers and priests of the churches or wise women, wizards, conjurers, sorcerers, charmers and other practitioners of 'popular magic'. It was Hume who pointed out in his *Natural History of Religion* that 'in proportion as any man's course of life is governed by accident, we always find that he increases in superstition' (Wollheim 1963: 42). In Hume's terms, the eighteenth century must have heralded a lessening of the need for 'superstition'.

The Self-sufficient Universe

This drive towards 'self-sufficiency' needed more than a grounding in the social and political developments of the time. It required an intellectual underpinning. Fundamental to the change in outlook was the end of animistic thinking and the rise of the mechanical philosophy associated with Newtonian science.

To an important strand of early modern thinking the heavenly bodies were alive, as was the earth. The universe was not a huge reservoir of 'dead matter' with very occasional signs of life; it was 'a pulsating mass of vital influences and invisible spirits'. In such circumstances, 'it was only necessary that the magician should devise the appropriate technique to capture them. He could then do wonders' (Thomas 1973: 266). 'Wonders', of course, suggests miracles. But what the magician believed himself and was believed by others to be doing was science.

In Chapter 1 I showed how this point can be illustrated using the example of the weapon-salve. This was the belief that a wound could be cured if the weapon that caused it, such as a knife or dagger, was 'anointed' (plunged into a special ointment). In the twenty-first century such an idea seems about as unscientific as it possible to get. At the time, however, many would have seen this as a 'scientific' procedure. Treating the weapon in this way would release vital spirits trapped in the congealed blood. These would then be able to reunite themselves with the victim and heal the wound. Hence when Sir Kenelm Digby wrote about the weapon-salve in 1658, he claimed that such a cure could be 'accomplished naturally and without any magic' (Thomas 1973: 225).

To Neoplatonic thinking each human being was a 'small universe'; just as the universe was made up of live beings, the stars, so live beings were each a universe writ small. The 'magician' who could tap into this hierarchical spirit world, for instance by studying astrology, was not acting against scientific law; that person was being a good scientist. The cosmos was an organic unity in which every part bore a relationship to the rest, including colours, letters and numbers. Such a way of thinking was not to last, although it could be argued that it anticipated some modern attempts to reduce the universe to a single mathematical formula. But whilst it was dominant in contemporary thinking, it could give to activities like palmistry or physiognomy a 'scientific' status. The individual human is a miniature world; the individual palm or face is a miniature human. The belief in 'signatures' was a similar indication of 'natural harmony'. If a root was shaped like a foot it must be a cure for gout. If a plant was yellow it must be a treatment for jaundice. Analogies and correspondences were everywhere.

It was the mechanistic science associated with Newton that drove this perspective away and instead established an idea of the physical universe as a self-sufficient product of divine craftsmanship. After Newton, it is possible for William Paley in his *Natural Theology* (1838: vol. 4) to advance the notion of the world as akin to an intricately designed watch, and to imply that the creator is a craftsman who effectively stands outside his work. The watch is a self-sufficient piece of craftsmanship that can proceed of its own accord. But a century earlier it would have been natural to think of spirits animating (indeed being) every cog and wheel. To influence those spirits by charms and spells would be at once to practise magic and to practise science. Hence the alchemist was one with the chemist and the biologist (for metals were living organisms that could grow like plants, so to believe that one might 'grow gold' was a matter of scientific conviction), and the astronomer was one with the astrologer (astronomy studying the movements of the planets/heavenly beings and astrology the effects of those movements on earth).

What happens during the century that ushers in the Enlightenment and makes an analogy like that of Paley possible is what Weber (1961, 1965) called the 'disenchantment' of the world. Hobbes and Descartes were challenging the notion of 'incorporeal substances', while Robert Boyle's chemical discoveries were undermining alchemy. Some initial forays into the notion of magnetism and electricity as a movement of particles were eliminating the notion of occult influences at work. William Harvey's insight into the circulation of the blood was at last beginning to improve the knowledge of anatomy and undermine the old 'humoral physiognomy' which linked a balance of humours in the body to the phases of the moon. Telescopes were undermining the astrologist's insistence upon the 'perfection' of the heavenly bodies in terms of form and movement, showing them, for instance, to be blemished by sunspots, comets and the rugged surface of the moon.

What is interesting is that none of these insights was of much practical significance in terms of making human life easier. Harvey's insights didn't lead to any improvement in treatment, in the way that the discovery of anaesthetics or vaccination did. Nothing practical was to be gained by looking at the stars through a telescope, by talking in terms of gravity or by refusing to admit that a substance could be incorporeal. Although, as I have tried to indicate, life did become easier during the century in question, thinkers like Newton, Descartes, Harvey and Boyle did very little to make it so. What they did by 'disenchanting' the world was to make possible the 'technological' advances of the future. Weber's point is that without the century of 'disenchantment' before 1750, the century of industrial revolution after 1750 could not have happened.

The Enlightenment therefore represented both a reduction in what Hume calls 'a life governed by accident', by which he largely means sudden misfortune, and a gradual working through to a view of the physical universe which established it as self-sufficient (though still very much the work of God; the watch cannot make itself, even though once made it is independent of its designer – assuming it is self-winding and doesn't go wrong). As a result, constant or even occasional divine 'intervention' was required neither by practical need nor by intellectual conviction. God was reduced to creator (in the sense of beginner) of the universe, and sustainer in the sense of detached observer.

Miracles as Natural Events or Examples of Deception

The eighteenth century saw writers emerge whose scepticism concerning miracles was as 'advanced' as anything the twenty-first century could offer. Alongside Hume's 'principle' that lying or deception on the part of witnesses to a miracle must always be more credible than a miracle taking place, which we discussed in Chapter 2, we have Voltaire (1694–1778) ridiculing miracles such as that of Jesus turning water into wine at a party where people were already drunk, or sending devils into pigs and causing them to behave like lemmings, in a country where, according to Voltaire, pigs weren't even raised.[3] Hermann Reimarus (1694–1768), in a manuscript kept unpublished during his lifetime,[4] accused the apostles of fraud and declared the Resurrection a trick. A similar position was taken up by the Cambridge don Thomas Woolston, eventually indicted for blasphemy. In his six discourses on miracles, published between 1717 and 1729, he attacked the trustworthiness of both Christ and the apostles, provoking Bishop Thomas Sherlock's reply, *Tryal of the Witnesses of the Resurrection* (1729). Sherlock's attempt to describe an imaginary trial of the apostles on a charge of fraud earned the description 'Old Bailey theology', levelled by Dr Johnson. Nearly three hundred years later, exactly the same charge might be levelled against those numerous 'evangelical' or 'fundamentalist' tracts which continue to do precisely the same thing with the texts, as I discuss in the next chapter.

If the miracles weren't tricks or frauds, they were at the very least natural events that had been misunderstood. As early as 1683 an anonymous author (possibly the Deist Charles Blount) wrote a pamphlet entitled *Miracles no violations of the Laws of Nature* which was closely based on, if not a translation of, Spinoza's *Tractatus Theologico-Politicus*.[5] The idea that a miracle could have a purely scientific explanation was one which a number of people defended during the late seventeenth and eighteenth centuries, including the astronomer Halley, who claimed that there was a scientific explanation of the flood, and the botanist Nehemiah Grew, who denied that the biblical miracles had 'supernatural 'causes.

The 'natural explanation' approach was one adopted by Heinrich Paulus, a professor at Heidelberg.[6] His aim was to undermine Reimarus' suggestion of 'fraud' by re-presenting the miracles as 'natural events'. Jesus walking on water was standing on the shore, but a mist confused the disciples as to where he actually was. Jesus 'resurrected' was a man entombed while still alive and then revived by an earthquake. In what is almost a reversal of Hume's 'principle' discussed in Chapter 2, one might argue that such 'explanations' are more incredible than the miracles they purport to explain.

These writers remain theists. Though some might argue that none of these thinkers could have been entirely honest about the extent of his scepticism, it is arguable that Hume, Voltaire and Reimarus, the foremost representatives of Deism in Britain, France and Germany, combine an eighteenth-century appreciation of God as designer of the world with an equally eighteenth-century conviction that God would never tamper with what had been made, however imperfect it was (and certainly Voltaire as the author of *Candide* and Hume as the author of Part XI of the *Dialogues Concerning Natural Religion* were convinced about its moral imperfections).

What really suffers with these thinkers is not the existence of God but the existence of miracles. The 'mechanical' universe effectively excludes God from interfering, even as it praises God for the workmanship involved in creating. In many ways it is best exemplified in Spinoza, writing some fifty to a hundred years earlier. The 'vulgar', Spinoza suggests in his *Tractatus* (1862: 120f.), see the unusual as a special manifestation of God's activity, whilst when they see what works in the customary manner they assume that God is doing nothing. It could be the outlook of a Peacocke or a Polkinghorne over three hundred years later, though they might refrain from references to the 'vulgar'. All around is the beauty and complexity of the physical universe, where people are blind to God's handiwork; yet they run at the drop of a hat to admire some weeping statue.

Of course the Deist position came in for some sharp criticism in the nineteenth century. We find writers like Gore, Trench and Illingworth[7] stressing the progressive and evolutionary nature of God's revelation, from inorganic life to human personality. The mechanical has now become the biological and the stress is upon ever greater degrees of complexity. Moreover, much in the manner of twenty-first century 'scientist-theologians' like Polkinghorne and Peacocke, we find the 'modernist' and 'immanentalist' movements stressing that God was everywhere, and that the distinction between nature and supernature, which allowed God only occasional interference from the supernatural beyond, should be avoided. But the 'immanentalism' of some of the modernists, like Peacocke's panentheism, still leaves us with a self-sufficient whole in which there is only general divine action and never specific divine action. 'Miracles', in the sense of special divine actions, remain excluded.

The Rush to Cessationism

Some hoped that they could reach a compromise position whereby miracles were essentially abolished in the medieval and contemporary world, but retained for the biblical period. Early Christian writers had delighted in telling the Jews that the spirit of prophecy, which had ceased with the death of the last prophets because of the 'sins of Israel', had been poured out again with the coming of Christ. In a similar manner some Protestant thinkers were attracted to the idea that the miraculous taps, switched off when the last prophet died and switched on again with the coming of Christ, were switched off once more as soon as the medieval church showed signs of appearing like a cloud on the horizon.

This position can be seen in Middleton's *Free inquiry into the miraculous powers, which are supposed to have subsisted in the Christian church, from the earliest ages, through several successive centuries* (1748). The point of the book is all in the title. On the surface it wishes to affirm the reality of biblical miracles, while denying those of the church. But the reality is that it brings to the study of all miracles canons of criticism, which might perfectly well be applied as much to miracles of the apostolic as of the post-apostolic period. Why should one pooh-pooh the idea of Thomas Becket turning water into wine at the Pope's table, but not Jesus doing so at a wedding party? Surely one should either affirm both or deny both.

The same problem occurs in a fascinating way in Newman's writings in the nineteenth century.[8] Newman travelled from the Church of England to the Church of Rome in the course of his lifetime. He published two essays on miracles. The first essay tries to distinguish between the biblical miracles and those of the church, which are seen as 'unmeaning, extravagant and useless'.[9] The second essay is full of the continuity between the two. Did not Elisha's bones heal a man? If so, why should the miracles associated with relics of the saints be seen as 'superstitious'? Did not St Peter's shadow and St Paul's handkerchief work miracles according to the Acts of the Apostles? Why then not a piece of linen which was once wrapped around the body of a saint? Newman is here adopting a position reflecting a Catholic doctrine of continuous inspiration, according to which the miraculous taps are not switched off in the post-biblical period. Yet it is difficult to believe that the later Newman didn't have the more logical position. Surely the medieval miracles are not different in kind from those of the biblical period. Why, then, should they be called 'unmeaning, extravagant and useless' in comparison with their forebears?

It is interesting, in this context, to consider the post-Enlightenment group of 'Cessationists',[10] who believed that the 'age of miracles' had indeed come to an end, though they placed the end earlier than the conversion of Constantine and the 'triumph' of Christianity in the early fourth century. It might be dated around the death of the last of the apostles or the death of the next generation which the apostles personally empowered with 'charismata'. These Cessationists (so-called, obviously, because they believe that at a certain point in history miracles ceased), argued that miracles played the role of essential 'scaffolding' while the fundamental doctrines and structures of Christianity were being erected (particularly the New Testament). But once the building had been erected, perhaps around 200 CE, it was time to take the scaffolding away. A favourite image quoted in Cessationist literature is that of Gregory the Great (540–604), where he compares the miracles necessary for nourishing the church in its beginnings to the water necessary for nourishing a shrub in the early days of planting. Once it has firm roots in the ground, the shrub no longer has need of special watering and can rely on nature.

Apart from anything else, such a view is a profound example of the Euro-centric outlook affecting so much Christian writing. The religion had established itself in the former Roman Empire, so the assumption is that it had established itself all over the world.

Moreover, Cessationism was also very much a Protestant viewpoint born of what it saw as the Protestant Reformers' protests against a corrupt medieval church. It was certainly in the interest of the Reformers, if not to embrace outright Cessationism, at least to play down the role of miracles in the post-biblical period. The idea that the house was already built, or the shrub already planted, suited those for whom the supreme authority in the Christian faith was the Bible, whose texts were all written by the end of the second century after Christ (though the texts did not yet constitute, as we have seen, a fixed canon universally accepted by Christians). Those to whom the supreme authority was the church, on the other hand, recognized that they were dealing with an evolving ecclesiastical establishment which was expanding into the different parts of the former Roman Empire and was continuing to define itself in terms of both organization and doctrine right through the medieval period.

But the main problem for Cessationism was how it was to survive the rationalist critique of the Enlightenment. The Protestant idea of the Reformers restoring 'Biblical Christianity' after the Catholic 'Dark Ages' certainly formed part of a chain of development leading to the Enlightenment emphasis upon reason pitted against superstition. Many Enlightenment thinkers, however, recognized that the 'rational' arguments of the Reformers against post-biblical miracles could equally well be used against those recorded in the Bible itself – as we have seen in the case of Middleton. Before very long the Enlightenment was bound to throw out the biblical baby with the post-biblical bath water, as indeed by the late twentieth century it was doing from firmly within the walls of Christian apologetic.

Conclusions

Against this background I believe that it is easy to see why the period leading up to our own day has had so many powerful advocates of the view that religion is a product of insufficient human control of the social, cultural and political environment. The modern period is familiar with Freud's idea (1961: vol. XXI) that our relation to God is modelled on an infantile dependence upon a father who is both tyrant and benefactor. The image is of human maturity and dependence upon God as incompatible. The former can only emerge through overthrowing the latter. A similar presumption runs through the thought of that other great influence upon modern thought, Karl Marx,[11] who claims that the real dependence of one class upon another can only be clearly perceived when the idea of the dependence of all people upon God is shown to be false. These two giants of late nineteenth and twentieth century thought stand in a certain tradition with earlier thinkers going back to the Reformation – thinkers who by no means believed that shaking off human dependence on the 'false consciousness' of medievalism required the end of belief in God. It was the Reformers who insisted (without using such terminology) upon the manipulation of minds by a 'priestly class' who claimed to be the officially sanctioned mediators of God's power which was available to all through Holy Scripture.

Moreover, like the revolutionaries of early twentieth-century Russia, the Reformers had their own uncontrollably fissiparous tendencies. Unsurprisingly, a 'vanguard of the proletariat' emerged to manage and interpret truths which ordinary Christians might be unable to appreciate, leading to a new 'class' of biblically embedded mediators without whom the Word of God could not be received. Both Papists and Puritans could be accused of manipulating reality in their own interests.

From the perspective of religion as manipulation, a claim to 'miracles' can only be seen as a means of self-promotion taking advantage of a credulous age. God is not denied in the 'disenchanted' world of the Enlightenment, but God is certainly not allowed to intervene! For one thing, there is nothing for God to do – a perspective aptly reflected in Laplace's comment to Napoleon when asked whether he could spy God through his telescope, 'I have no need of that hypothesis.' Further questions over whether there are still 'gaps' somewhere for God to fill, for instance concerning the doctrine of evolution in the nineteenth century, are invariably answered in the negative. The view is that whatever God did by way of miraculous interference would be hijacked by human beings and made into the vehicle of their own self-aggrandisement – an extension of the Reformers' critique of the medieval church.

Whatever the Cessationists might try to do to isolate the biblical miracles from what is going on, they too are bound to come under the ban. Hence the biblical stories of miracles are either frauds or (this was less upsetting to believers in the truth of scripture) they described purely natural occurrences like Jesus walking on a sandbank or a fog-covered shoreline.

God is still there as a creator and a (distant) sustainer, and God's creation can still be taken as a whole and admired as a 'miracle' (a cause of wonder). The Enlightenment is not short of enthusiasm for the physical universe taken as a whole. Human beings can still believe in this deus ex machina and they may even rationalize the absence of miracles in terms of a demand for maturity. The German twentieth-century theologian Dietrich Bonhoeffer summed this up in terms of the need to live 'etsi Deus non daretur' – as if there was no God.[12] God was teaching us how to live without God. The 'disenchanted' world became the proper one in which we could learn to live *with* God by learning to live *without* God.

Yet as we shall see in the third part of this book, the modern world isn't quite as 'disenchanted' as it might seem, and the brave stand taken by Bonhoeffer against the religious manipulators of his time does not solve our problems.

The last three chapters have attempted to examine miracles from the time of Jesus to the present day. In one sense it has been a terribly limited perspective – that of the Christian tradition only, and clearly written from an Anglican/English perspective. Yet even such a limited perspective can perhaps throw some light upon the way in which miracles have been interpreted. I have tried to show how a claim to work or even observe miracles can be associated with a claim to authority. This may be the authority of an individual like Paul ('Have I not seen the Lord?') or it may be the authority of a community. The early Christians claimed that God showed favour to them with miracles, just as God showed disfavour by ceasing to provide miracles for the Jews. Over a millennium later, Puritans and Catholics in England squabbled over who had true miraculous powers – the 'real magic' – and later still the Cessationists tried to argue that miracles ceased after the Bible had been written because everything important in Christianity was now established. The medieval church became an aberration starved of miracles, although of course from another perspective the medieval church abounded in miracles, showing God's continual support for the church as the vehicle of God's continuing inspiration. Within that miraculous environment, there were arguments as to who could perform miracles; charismatic individuals were dangerous bearers of such powers, and there were struggles to contain them within the institutional forms of medieval Christianity. Miracles have been part of the religious power games played out through two millennia of Christian history – not to mention a vehicle of economic progress and a key element in a successful business start-up.

In the post-Reformation period of 'disenchantment', belief in miracles ceased to be a necessary ingredient for managing one's life in an uncertain world. However, as I shall try to show in Chapter 12, it would be a great mistake to think that claims concerning miracles have died out in the technologically sophisticated twenty-first century, where everyone is supposedly in control of their lives.

Such a tour of Christianity may leave us a little sceptical and sour where miracles are concerned, and yet I do not see this as a necessary conclusion. That there would be false, self-interested or merely cynical claims to miracles is something predicted by Christ himself. From a very early period miracles were stripped of their religious significance and incorporated into the weaponry of various groups vying for power. As Jesus himself foresaw, the signs of the Kingdom could very easily be transformed into instruments of domination. The Pharisee asking for a 'sign' lived on in Christian tradition, and each generation became one that kept asking for a sign, but to whom no sign would be given.

Notes

1   Lohse's book still provides an excellent Cook's Tour of Christian doctrine.
2   He makes the point in Chapter 44 of *Leviathan* (1968), first published in 1651.
3   Voltaire's early *Traite de Metaphysique*, written in 1734, offers a very Paley-like argument for the existence of God. Despite all the ribald undermining of the Bible and the church in Voltaire's later life, it is not clear that he didn't hold on, like other

Deists, to a belief in God as the designer of the universe. There was no problem believing that God made the universe; the problem was that God might then seek to interfere in it further.

4   The work was called *An Apology for the Rational Worshippers of God* – illustrating the fact that Reimarus by no means felt his arguments undermined belief in God.

5   Spinoza's *Tractatus* had been published in 1670, 13 years before Blount's work.

6   Interestingly, one of the students of Heinrich Paulus at Heidelberg was Ludwig Feuerbach.

7   Charles Gore in his *Bampton Lectures* of 1891, J.R. Illingworth in his *Divine Immanence* of 1898 (compare Peacocke's panentheism today), R.C. Trench in an earlier work of 1846, *Notes on the Miracles of Our Lord.*

8   Newman's first essay appeared in 1825 and his second in 1842. His conversion to Roman Catholicism finally came in 1845, but a more Catholic perspective, allowing for continuity between the biblical and post-biblical miracles, is visible in the second essay.

9   Despite this remark in the first essay, Newman himself published the two essays together in a new edition in 1870, claiming that taken together they represent a consistent position on miracles. It is difficult to agree with this.

10   'Cessationism' is associated in particular with the thought of B.B. Warfield, a Calvinist professor at Princeton Seminary at the turn of the nineteenth and twentieth centuries. His doctrines are most clearly set out in his *Counterfeit Miracles* (1918). For a useful study of cessationism and a critical review of its doctrines, see Jon Ruthven (1993).

11   The collection *On Religion* (1957) remains an invaluable selection of Marx's writings on religion.

12   A good (and enthusiastic) summary of Bonhoeffer is given in the chapter entitled 'The End of theism?', in Robinson (1963), pp. 29–44. Bonhoeffer's attempt to distance 'Christianity' from 'religion' could be compared to the attempt to maintain belief in God in a 'disenchanted' world.

Chapter 9

Christianity and
the Miracle of Resurrection

In the last three chapters I traced the role of miracles in the history of Christianity. In the next two chapters I wish to focus on one particular Christian miracle, the resurrection of Jesus. In this chapter the focus will be more historical and philosophical, considering what 'resurrection' means and what the evidence for this miracle might be. The following chapter will be theological, in the sense that it will ask what it means for God to perform a miracle upon God (assuming that Jesus is God the Son, as Christian orthodoxy affirms). This will enable me to conclude with some further observations about the importance of special divine actions, once again challenging the view that God's general providential activity is a sufficient and even more desirable way of relating God to the world.

Resurrection and Immortality

There is one clear reason for devoting space to the miracle of resurrection. It is that resurrection is the core of Christian belief. This is true of the resurrection of Jesus – St Paul argues that 'if the Messiah is not raised, our proclamation and your faith are both empty' (1 Corinthians 15:14) – but it is also true of our own resurrection. According to Paul, without belief in resurrection Christianity collapses both as a system of belief and as a system of ethics – 'if the dead are not raised, "let us eat and drink, for tomorrow we die"' (1 Corinthians 15:32).

I will begin by examining Christian belief in life after death in terms of a contrast between the terms 'resurrection' and 'immortality'. I will then go on to consider the evidence for the resurrection of Jesus and the implications for the resurrection of human beings as a miracle located in an indefinite future. Can Christians position themselves as believers in a miracle which, unlike for instance the blind receiving their sight or the lame walking, can only be perceived on 'the other side of death' and is therefore cut off from present experience?

When examining Christian belief in life after death, it is often argued that 'resurrection' and 'immortality' must be distinguished, with Christian belief more closely aligned with the former concept.[1] The notion of 'immortality', the argument goes, implies that you contain within your body a soul which continues to exist after death. The famous philosopher Socrates, who committed suicide by taking hemlock according to Plato's account in the *Phaedo*, believed that he would escape the 'disposable covering', the body, and proceed Houdini-like into the afterlife. The 'immortal soul' would leave the body like a snake which has sloughed off its skin. It is as if at death the body releases the soul which has been its captive during life. Writers in the Platonic tradition frequently saw the body as a 'tomb' (the Greek words 'soma' (body) and 'sema' (tomb) were often punned with one another), so that death, far from leading *to* the tomb, provided the immortal soul with its first opportunity to escape it.

Unsurprisingly, such images tend to downplay the physical or material; the body is left behind at death and has no part to play in whatever happens afterwards. It is merely your 'remains'. This downplaying of the material can be seen in the various ideas of the Gnostics, who lapped at the edges of orthodox Christianity during the early Church period. Broadly speaking, the Gnostics believed that our souls were like sparks of divine light trapped inside our bodies, waiting for liberation at death. Some Gnostics went so far as to distinguish between a creator-god, who was evil and made the material world we currently suffer from, and a redeemer-god who would release us from this 'evil' world at death. Such dualism solved the 'problem of evil' by attributing all our bodily ills to the inferior god from whom the redeemer god would liberate us.

This view of 'immortality' is then contrasted with belief in 'resurrection'. In the case of 'resurrection', life after death is in bodily form and Christian belief is usually associated with resurrection of the body. A particular aspect of Christian belief in Jesus' resurrection makes this difference from immortality clear, and that is the tradition of the empty tomb. The body has gone. If Christians believed that the soul could simply escape the body at death, and that this soul was all that mattered in the afterlife (as in the Platonic soma/sema approach described above), they could have pointed to Jesus' corpse and said 'it's just his remains. He's elsewhere.' Note that in saying this I am not trying to decide the complex historical issues around whether the body was actually there, or was stolen by the disciples, or somehow survived the agony of crucifixion (as imagined in D.H. Lawrence's novel *The Man Who Died*), or whether it is significant that the empty tomb was not explicitly mentioned by St Paul. I am trying to suggest that whatever actually happened, there is an important philosophical point to be made in the claim concerning the empty tomb, namely that Jesus' resurrection must be bodily resurrection. Whatever happened had to involve the corpse. The body was not 'a tomb within a tomb'; it was part of whatever had happened to Jesus himself when he rose from the dead. Whether or not the tomb was empty was something that mattered.

A second implication of the distinction between 'immortality' and 'resurrection' is the fact that resurrection requires a miracle; immortality does not, at least in the sense of a special act of God. If we have immortal souls locked inside us which spring into action when we die, then we have within ourselves, as part of our natural resources as humans, the means of surviving death. It could even be said that we proceed to the afterlife according to a 'law of nature'. We carry on without any divine interference. Resurrection, on the other hand, implies that we have to wait for God to act and raise us from the dead. In the famous image of St Paul in 1 Corinthians 15, he talks of the trumpet sounding and the dead being raised incorruptible (v. 52). They do not raise themselves. Another frequently used image is that of the dead as 'sleeping', but once again they do not wake of their own accord but are awakened by the Lord (for example 1 Thessalonians 4:14–16, where Christ is described descending from heaven with the trumpet of God and the voice of an archangel, which is doubtless a noise sufficient to 'wake the dead'). It is not as if our souls leave our bodies and go on the journey 'to a better place'. It is that Christ comes to us – we are unable to go anywhere on our own at death – and gives us new life. We are raised; we cannot bring ourselves back to life. Not even the dead Jesus, it must be presumed, can do this. He has to rely on the father (the implications of this belief are discussed in the next chapter). Once again, then, 'resurrection' rather than 'immortality' appears to come closer to Christian belief about life after death. It is not a life we can move on to from our own natural resources; it is new life that has to be given from God.

A third point about the Christian belief in life after death concerns the fact that it must satisfy the requirements of continuity of identity. Thus the immortality of my soul can be of no interest to me unless it is 'my' immortality; a soul which burst out of me at death like an alien creature in a science fiction film would not satisfy the requirements for my living again. Immortality of the soul must be immortality of the self. Or, to talk in terms of 'resurrection', if I am raised from the dead, the one who lives on must be 'me'. If we are destined for a Last Judgement and reward or punishment, then it must clearly be 'we' who are punished or rewarded. The process of transformation after death cannot destroy our identities or judgement becomes meaningless.

It seems to me that it is this aspect of the belief in life after death which causes the most difficulties for the New Testament writers. The issues here are complex – not least in a postmodernist world that is suspicious of the self's continuity at different points in our lives, let alone through death. On the whole the New Testament belief in life after death involves 'continuity through change' and involves a body, although not necessarily the body we had during our earthly lives. But it is not clear that it has a consistent view, despite the Herculean efforts of Wright's recent tome (2003) to demonstrate that it has. The next section of this chapter tries to specify more clearly what this 'continuity through change' might mean.

Resurrection and Personal Identity

That resurrection involves transformation, and not just restoration, of our bodies points up an essential difference between a miracle like the raising of Lazarus (described in John 11) and a miracle like the raising of Jesus (described in John 20). The raising of Lazarus or of Jairus' daughter, as recorded in the synoptic gospels, brings them back to the life they were leading before death. It is effectively a miraculous resuscitation rather than resurrection. A cynic could say that they have the dubious distinction of being able to die twice. The resurrection of Jesus, however, does not just bring him back to the life he knew when he was alive, but transforms him into new life. Paul thinks in the same manner of our own resurrection. Unlike Jairus and Lazarus, the risen Jesus will not die again; nor will we when we are raised from the dead. These resurrections are a victory over death; the raising of Lazarus is a mere postponement, and by the year 100 CE one may presume that the body of Lazarus was rotting all over again.

In his carefully crafted account John points up these differences in terms of the graveclothes. Lazarus emerges from the tomb bound hand and foot with graveclothes, and his face is wrapped in a cloth (John 11:44). He is still bound by the constraints of the world he was once living in and now lives in again. But when Jesus is raised the linen cloths are left lying in the tomb (John 20:6), and the handkerchief that had been round his head is 'folded together in a place by itself' (John 20:7). Jesus has not been brought back to the state he was in before death. He is not what he was, but has been glorified. He is presented as looking different (Mary Magdalene thinks he is the gardener, John 20:15) and when in Luke's gospel the disciples finally realize that the man who has been with them on the road to Emmaus is Jesus, he vanishes from their sight (Luke 24:31).

At the same time, however, as they make clear how Jesus as raised from the dead has been more than resuscitated, the gospels also make clear that he still has a body. It is a body which (in the account from John's gospel, for instance) can be touched by doubting Thomas (John 20:27). In Luke's account Jesus shows the disciples his hands and feet (Luke 24:40), eats fish (Luke 24:43) and specifically distinguishes his risen presence from that of a spirit ('a spirit does not have flesh and bones, as you see I have' – Luke 24:39). The risen Christ is transformed and glorified, but he is still a glorified body, one that remains with the disciples until it is removed at the ascension.

It may be that the images of resurrection offered in the gospels appear superficially to clash – Thomas may touch, Mary Magdalene may not; Jesus reveals himself and then promptly vanishes; the risen Christ terrifies the disciples by appearing suddenly in their midst (Luke 24:36–7), but stresses that he is not a disembodied spirit and eats fish. But the point of this apparent confusion is to stress the continuity through change which is the essential characteristic of resurrection. Eating and touching represent continuity; sudden appearance and disappearance, or the fear that comes upon the disciples when they encounter Jesus again (Matthew 28:10, Luke 24:37) represent change. But what is changed, transformed and glorified is a body. Spirits leave their bodies behind when they come back from the dead; the risen Christ does not and nor, by implication, will we at the time of our own resurrection.

But if we are not to leave our bodies behind at the resurrection, what will they be like? We know what restored sight or even walking on water would be like – but what is it like to live on after death with a glorified body? Does such a body eat? The risen body of Jesus apparently does. Does this mean it feels hungry? How does it digest the food? Does the food need to be let out as well as in? Doubtless these will be seen as impossible or reductionist questions to ask from 'this side' of resurrection. But if so, just what do those who talk about a resurrected or glorified or spiritual body mean by the word 'body'?

It might seem that it is unnecessary to concern ourselves with such questions when talking about life after death. Instead we could simply adopt a frequently used image to convey the Christian idea of resurrection, namely that it is a miraculous act of recreation whose only parallel is the miraculous act of creation itself. The first creation was, so far as most scholars are concerned, 'ex nihilo' – out of nothing – which means that the material from which we were made did nothing to contribute to or constrain its creation. In the same way, the argument goes, the material of our recreation, decaying bones or scattered ashes, can do nothing to affect our miraculous resurrection. It is as if in trying to think about how we might have bodies at the resurrection, we were simply being naive about the power of God. If God made the world from nothing, why can't the Deity remake someone by working on decaying tissue, irreversibly damaged brains, old bones, dust and ashes or a few molecules scattered around the universe, and then turn them into whatever God wants?

The trouble is that this analogy between resurrection and creation is inadequate in one crucial respect. Certainly we cannot resurrect ourselves any more than the world could make itself – I have already tried to emphasize this aspect of 'resurrection' as opposed to 'immortality'. But what we become at the resurrection must be 'us', continuous enough with the persons who lived here on earth to be, for instance, susceptible to a last judgement (how can the afterlife involve judgement if it is not we who are judged and presumably recognize the validity of this judgement in relation to our past lives?). Our resurrected bodies must bear a continuity with our own bodily past which is not demanded of the first creation 'out of nothing'. It is precisely this constraint, the constraint of the fact that God, in acting to raise the dead, is acting upon people with lives already lived and characters already formed, that makes for difficulties in the concept of resurrection and leads us to talk of some continuity through death of our 'physical humanity'. And it is this constraint which rescues, it seems to me, the notion of 'immortality' as bearing a valid constraint upon Christian belief in resurrection. For at least in speaking of an immortal soul or self we recognize that what is raised from the dead must be 'us'.

The point is illustrated if we consider three different images offered in the New Testament to describe resurrection. One of Paul's favourites is that of putting on, clothing or (in more philosophical terms) addition:

> For this corruptible [body] must clothe itself with incorruptibility; and this mortal [body] must clothe itself with immortality.
>
> (1 Corinthians 15:53–4)

The following passage also has this sense of 'putting on', but it is described in a slightly different manner:

> For we know that if the earthly frame that houses us today should be demolished, we possess a building which God has provided – a house not made by human hands, eternal and in heaven. In this present body we do indeed groan; we yearn to have our

heavenly habitation put on over this one – in the hope that, being thus clothed, we shall not find ourselves naked. We groan indeed, we who are enclosed within this earthly frame; we are oppressed because we do not want to have the old body stripped off. Rather our desire is to have the new body put on over it, so that our mortal part may be absorbed into life immortal.

(2 Corinthians 5:1–4, NEB)

This second text from 2 Corinthians is very difficult. It must always be remembered that these are not intended to be philosophical descriptions of life after death. At the back of Paul's mind is the religious imagery of Adam naked in the garden of Eden, the first man who sinned, in comparison to the new man or second Adam, the sinless Christ who redeems. Nevertheless, there is an implicit description of bodily resurrection which thinks both of 'addition' – we who are in this tent wanting to be further clothed – and of something more like 'exchange' – getting rid of the earthly frame and replacing it with a building made in heaven provided by God (see Moule 1966).

Both of these images, however, run into difficulties when we try to analyse their value philosophically as descriptions of life after death. For 'addition' and 'exchange' imply no change to whatever adds or exchanges. They are essentially external changes. If the mortal body 'puts on' immortality, it remains a mortal body. If it exchanges one 'dwelling' for another, then it remains the same inside both 'houses'. These images stress the newness of resurrection and the fact that we depend upon God to raise us. Hence the attraction of the idea of clothing the naked, with its sense of vulnerability and dependence and the rescue which comes at the mercy of another who enables us to put on something completely new. But they arguably fall short in understanding how in the process we are changed – and this may in part account for the convoluted nature of Paul's prose.

A third image used to convey the idea of resurrection is that of the seed and the corn. We find it in John's gospel:

unless a grain of wheat falls into the ground and dies, it remains alone; but if it dies, it produces much grain

(John 12:24)

and it is also present in Paul, in the extended metaphor of 1 Corinthians 15:36–44, beginning with the observation that

What you sow is not made alive unless it dies.

Apart from the obvious parallel between planting a seed and burying a corpse, the biological metaphor conveys the 'continuity through change' idea much better than addition or exchange, because it clearly suggests an alteration that is not merely external – 'putting on' something new. It is a total transformation. Interestingly, however, it is a metaphor much closer to 'immortality' than 'resurrection', since the seed becomes a plant through a natural process requiring no external interference. It is in the nature of seeds to become plants, whereas it is not in the nature of mortal bodies to 'put on' immortality.

These different images highlight some of the difficulties involved in making sense of resurrection. On the one hand it must involve an act of God breaking into the natural order and raising the dead who cannot raise themselves. On the other hand it must preserve the continuity of what is acted upon – hence the attraction of the seed/grain metaphor.

In this first section of the chapter I have tried to establish three things about the nature of the resurrection in order to define what exactly the miracle entails. I have tried to argue that it involves, first, life in bodily form, not the escape of some immortal part of us which leaves behind our 'mortal remains' and wends its own, separate immortal way to heaven. It involves, second, a miracle, a special act of God which does to us what we cannot do to ourselves. In the case of the resurrection of Jesus, the father acts upon the son, both of them divine, a concept which I explore further in the next chapter. Third, I have stressed that the miracle of resurrection involves not bringing people back to the life they once knew but transforming them into new life. In this sense the miracle of Jesus' resurrection, or that of ours, is quite different from the raising of Lazarus, of the Widow of Nain's son or of Jairus' daughter. These latter are essentially healing miracles; they are not a case of resurrection. However, I have also tried to stress that this transformation is of 'them', in other words that there must be an element of continuity between what they were in their earthly life and what they are at the resurrection. This condition of continuity, it seems to me, is protected by the idea of 'immortality' and means that a simple contrast between the concepts of 'immortality' (bad) and 'resurrection' (good) will not do. It would be better to say that Christians believe in an immortality of the bodily self made possible through a special act of God, the miracle of resurrection, rather than through their own human resources.[2] The notion of a special act of God, central to my understanding of miracle, remains essential. Resurrection is not something that people can do to themselves.

Having tried to establish what is meant by 'resurrection', including the question of what the biblical texts mean when they talk about the resurrection of Jesus, I now move on to a consideration of how the biblical texts may be interpreted. Can we approach any kind of 'balance of probability', to quote the conclusion of a recent study of Jesus' resurrection (Swinburne 2003: 201–3), about their reliability?

The Courtroom Drama Approach

One preliminary observation needs to be made, which I touch upon elsewhere in this book. We must avoid assuming that primitive people were innately 'credulous'. It is important not to patronize the past and not to assume that before 'modern science' and the formulation of 'laws of nature' a kind of anarchy prevailed in which it was impossible to disbelieve miracle stories. On the contrary, people in the ancient world regularly challenged such stories, not least because miracle-workers were laying claim to an authority which rivals naturally wished to challenge. The very fact that Matthew records an account of soldiers being bribed to say that the disciples came during the night and stole the body (Matthew 28:11–15) shows that people were perfectly capable of finding alternative, 'natural' explanations of what had happened to the corpse of Jesus.

Having said that, there are several different ways in which the resurrection has been handled by scholars, and I want to consider some of them before trying to reach some conclusions about both the nature and the probability of this miracle.

The first approach has been to treat the resurrection of Jesus as if it was a case to be tried in court. In a strange reversal of the usual murder case, it is the fact that someone has come back from the dead that is on trial. The accounts of the evangelists and Paul are assessed as 'evidence' and a 'judgment' is made.

This approach can be traced back to the eighteenth century and Bishop Thomas Sherlock's *Trial of the Witnesses of the Resurrection* (1729), a rejoinder to the Cambridge don Thomas Woolston's *Six Discourses on Miracles* (1717–29). It was an imaginary trial of the apostles on a charge of fraud (Woolston had accused the disciples of fraud by stealing the body of Christ from the sepulchre), and was part of a genre which the great Dr Johnson dubbed 'Old Bailey theology'. Nowadays such an approach tends to be adopted, if at all, by fundamentalist commentators who take it for granted that whatever each evangelist writes must be intended as a literal statement, even if it turns out to have been mistaken. As a result, of course, such commentators are faced by an apparent contradiction in the accounts given by the various 'witnesses' – for instance whether Jesus is raised after three days or on the third day. However, these apparent differences can be made to count in their favour, for instance by proving that there was no collusion between them. Had they all said the same thing, the statements would have been far less credible. Genuine witnesses always have a different 'take' on events, especially unexpected and extraordinary ones. On the other hand, such an 'explanation' of discrepancies in the accounts is hard to square with the notion of 'biblical infallibility'.

The trouble with this approach, quite apart from the fact that it is inherently unconvincing (would you really applaud the trustworthiness of witnesses who differed from one another concerning the date of a murder?), is that it has no understanding of the evangelists as editorializing writers who reflect the traditions of different communities and commend a particular theological viewpoint. This is not to say that there is no historical basis for what they write – there must be. But they did not, when they wrote the gospels, write as if they were producing statements for use in a courtroom.

Take, for instance, the sort of commentary that remarks how Matthew, the most 'Jewish' gospel, places the final appearance of the risen Jesus to the disciples in Galilee, to show that the good news is to be proclaimed to the whole world. This suggestion of a theological purpose may mean that the evangelist describes Jesus as appearing in Galilee without knowing whether he actually did. Such an editorial decision does not mean that he can be accused of deception or invention. He was writing in the literary traditions of his time. Since the aim of any good biblical scholar is to be faithful to the Bible, he or she has to be faithful to the biblical traditions of writing which were certainly not those of modern-day courtroom dramas.

The same point could be made of Luke, the most 'Gentile' of gospels, which ends in Jerusalem in order to show that this 'good news' (gospel) is nevertheless the fulfilment of Judaism. Once again, it is not necessary to say that such appearances must be seen as 'invented'. It could be that the risen Jesus appeared in both Galilee and Jerusalem, with each gospel writer choosing to highlight a selection of 'real appearances'. But even if Luke only knew that Jesus had risen from the dead and appeared to some of his followers, he might well have placed some of those appearances in Jerusalem for precisely the theological reason which I have tried to outline. Treating the gospel writers as witnesses taking the stand simply misses the point of what they are doing.

Resurrection Experiences as 'Natural Events'

The second approach is to turn attention away from whatever went on with corpses, tombs and sleeping soldiers, and to concentrate instead on the resurrection experiences. This approach is interesting, and itself needs to be divided into three different strands.

The first strand can be associated with a fascinating book by Michael Perry called *The Easter Enigma* (1959). Perry interpreted the appearances of the risen Jesus in terms of what he believed could be inferred from our knowledge of the paranormal and psychical research. He took the view that the dead sometimes made contact with the living by causing those still alive to project an image of themselves. This was, as it were, their way of getting in touch. The appearances of Jesus thus become a further instance of appearances which many others have caused to be projected of themselves. In Perry's analysis the Pauline experience on the road to Damascus becomes, not the exception to the other 'appearances', but the model in terms of which all the rest should be viewed. Jesus causes Paul to see and to hear him; he causes Thomas to touch him; he causes the disciples to see him eating. In the manner of other cases where the dead make contact, Jesus manifests himself all of a sudden and vanishes all of a sudden (Luke 24:31, 36). All this can be maintained without any reference to the empty tomb – indeed this is the one aspect of the tradition which is liable to be lost in Perry's analysis, since other apparent cases of the dead getting in contact do not involve their corpses getting up and walking.

Perry's account is interesting because it effectively allows the appearances of the risen Jesus to be viewed as an instance of 'natural law', at least if 'natural law' is defined in a broad enough manner to include psychic phenomena. Rather like those who argue that Jesus walking on water is 'proved' by the occurrence of sandbanks in that part of the world, Perry keeps the apparent reliability of the text at the expense of losing the miracle. His book shows that even where the 'greatest miracle of all' is concerned it is possible to 'accept' it as one of those things that happen, not as a violation of a natural law but as an illustration of a natural law. It is a point that reminds us of how when defining a miracle as 'a violation of a natural law' or as something that is beyond the powers of human beings to accomplish, we have to be clear what those natural laws are or what the limitations of those human powers are.

In Chapter 8, I consider the way in which some people believed in the weapon-salve not as a miracle but as a scientific procedure. Perry illustrates that it is even possible to contain the resurrection within the bounds of what is 'scientific', namely as an illustration of the way in which the dead make contact with the living. His case also illustrates the point that there is always a debate over what is scientific, be it the controversy over Neoplatonic animism in the seventeenth century or that over psychical research in the twentieth.

Resurrection Experiences as Proof of Jesus' Resurrection

The second strand of thinking which focuses on the resurrection experiences is based on a desire to avoid the uncertainties surrounding the 'events leading up' to something that cannot be denied, namely the faith of the disciples. A number of authors have fixed on the fact that whatever the doubts over what happened to the body of Jesus, one thing is undeniable and that is the conviction on the part of the disciples and numerous others that he had risen from the dead. They therefore try to locate the resurrection here, in the 'Easter faith', where there are no difficult questions concerning claims about a body being raised from the dead.

Sometimes this simply means arguing that 'something must have happened' in order to generate such enthusiasm and conviction on the part of Jesus' followers – how otherwise would the disciples who took flight at Jesus' arrest have regrouped and become convinced that the gospel must be proclaimed to the ends of the earth? The evidence for the resurrection therefore becomes the belief that it had taken place.

In general terms such an argument can hardly convince. Martyrs create movements, which is why many oppressive regimes prefer to imprison or otherwise marginalize rather than kill their opponents. In specific terms, however, the argument is more plausible. Given Jesus' claims about himself during his life, it could be said, only his resurrection would have made his ministry seem credible. Most martyrs, after all, do not predict that they will rise from the dead, except in the sense that they will live on in the commitment of others to the movement they are dying for. But all this begs questions about what Jesus actually claimed about himself during his ministry, and the way in which the gospel accounts of his claims should be unpicked. It is perfectly possible to argue that the gospel writers described a Jesus who claimed that he would rise from the dead when they were writing more than a generation after his death, but that this was simply the result of the rise of Christianity following the 'great deception' of the disciples stealing the body and 'creating' the resurrection story. That Jesus himself claimed that he would rise from the dead could still be denied. In the jargon of New Testament studies, all references to it in the various texts could be dismissed as 'later interpolations'.

The more it seems credible that without the resurrection Jesus' life is worth nothing, the more motivation there is for deception. I am not trying to claim that such a deception took place. I am claiming that the argument that without believing Jesus was raised from the dead, his followers could never have got together to launch the new movement after his death, cuts both ways. It could mean that he did indeed rise from the dead. It could also mean that those followers had every reason for making it seem that he did. As a consequence it seems to me that the uncertainty generated by any consideration of history remains – in this case uncertainty about what Jesus actually claimed about himself. The faith of the disciples is clearly a significant factor in considering the resurrection, but it does not remove the necessity of examining historical issues concerning the events that took place to promote that faith.

Resurrection Experiences as the Content of Jesus' Resurrection

The third strand of thinking which focuses on the resurrection experiences, rather than on the events that might or might not have given rise to them, is a more systematic attempt to bypass history altogether as too weak a foundation for faith. Rather than speaking of faith 'in' the resurrection, this strand believes that the Easter faith *is* the resurrection. 'Jesus is risen' effectively means 'Jesus proclaims himself to me now'.[3] Where the second strand merely saw the faith of the disciples as decisive evidence for the truth of the resurrection, this strand seeks to identify it with the resurrection.

As with the other strands, this approach focuses upon the reported experiences of the risen Christ and upon that of Paul in particular. It is certainly interesting that when Paul lists, in 1 Corinthians 15:5–8, the various appearances of the risen Jesus, he includes among them his own experience on the Damascus Road. In principle such an encounter with Christ could therefore happen to anyone at any time, since for Paul the 'appearances' are not limited to the 40 days between resurrection and ascension during which Jesus was still a bodily presence on earth. Paul himself, though he mentions the burial of Jesus (1 Corinthians 15:4) makes no mention of the empty tomb, an omission which some scholars see as significant (though others claim that Paul 'implicitly affirms' the empty tomb). Could it be that for Paul the encounter with Jesus on the road to Damascus – the light shining all around and the voice saying 'Saul, Saul, why are you persecuting me?' (Acts 9: 4–7) – was a direct experience of the risen Christ that made questions along the lines of 'what happened to the body' redundant? Unlike the public appearances to the disciples before the ascension recorded in the gospels, this has more the character of a private vision in which those who were with Paul could not participate (in Acts 9:7 they hear a voice but see no one; when Paul retells the story in Acts 22:9 they see the light but hear nothing – but in either case his companions are effectively excluded from what is going on). If 'Jesus is risen' means that 'I experience him as risen now', perhaps through a Damascus Road-type of experience of my own, what does it matter that I have difficulty making sense of the circumstances through which he died and was raised? It is as if the unexpected guest were to say: 'Here I am, so why worry about how I got here?'

The attraction of this position is that it apparently removes the believer from all those nagging doubts associated with considerations of historicity. They become irrelevant. The Easter faith is based on itself. Whatever happened in the past, whatever went on with corpses, tombs and sleeping soldiers, is unimportant. But is it really a way of, in Bultmann's words, ensuring that 'the historical problem is not of interest to Christian belief in the resurrection' (1972: 41)? Let us accept for the moment that Paul's experience on the Damascus Road was a 'resurrection appearance' in which the risen Christ made himself known to him in a vision. Does this bypass all the historical questions and the uncertainties associated with them? Those who want to say that direct contact with the risen Jesus, whether in the case of Paul or in the case of Christians now, avoids questions of history, forget that the very first thing such 'direct contact' would raise would be a historical question – namely 'Is this really Jesus of Nazareth who was crucified?' The 'Here I am, so why worry about how I got here?' approach would be confronted by 'How do I know it's you?'

People who wish to replace the uncertainties of historical research with the certainties of personal experience forget that personal experience does not deliver certainty. The only thing that I can say with absolute certainty is 'there is an experience' or perhaps 'I am having an experience'. Saying that my experience is 'of Jesus' or of 'the risen Jesus', however, immediately brings me into the public arena where someone is perfectly able to argue that I am mistaken, not of course concerning the fact that I have an experience, but concerning what my experience is of. Probably no argument has been more resisted by Christians, anxious to huddle inside the tent of their personal contact with the 'living Jesus', than this. Nevertheless the point remains that what I can say with absolute certainty is entirely trivial – namely that I am experiencing. What I can say that is significant – I am experiencing Jesus – is always open to doubt.

Even if we choose to locate the 'miracle of resurrection' in the appearances to the disciples and to Paul, this does not bypass the questions concerning 'what happened' to the body but rather makes them even more significant. We might want to say that Perry is wrong to give the appearances the quasi-scientific status he does; rather, these are genuine 'miracles' in which Jesus causes, for instance, Paul to have a blinding vision of him. But even if that is so, it only makes more urgent the issues surrounding his death and its aftermath. When Paul receives the vision of Christ, his first question is 'Tell me Lord, who you are' (Acts 9:5). If he is to believe that the one who has appeared to him on the Damascus Road is Jesus of Nazareth who lived, died and was buried, then he is bound to be confronted by the question of another miracle, the one that brought Christ back from the dead. Indeed Paul is profoundly aware of the significance of Jesus' life and ministry as something he did not share and which to some extent undermines his claim to be an apostle – the appearance to him was, after all, to one 'untimely born' (1 Corinthians 15:8).[4]

The approach which I have described as defining the resurrection in terms of the Easter faith has a very unfortunate consequence. It leads to a belittling of the whole historical enterprise, which is removed from the process of achieving or deepening Christian faith. Lessing's dictum that 'accidental truths of history can never become the proof of necessary truths of reason' (1957: 53) has led to a belief that anything to do with the 'quest of the historical Jesus', be it his life, his teaching or his death and resurrection, is irrelevant to Christian belief, which must rest on firmer foundations than historical possibility or even probability. Arguably such an attitude has brought about a failure to engage with matters of history that has both enraged sceptics and weakened the apologetic case for Christianity.

The idea that faith cannot rest on uncertainty begs certain questions about faith. It is perfectly possible to argue that notions like 'faith', 'belief' and 'trust' only make sense where there is *un*certainty. If the miracle of Jesus' resurrection is and will always remain, this side of death, something of which even the believer must remain uncertain, that need not mean that it is impossible to have faith in Christ as risen. It could simply mean that Christ has chosen to make himself known in the temporary, ambiguous and fleeting arena of vulnerable human life, and faith in him means accepting the uncertainty of our knowledge concerning the past.

If Christians accept doubt as a part of their faith,[5] then lack of certainty ceases to be a problem. Unfortunately for many of them such acceptance is impossible, perhaps because it was psychological insecurity that drove them to belief in the first place (see Towler 1984: 99–109).

Acceptance of Historical Uncertainty

Which brings me to the third approach. This accepts that uncertainty is an inherent feature of any historical investigation. A suggestion such as that the disciples or other followers of Jesus stole the body cannot be proved true or false. According to this third approach it has to be admitted that proof, either in the strong sense of logical demonstration as in mathematical theorems, or in the weaker sense of 'proof beyond reasonable doubt' as in a court of law, is simply not attainable. Doubt cannot be banished through some direct personal onslaught by the risen Christ upon those he favours; doubt is to be accepted rather than fled from. Swinburne's 'balance of probability' may seem like a weak-kneed alternative to the other options, but that might be precisely what makes it appropriate to the working of God in relation to humanity. This seemingly inescapable fact, namely that in dealing with the lynchpin of Christian faith, the miracle of Christ's resurrection, we are dealing with a series of events that we can never affirm as more than 'probable', might be a part of God's design. It is consistent with God's decision to be made known in the life of a vulnerable and (in some senses of the words) weak and dependent human being. I shall seek to expand this point further in the next chapter.

There is no doubt that the sorts of concerns Hume voiced over the reliability of witnesses can be brought into consideration where the resurrection is concerned. Acts 10:40–41 has Peter recounting that God raised Jesus on the third day and 'showed him openly'. 'Showed him openly' does not, however, appear to mean showed him publicly. Verse 41 explains that God showed him 'not to all the people, but to witnesses chosen before by God, even to us who ate and drank with him after he rose from the dead'. The risen Jesus does not, then, appear to people like Caiaphas or Herod. The risen Jesus comes quietly and modestly back to his own before ascending. There is a hint of something more suggestive of a 'mass rally' in Paul's account of Jesus' appearance to 'over 500 brethren at once' (1 Corinthians 15:6), presumably some kind of early 'church' assembly, but there is no passage in the gospel accounts referring to this event. If Acts 1:3 talks of Jesus presenting himself alive after his suffering 'by many infallible proofs', then not many of them seem to have been handed down in the gospel records.

During his life Jesus performed miracles openly (though he often asked those who were healed not to tell anyone of what had been done to them) and acquired a reputation outside the ranks of his supporters for his wonder-working. Josephus refers to him in his *Antiquities* as 'a doer of startling deeds'. But the most startling deed of all is made known only to those closest to him.

The fact that the risen Christ only appears to those who might be thought to desire his resurrection (Paul may be an exception in this respect, though someone could always employ the catch-all argument that he unconsciously desired it) might seem to weaken the case for its credibility and increase the strength of the argument that it was a case of wish-fulfilment, or some kind of 'Che lives' determination to make the work and influence of the dead Jesus survive him. At the same time it is clear that the resurrection appearances are linked to the specific task of commissioning the apostles and sending the Holy Spirit to maintain their faith after Christ is no longer bodily present. I would return to the argument that Jesus refuses demonstrations of power, 'signs' for the Pharisees, and in submitting to the cross refuses the power which might save himself. To emerge from the tomb like a Jack-in-the-box for a 'told-you-so' demonstration to his opponents that they were wrong would hardly be consistent with this approach. The deliberate policy of weakness and self-giving surrounding the way of the cross, it is important to recognize, is not simply overridden by the resurrection.

I would argue that this is the theological context within which it is possible to make sense of Swinburne when he defends the lack of evidence for Jesus' resurrection on the grounds that God must not 'make his presence and his intentions for us too obvious' (2003: 172). The restricted number of appearances is about maintaining what Swinburne likes to call an 'epistemic distance' between God and humanity. This is how Swinburne seeks to make a virtue out of what Hume might have considered a vice, namely the relative lack of witnesses and the absence of any disinterested ones. He assures us that we will have 'quite a bit of evidence' but not 'the overwhelming evidence that would make free choice impossible' (2003: 173).

Stated in such a way, Swinburne's position could easily be open to parody. The more incredible Christianity becomes, the more its supporters trumpet God's wisdom in leaving us room to choose for ourselves! But taken within an overall context that understands how Jesus' miracles are not intended to be demonstrations of overwhelming divine force beating his opponents into submission, it seems to me logical that the resurrection would not subvert that strategy with some explosive display of force majeure.

The Significance of the Empty Tomb

From all that I have said concerning the essential role of the body in resurrection, it will be clear that my own view is that the empty tomb must be considered an integral part of the narrative of Jesus' resurrection. This is not a case of a 'soul' proving that it has successfully escaped all bodily constraints, leaving its useless 'shell' behind.

There are many theologians who claim that it would be easier to sustain belief in the resurrection of Jesus by jettisoning belief in the empty tomb. They argue that the empty tomb is not explicitly affirmed by Paul and that it is harder to believe in than the appearances of the risen Jesus. As I have tried to outline in the second half of this chapter, they seek to make the 'direct contact' between the risen Jesus and the believer – whether a first-century apostle or a twenty-first-century follower – something that overrides historical considerations concerning what happened to the body.[6] I have tried to argue that it cannot override these considerations.

It is perfectly true that the empty tomb is 'harder to believe in' in the sense that it requires acceptance of a miracle. As I have already said in relation to Perry's book, the appearances could be seen as examples of a scientific law, providing that 'science' is given a wide enough definition. The empty tomb, on the other hand, cannot be seen as an instance of any law (providing that it is accepted that Jesus died, that the tomb was correctly identified and that the body was not stolen). Moreover, focusing on the appearances alone allows for all those interpretations of 'resurrection' which talk about the disciples stirring themselves to overcome their depression and to 'believe'. The Easter faith ceases to be faith *in* a miracle and becomes *itself* the 'miracle'. But it seems to me that without the empty tomb these 'visions' of the 'risen Jesus' would not have been convincing. The question would have arisen as to whether they were delusions. They would not have been sufficient evidence in themselves that he had been raised to life.

People are wary of admitting the empty tomb to the story of the resurrection, because they fear that as a claimed fact of history it cannot be certain. That is true. Each of the three explanations given above – that Jesus didn't die, that there was confusion over the tomb he was laid in and that his body was stolen – is a possible alternative to resurrection. I would not myself consider them plausible, but that is itself a matter for debate and many historians would find one or more of these alternatives perfectly convincing.[7] Yet it seems to me that without an empty tomb the resurrection of Jesus as the resurrection of his body makes no sense. If that means that I have to face the fact that there are alternative explanations concerning what happened to his body than my own, and that I can never be certain I am right, then I would argue that this uncertainty is part of the logic of incarnation itself, where the divine surrenders itself to be part of human life with all its ambiguity. The next chapter will try to put some theological muscle behind this claim.

Swinburne (2003: 152ff.) is sceptical of the idea that the first gospel, that of St Mark, ended at verse 8 with the women fleeing from the tomb having found it empty. It is certainly interesting that scholars find it easier to accept appearances without an empty tomb than an empty tomb without appearances. Yet it seems to me that the 'shorter ending' of Mark is perfectly plausible. It ends with a preposition, which is unusual in Greek, but might that not have been an effective way of saying that words fail in describing what has happened? It ends in uncertainty and confusion, but uncertainty and confusion pepper the whole gospel, where the disciples believe and fail to believe, where Jesus is misunderstood even by the inner cabinet of his adherents and where he goes to his death betrayed. The author of St Mark's gospel refuses to end with the sort of triumphant display which would usurp all that had been said during Jesus' ministry. If there was a miracle, if at this one point in history there was a special act of God, then for the women to run from the tomb afraid, rather than standing wildly clapping Jesus' success, is a measure of their appreciation of what had gone before, including the long-drawn-out agony of the cross. And if, to return to the point where this chapter began, resurrection is a miracle that cannot be perceived on this side of death and is cut off from our present experience, then the words to describe it are bound to fail. Whatever the other gospels (or the 'longer ending' of Mark) describe the followers of Christ as seeing, here they are confronted with that of which they cannot speak and must be silent. The empty tomb and the broken sentence to end the gospel are metaphors of human inability to encapsulate God, even the God who deliberately becomes incarnate as a human. The women are afraid as in the Hebrew Bible those who approach the presence of God on the mountain are afraid. But what inspires that fear is God's presence, not God's absence, God's presence in the miracle of Christ's resurrection, which is first made known not in what is but in what is not, in the fact that the torn body they have come to anoint is no longer there.[8]

Notes

1   See the argument of the philosopher P.T. Geach (1969), ch. 2, 'Immortality', pp. 17–29. It is interesting to compare the view of Geach as a theist with the similar arguments of the atheist Bernard Williams (1973). Both favour the idea of bodily continuity as a necessary condition of personal identity, with the implication that it is a necessary condition of life after death.

2   In this sense it is possible to understand and concur with the title of A.E. Taylor's *The Christian Hope of Immortality* (1946).

3   This is the position which I would associate with Bultmann (1972: 41) where he writes that 'the historical problem is not of interest to Christian belief in the resurrection' and that 'faith in the resurrection is really the same thing as faith in the saving power of the cross'.

4   See Rowland (1982: 376) for this interpretation of the appearance to Paul as to one 'untimely born'.

5 As suggested by the poet Tennyson when he wrote:

> There lives more faith in honest doubt,
> (Believe me), than in half the creeds.

6 There are many examples of this approach. One of the most readable is that by Peter Selby (1976). Selby's approach is clear from the title, *Look for the Living: The Corporate Nature of Resurrection Faith*. The faith awakened by the risen Christ in the community of those who follow him makes 'poking around in tombs' looking for bodies (or their absence) a redundant and even faithless activity. Another writer in this vein is Willi Marxsen, who contributed 'The Resurrection of Jesus as a Historical and Theological Problem' to Moule (1968). Once again a lot can be read from the title of Moule's volume, *The Significance of the Message of the Resurrection for Faith in Jesus Christ*. What is significant for faith is the 'message' rather than the 'reality' of the resurrection, leaving open the question of whether the message is about anything that actually happened.

7 Like Swinburne, I do think there is significance in the fact that the Christians were accused by their opponents of having stolen the body. This indicates that it was not possible to suggest that they had mistaken the tomb or simply to go to the tomb and identify its contents. But this observation cannot, of course, prove those opponents wrong in their arguments.

8 A sympathetic view of the 'shorter ending' can be found in Morna Hooker (1991).

Chapter 10

Jesus' Resurrection and the Nature of God

The last chapter examined some of the issues involved in defining the miracle of Jesus' resurrection and assessing the evidence for it. In this chapter I want to examine the implications of the resurrection of Jesus for Christian belief in God. The chapter will therefore concentrate upon an issue that is implicit at every stage of the argument concerning miracles, namely what sort of God would carry them out.

The Resurrection of Jesus as a Revelation of God

One of the most interesting implications of orthodox Christian views concerning the divinity of both the father and the son is that they require us to believe that the miracle of Jesus' resurrection was a healing internal to God. If Jesus is thought of not as a man filled with the Holy Spirit but as God the Son, the second person of the Trinity, then the death of Jesus is a death within the tripersonal unity of God.

This is extremely significant for Christian doctrine. For say that Jesus was a man filled with the Holy Spirit, or a great prophet, or a wise teacher blessed by God, or anything that falls short of the traditional doctrine of the incarnation and the idea that 'God was in Christus',[1] and you have a doctrine that is compatible with an apparently straightforward theistic notion of a God who acts as some kind of cheerleader from above for the man Jesus.

Other understandings of the significance of Jesus' life, death and resurrection, on the other hand – ones that would generally be considered more 'orthodox' – extend the involvement of God in the life of Jesus from external approval to actual presence. This requires us to consider what sort of a Deity could possibly be fully present in a vulnerable human life and then, when that life is snuffed out, reconstitute itself through its own death. What sort of a God could possibly pass through all the hoops that orthodox views of the incarnation, death and resurrection of Jesus 'God and man' throw up for such a deity?[2]

A view of God as substantially present in the life, death and resurrection of Jesus of Nazareth creates enormous problems in making sense either of Jesus as 'God and man' or of God as 'father, son and spirit'. Though justice cannot be done here to the huge debate surrounding these doctrinal issues, an attempt needs to be made in order to introduce these problems. The advantage of doing so is that if the resurrection as a miracle 'at the heart of God' is explained further – though this is perhaps over-confident – something might be conveyed of the extraordinary and exciting concept of God which is delivered by 'orthodox' Christianity.

From the very beginning Christianity had to show how the son could be different from the father and yet together with the father form one single God. As soon as the religion decided to reject any notion that Jesus was merely a spirit-filled man, or a divine being but not 'as' divine as the father (the so-called Arian heresy), it faced the criticism that it believed in two gods, the father and the son. Later, with the proclamation of the divinity of the spirit, it became a challenge to say how it believed in three divine 'persons' who were not three separate gods but formed one God who was 'three-in-one'.

Having rejected 'subordinationism', the idea that either son or spirit were inferior to the father, orthodoxy had to maintain itself against what it saw as being two equal and opposite pitfalls. The first pitfall was tritheism, the belief in three gods, the idea that Christianity was a polytheistic religion pretending to be monotheistic. The second pitfall was modalism, which essentially saw 'father', 'son' and 'spirit' as three 'modes of being' of the one God, perhaps like three different parts in a play. This didn't work either. Father, son and spirit couldn't be three different roles, appearances or presentations of the one God. But nor could they be three gods. The attempt to pitch orthodoxy's tent between these two 'extremes' is reflected in the language of the creeds. The Nicene Creed in 325 spoke of the father and the son as 'homoousios', 'of one substance'. Later creeds went on to develop this into the notion of God as three 'persons' ('hypostases' in Greek, 'personae' in Latin), in one substance ('ousia' in Greek, 'substantia' in Latin). The fact that the Greek and Latin words arguably do not mean the same thing has contributed to the complex arguments over these credal formulations.[3]

The danger of such formulae, beyond the problems of achieving a precise understanding of their terms, is that they only define themselves negatively. They are formulated expressly to rule out something that they don't want to say, but it's not at all clear what they *do* want to say. Hence the importance of those theologians who tried, after the creeds had been formulated, to reach a positive understanding of God through the 'three-in-one' nature of the divine, rather than simply seeing it as a formula to be employed as a weapon in rooting out certain undesirable 'heresies'.

Being in Relation

One such theologian was Richard of St Victor in the twelfth century, who claimed that in God the very concept of 'person' is defined by means of relation. Linking the divine persons to their mutual relations was not in itself new. From as early as the Cappadocians in the fourth century, the point was being made that it was impossible to speak of the 'son' without speaking of the 'father'. Speaking of the one 'co-designates' the other, said Basil of Caesarea, for the obvious reason that to define someone as 'son' immediately raises the question: 'Son of whom?' Augustine explored the notion of the persons of the Trinity being understood in terms of their relations too, while it could be argued that the common patristic term 'perichoresis', used to describe the mutual indwelling of father, son and spirit, also conveyed this point.

But Richard of St Victor's definition may have achieved a greater formality by arguing that in the case of father, son and spirit the relations of each divine person to the others is what defines them and makes them the persons they are. The clearest statement of this position, however, comes from Aquinas in his *Summa* (Ia 27–43), when he explores the notion of 'substantial relations'.

In the case of ourselves as human beings, it is fair to say that our relations to others make us only part of what we are. We can exist independently apart from other humans, even those closest to us – we don't need these relations in order to exist as separate entities. Certainly a father who loses a son may say 'a part of me has died'. But this is only true to an extent. The father will live on after the death of a son and there will be other relations to affect him. Such language makes the point that in the case of human beings as social and communicating animals, what happens to others affects us and helps to form us. We are what we are only in relation to other people. But still we could live apart from them.

In God, however, Aquinas suggests, the mutual dependence between father, son and spirit is absolute. In this case father, son and spirit are not just 'affected by' their mutual relations. Those relations make them what they are. The divine persons are fully constituted by their relations to one another. The substance of what they are lies in these relations. In the case of the divine being, therefore, the father who loses the son not only loses 'a part' of himself but his very substance is destroyed. The mystery of God's 'being-in-relation' entails that the death of Jesus disrupts the nature of God far more than the death of a son would disrupt the being of a human father.

Aquinas' exploration of 'real subsistent relations' has been criticized.[4] But one aspect of Christianity is illustrated very clearly by his formulation of divine person as relation. If we take the view that Jesus was simply a man inspired by God and not himself God the son, then God remains at a distance from the events in Jesus' life, however much what happens to the great prophet from Nazareth pains or disturbs the Deity. But if we take the orthodox view that Jesus was God the son, then the tragic events of his life are part of the Godness of God, they are part of God's eternal being as (maybe even struggle to be) God. All at once an 'orthodox' Christology has delivered us a radical and exciting theology. The straining inner 'perichoresis' of the divine persons, derived from God's presence in Christ, turns God's immutability into something 'dynamic', the immutability of the waterfall rather than the rock, constantly changing even while it is ever the same.[5]

In the early nineteenth century this understanding was reinterpreted in Hegel's philosophy of religion, which once again argued that God's unity can only be understood in terms of the reciprocity of the divine persons. The Hegelian dialectic of a complex unity which accepts and yet at a higher level overcomes difference (the difficult notion of 'aufhebung') seemed to fit well with the 'complex unity' of God as father, son and spirit. Once more the exciting implications of Hegel's approach lay in the doctrine of God which it derived from God's involvement in the life of humanity in general and Jesus in particular.[6]

Such metaphors or analogies do not 'solve' the problem of understanding God as Trinity, but they do at least help to illustrate how Christian theology has tried to look for answers. The notion of 'substantial relations' has the attraction of suggesting both the natural and the moral characteristics of God. On the one hand, it points to the fact that because each divine person is exhaustively defined in terms of the other two, the three persons do not constitute three separate independent entities and therefore this interpretation does not fall into the trap of tritheism. On the other hand, it highlights the mutual self-giving which is the nature of God as love. It is precisely because three human beings are less able to give themselves to each other than are the three persons of the Trinity that they form three separate beings. The divine being alone can maintain itself as a complex unity of distinct persons.[7]

The Problem of Christology

If we now move from the doctrine of God to the doctrine of Christ in Christian theology, we see a similar pattern of argument emerging. Where the Trinity was seen in terms of the participation of a plurality of persons in one nature or substance, the problem of Christology was defined as the unification of two natures in a single person. Christ had to be fully human and fully divine (*vere deus*, *vere homo*) and yet a single person. Yet how were the divine and human able to meet, still less to mingle, in one person?

Mingling was strongly excluded because it might produce some 'third nature', a hybrid that was neither human nor divine but produced by mixing the two. It was in these terms that Theodoret rejected Gregory of Nazianzus' fourth-century image of Christ's human nature dissolving in his divine nature like a drop of vinegar in the ocean (though Theodoret made it honey rather than vinegar).[8]

The problem faced by the church in its first major formulation of belief, the Council of Chalcedon in 451, was that of how to speak of Christ as one and the same person (hypostasis) 'in two natures' (*en duo physein*), the divine and human in a single person.

As with the Trinity, so also in the case of the doctrine of Christ there is a feeling that the formula agreed upon – in this case the Council of Chalcedon speaking of one person in two natures which remained 'without confusion, without change, without division, without separation' and yet indivisible – was designed more to exclude what was wrong than to explain what was right. The first of the two 'heresies' to be excluded was the tendency to undermine the human nature of Christ, for instance by denying him a human soul or mind and defining Jesus God and man as the divine 'logos' inside a fleshly, human shell. This was associated with Apollinarius of Laodicea and, in terms of location, with the 'Alexandrian' school. The second 'heresy' to be excluded emphasized the fully human nature of Christ, but in such a way as to compromise the unity of his person. This was a failing associated with certain representatives of the Antiochene school.

Chalcedon was not a very successful compromise between these two extremes, and led to the first great confessional schism in Christian history, with the 'oriental orthodox' in Syria, Egypt and Palestine maintaining that Christ could only have one nature (hence the term 'monophysite') and insisting that two natures effectively meant two Christs rather than one. Weakened by this rift, the areas of monophysite Christianity never had the impact they might have done on the rest of Christendom because they were overrun by Islam in the seventh century. This arguably meant that the balance of opinion in the Christian world was tilted towards the Antiochene position more by force of arms than by reason. When in 681 the Council of Constantinople adopted the 'dyothelitic' position that there were two separate wills in the person of Christ, many people decided that the matter had been resolved in such a way as to compromise the unity of Christ's person.[9]

The ideas offered during the Middle Ages – the 'assumptus' of Abelard, which seemed too much like Apollinarius and the idea of the divine logos assuming a shell-like human flesh, the 'habitus' of Lombard which again suggested that humanity was mere clothing for the divine, or even Aquinas' notion of the human nature 'subsisting' in the logos – seemed to move in the other, Alexandrian direction, compromising the completeness of Christ's human nature.

Trying to formulate a satisfactory Christology is as difficult as trying to formulate a satisfactory doctrine of God, but it might be helpful to look in the same theological area for assistance as we did in the case of the Trinity. In that case it was the relations between the persons that seemed to provide the best clue to understanding the nature of God. In the case of Christ the same approach can be made. It is the relation between the human and divine natures that is the most helpful starting point.

Relations between the Two Natures of Christ

Jesus of Nazareth lives in complete dependence upon and self-surrender to the will of the father ('thy will, not mine, be done' – the famous cry from Gethsemane). This living in dedication to the will of another is not what is rewarded with 'eternal sonship' as a prize for good behaviour – it *is* that eternal sonship. It is precisely as one who lives in accordance with the will of the father that Christ articulates the eternal being of the son. For this reason it is possible to agree up to a point with David Brown when he writes that 'His words and actions [those of Jesus] display confusion or reticence about whether his relationship with the divine is external or internal to his person, with him sometimes clearly referring his actions to his father and at other times apparently speaking in his own right' (1985: 119–20).

But surely it is precisely this relationship that Jesus has to work out during the course of his ministry. This is the point of what we may suppose is a difficult and even agonizing exploration of who he is in the life of Jesus. It is reflected in sayings such as 'I am not myself the source of the words I speak to you: it is the Father who dwells in me doing his own work. Believe me when I say that I am in the father and the father in me' (John 14:10–11). Jesus comes to see that living in complete submission to the father is more than an example of human devotion to God. It is in fact the eternal nature of God the Son. Jesus comes to the understanding that his obedience to the father is actually the life of God in human form. Hence Brown is right to continue the passage which I have quoted above by saying that 'such confusion about identity is in any case inherent in the type of religious experience in terms of which his life is most appropriately analysed'. Notwithstanding the Lucan picture of a self-confident child in the Temple, we may even speculate that this is something which Jesus took almost half a lifetime to make sense of to himself, beginning his ministry in early middle age.

If Jesus were merely a man inspired by God, then his self-surrender would not be a direct revelation of the nature of God. The God above might approve of this self-surrender, but God would not *be* it. But if the self-surrender of the son to the father, visible in the life of Jesus, is something that takes place within the life of God, then this self-surrender *is* God, the God in whom there is an eternal being-in-relation.

The traditional discussion in relation to two natures and possibly even (as in the 681 formulation) two wills in one person is thus in danger of missing the point. The point is not that there are two separate natures struggling to fit together within 'one person', as if the problem were one of squeezing a quart into a pint pot. Nor can there be two separate wills operating – however harmoniously – within one person. Rather, there is one nature which is human and one will which is human. But as that human nature grows in awareness of its relation to the father, and as that human will finds itself living in accordance with the father's demands, it comes to perceive (as Brown puts it) that this relation is not just an 'external' one between a human being and God; it is internal to the life of God. Thus the human will to obey becomes the will of the son in relation to the father that is part of the eternal life of God. It does not become another will; the will of the man and the will of the son in relation to the father are the same. Jesus' human nature is not superimposed upon or somehow coexistent with or adjacent to the divine nature. It *is* that nature. The monophysite and 'monothelitic' position is correct, but not in the terms in which it is usually defended. There is not a single divine will and nature in Christ, nor a single human will and nature. There is the single human will and nature of a man who in the course of his life realizes that it is also the will and nature of God the son. To go back to Brown's terminology, the external association between the human person and God is also an association internal to the life of God. In these terms our doctrine of Christ attempts to reinforce the notion of being-in-relation which we adopted in connection with our doctrine of God.[10]

To recap the argument thus far. I have tried to consider what sort of a God could jump through all the hoops required by the belief that this God became flesh, died and was raised from the dead. Trying to answer that question led to a particular understanding of the nature of God as Trinity and a particular understanding of the nature of Christ as divine and human. The two understandings are inseparable, because according to the argument put forward here Jesus grasps the significance of his own life as a human being only insofar as he perceives it to be part of the eternal life of God. The individual man dedicating himself to the father is drawn into the being-in-relation of father, son and spirit.

In the rest of this chapter I shall try to take this understanding of God and relate it to the question of miracles. Is the sort of God which has emerged from this discussion of Christology and the Trinity one who would perform miracles? Just as Swinburne is led in his recent book on the resurrection (2003) to considerations of 'God's reasons for incarnation' and 'The marks of an incarnate God', so I am driven by the resurrection to consider whether (to put it in a deliberately paradoxical way) the sort of God who would submit to death on the cross is the sort of God who would raise himself from the dead. As this chapter began by saying, the real challenge of an 'orthodox' Christology is its radical theology. The argument is that a God who has to do all that the doctrine of the incarnation, traditionally understood, demands of God will be far more challenging than a God who surveys approvingly from afar the goodness of various men and women below.

The doctrine of God and of Christ which has been formulated here around the notion of resurrection as a 'miracle in the heart of God' provides at least some assistance in the area of theodicy (for further development of this theme see Chapter 5). It makes it possible to argue that the pain of suffering, rejection and death seen in the life of Christ reaches into the heart of God and is not just something which the Deity sympathizes with from afar. This is a God who gets the divine hands dirty, suffers and even dies like a human being. As the theologian Juergen Moltmann (1974) explained in making sense of the title of his famous book *The Crucified God* (*Der Gekreuzigter Gott*), the death of Christ as a death of God the Son is a death within God.

The Concept of 'Kenosis'

But is this idea of God sustainable, whatever its value in terms of 'solidarity' between suffering humanity and the apparently co-suffering creator? Traditional attributes of God such as God's changelessness and omnipotence are brought under scrutiny by it, though it is certainly not clear that they are undermined.

It might be argued, for instance, that the fundamental notion of Christians concerning God is that 'God is love'. God as Love means unselfishness, giving of the self to another, and this is not just 'recommended' by God but played out in the divine being itself, in the being-in-relation of father, son and spirit and in the relation of Jesus to the father. Through the incarnation human history is caught up in that eternal relation of self-giving between father and son, but this need not imply any 'change' in God as love, nor need it mean that love ceases to be omnipotent.

The Hebrew and Greek Bibles (the 'Old' and 'New' Testaments) show a relationship between God and humanity played out in terms of a covenant with a chosen people made, broken and renewed, a love of God for human beings which is constantly offered if not constantly accepted. Many biblical scholars identify this love or faithfulness of God as the unchanging nature of the Deity. The history of God's relations to human beings and the reality of human sin means that this loving faithfulness brings pain to God and when (so far as Christians are concerned) it reaches its climax in Jesus of Nazareth then it brings suffering, death and even failure and disappointment into the heart of God.

To say that it challenges the 'Godness of God' to speak in such terms presupposes a certain understanding of theism, one that the God who is revealed in the biblical narrative arguably contradicts.[11] The God who was in Christ is omnipotent and yet suffers, is indestructible and yet experiences the death of Jesus as a death within God. Such language could be seen not as a denial of God's omnipotence but as a description of the omnipotence of God's love.

There is no doubt that this interpretation of the suffering God is deeply attractive to many theologians and has been played out in a number of explorations of the doctrine of 'kenosis', literally 'self-emptying'. Variations of 'kenotic' theology have been advanced both because they seem to express the self-giving at the heart of God and (connected to this) because they seem to provide a way through various Christological dilemmas. If we are to consider the idea of 'what sort of God' might suffer, die and rise again, then it will be worthwhile to explore this notion further.

The word 'kenosis' derives from a section of Philippians 2:5–11, the so-called 'Christological hymn' in which it is said that Christ does not count equality with God as something to be 'seized' or 'grasped' or 'prized' but rather 'empties himself', assuming the nature of a servant or slave. As such he bears human likeness and is obedient to the father even to death. As a result of his obedience the one who has 'emptied himself' is 'lifted up' and 'exalted' by the father.

The passage is open to many interpretations. Some commentators stress the idea that Christ is here being seen as the 'new Adam', who replaces the disobedience of the first man with the obedience of the second. From this perspective the passage need involve no more than an outline of how human life should be lived in obedience to God rather than selfishly. Other commentators feel that the passage gives support to the notion of 'incarnation', so that the life of Christ is to be understood not only as a perfect human life but as the life of a God who has made human existence a part of the divine. A 'kenotic' Christology stresses the voluntary surrender of power made by God the son in taking human form, precisely in order to show how the human can become part of the divine.

It is clear that a 'kenotic' Christology can be helpful in dealing with the sort of struggling Christology which says that Christ suffers the pain of the cross 'in his human nature' but triumphs over it 'in his divine nature', or that he feels pain, anger and temptation 'in his human nature' but a 'detached serenity' in his divine. Such Christologies shunt from one 'nature' to the other, allocating different 'experiences' to each, in a way that makes the unity of Christ's person unsustainable. A kenotic approach cuts through this kind of Christology, because the sort of experiences which it seems designed at all costs to protect the divine nature from having – doubt, pain, temptation – are now attributed freely even to the divine nature in its 'voluntary surrender' of power. Rather than it being an impossible humiliation for the divine nature of Christ to experience fear, uncertainty or pain, such a condition becomes the freely willed state of kenosis where the divine being sacrifices all the creator comforts of heaven.

A 'kenotic' Christology has been explored in a number of writings, including those of J.A. Baker (1975), W.H. Vanstone (1977), Paul Fiddes (1988) and most recently a collection of stimulating essays edited by John Polkinghorne (2001b). Traditionally the doctrine has been conceived in a 'weak' and a 'strong' form. The 'weak' form interprets the 'self-emptying' of the son in terms of concealing or refusing to use certain attributes. The 'strong' form conceives of the son abandoning these divine attributes even to the point of being unaware of having renounced them. His 'divinity' is something that has to be rediscovered during the course of his ministry, rather like a severe stroke victim rediscovering language. This is indeed close to what I suggested earlier concerning the time during which Jesus reflects upon and prepares his ministry.

Probably the best popular illustration of kenosis is Kierkegaard's parable of the king and the maiden (1962: ch. 2), in which a king seeks to win the love of a woman of lowly origins and, in order not to win her love for the wrong reason, disguises himself as a servant. Most commentators would probably see this as an example of the 'weak' version of princely advantages concealed, though some see it more as the 'strong' form of those advantages no longer even being recognized (for example Swinburne 2003: 45). Certainly the parable conveys more power in the 'strong' version, since it ceases to be a case of the rich man playing at being poor, stooping to conquer a woman's heart in a way that the twenty-first century is likely to see as highly condescending. According to the 'strong' version, the king as servant has no idea of his royal origins, and is therefore relieved of any patronizing assumption that 'humble maidens' need to be properly guided towards a 'proper' response to male advances.

The notion of kenosis has exercised a particular attraction for Lutheran theologians. The reasons for this make for fascinating reading, linked to eucharistic theology, thus illustrating once again the point that in theology one doctrinal question invariably raises a host of others. However, it is impossible to enter into these reasons here.[12] A line of development can be traced from the seventeenth-century Lutheran theologians who speak of 'concealing' attributes – the 'weak' version of the doctrine – to the nineteenth-century Lutheran kenotics who speak of 'renouncing' them (the 'strong' version).

As a purported solution to the problem of Christology, the doctrine of kenosis encounters difficulties if it is interpreted as implying an alteration in God the son. Whether the son hides certain attributes (like omnipotence and omniscience) or throws them away, the image is of someone who abandons the 'safety' of heaven and makes his way to earth. His situation changes. Though it might be possible to argue that this 'change' does not threaten the immutability of God the son, since he remains eternally the same in terms of attributes like love, justice and holiness, it is arguable that a doctrine of kenosis tied to Philippians 2:5–11, with its apparent 'journey' of the son from above to below, is more misleading than illuminating. For the 'self-emptying' of the son is more appropriately seen not as something which he does at a single moment when he becomes incarnate, but something which he does eternally as the son. In other words, kenosis is a more powerful image when placed in a trinitarian context of the eternal life of God, than when tied to the specific doctrine of incarnation.[13]

Besides the continuing output on a kenotic theme of Moltmann, the writer who more than any other explores this notion of kenosis as a description of God's eternal being as God (rather than God's 'special measures' for the act of incarnation) is Hans Urs von Balthasar (1990).[14] From Balthasar's perspective 'the inner life of the Trinity takes its impress from the reciprocal kenosis of the divine persons in relation to each other' (Moltmann 2001: 140).

I determined in this chapter to consider what sort of a God might become flesh, die and rise from the dead. I did not find it possible to answer that question without considering the nature of God as Trinity and of Christ as divine and human. I argued that Jesus grasps the significance of his own life as a human being only insofar as he perceives it to be part of the eternal life of God. The individual man dedicating himself to God discovers that he is part of the being-in-relation of father, son and spirit. He is part of a God who is eternally self-giving and self-emptying, a 'kenotic' God. By arguing in this way I would agree with those who claim that the doctrine of kenosis must be placed in a trinitarian context of the eternal life of God, rather than be tied to the specific doctrine of incarnation.

Kenosis and Miracles

If the doctrine of kenosis helps us to understand the nature of God, what does it suggest about the idea that God performs miracles? The emphasis upon self-emptying and freely chosen vulnerability, when widened from being a strategy adopted under the specific conditions of incarnation to being the eternal nature of God as God, might seem to push us towards the supposition that a miracle as an 'act of power' is at loggerheads with God as love. Miracles become divine actions that are at variance with the kenotic principle that God's power is qualified and limited (by God's own will).[15]

Does this mean that miracles are incompatible with a 'loving' God? Many theologians consider that they are. The more they think of God's willingness to be vulnerable, the less they find it conceivable that God would (so to speak) throw God's weight about in the world with miracles. It is, moreover, difficult to resist the notion that for some of these theologians a kenotic understanding provides a way of avoiding some of the troublesome issues raised by special acts of God. Many of the contributors to Polkinghorne's *The Work of Love: Creation as Kenosis* (2001b) are primarily scientist-theologians. In the contributions of writers like I.G. Barbour, John Polkinghorne and A.R. Peacocke great stress is placed upon the manner in which the work of creation requires God to qualify God's own power. They see a God who is self-limiting, self-emptying, vulnerable and self-giving as demanded by the very evolutionary processes which God has set in motion. As I describe in Chapter 3 on acts of God, these writers, in the manner of the best nineteenth-century immanentalists, have a very strong sense of the physical universe as itself a wonderful demonstration of God's creative skill, and they do not like to see such skill supplemented by occasional tampering. A kenotic theology seems to give their view the support of metaphysical necessity. It is the nature of God, they would say, to stand back and allow human beings the 'space' to make mistakes or even to be the cause of large-scale suffering.

Can miracles then be abolished? Can the Christ who reminds his disciples that legions of angels could be summoned to his support but refuses to do so (Matthew 26:53) be interpreted as ruling out special acts of God altogether? Christ versus Pilate is not like Moses versus Pharaoh. It is not a contest concerning who has the most powerful magic. The miracle about the absence of which the crucified Christ is taunted by those who pass by ('He saved others, but he cannot save himself' – Mark 15:31) does not occur. He dies. The arrest, humiliation and death of Jesus proceed without divine interference. The owner of the vineyard does not intervene to save his son. Is this not a means of showing that the ultimate revelation of God lies in the life of one who does nothing to save himself, who submits to human maltreatment and overcomes it only through that passive submission? Is not Jesus' refusal to save himself (or to call upon God to save him) a revelation of the eternal working of a God whose self-limitation within the logic of creation refuses all special actions? Surely the 'love that does not compel' must reject the sort of 'coercive demonstration of power' that a miracle must represent and therefore all acts of intervention are ruled out in our lives and the lives of others as they were apparently ruled out in the life of Christ.

But then comes the resurrection, the miracle 'within God'. Certainly the resurrection cannot be interpreted as a delayed-action production of the 'proof' which those who taunted Jesus as he hung on the cross demanded. Nevertheless, it still represents what (in the terms laid out by this interpretation of kenosis) must be called an 'act of power'. According to the interpretation which we arrived at in the previous chapter, Jesus is brought back to life by a special act of God and indeed this action becomes the mainstay of the new faith. In such a context, the constantly self-deprecating figure who is eternally withdrawn so that humanity can play out the full effects of its divinely willed freedom will not do.[16]

Sarah Coakley's essay in *The Work of Love* is particularly interesting, because she is willing to look more deeply into the assumption that is shared to a greater or lesser extent by all the contributors to the book, namely that 'humans should enjoy a type of freedom that places limitations on God's power and foreknowledge' (2001: 204–5). She describes one common 'visual picture' of that assumption. It is one of 'a (very big) divine figure backing out of the scene, or restraining his influence, in order that other (little) figures may exercise completely independent thinking and acting' (2001: 205). Coakley points out that to those schooled in psychoanalytic theory such a vision is 'deeply reminiscent … of the child's repudiation of the power of the mother' (2001: 205). She contrasts what she calls this 'incompatibilist' and perhaps masculinist view of human freedom in relation to God, according to which God must get out of the way in order for freedom to be enacted, with an alternative 'compatibilist' understanding which adopts 'views of freedom that do not attempt to abstract from the conditioning and even "determining" factors that continue to be in effect even as a "free" act is undertaken' (2001: 205). A religious interpretation more in line with this 'compatibilist' interpretation, she suggests (2001: 206), would be the mystical tradition of Julian of Norwich, presenting a divine desire that finds its completion in human responsiveness rather than being in competition with it – and a human desire, we may add, that finds its completion only in responding to God.

The argument about gender connotations which Coakley raises and discusses in more detail elsewhere (1997) is not one that I shall discuss here. However, it seems to me that the discussion of gender connotations does make an interesting point. It is very easy to assume that in talking of God 'withdrawing' and 'giving humanity space' one is replacing the 'dictatorial' God with one who is more 'empowering' and thereby 'learning the lessons of feminism'. The reality may not be so simple – nor the lessons to be learned. When Barbour, for instance, talks of a 'feminist' view of God as 'like a mother who empowers a child *in utero* and in subsequent life by working with other powers, not by displacing them' (2001: 15), it has to be asked whether this is really how mothers behave. Again, Swinburne comments that 'Like a good parent, a generous God has reason for not foisting on us a certain measure of knowledge and control' (1996: 53). This is all right so far as it goes, but if God were really a 'good parent' there would be times when God *did* foist such control on us, as I tried to argue in Chapter 5. Ironically, one of the only things which both Hick and Swinburne agree on, in Hall's fascinating account of their different approaches to hell, is the idea of 'epistemic distance' in order to allow humans 'true freedom' in relation to God (2003: 204).

Yet one of the obvious lessons to be learned from any consideration of theodicy, as I argue in Chapter 5, is that parents simply do not behave towards their children in the way that some versions of the 'kenotic God' are supposed to operate towards us. At certain crucial moments they simply override their children's wishes. Even without invoking the charge of being over-protective, they prevent children from doing certain things that would harm them. God, on the other hand, apparently allows things to happen to God's children which a mother – or a father – would fight tooth and nail to prevent happening to their child. Doubtless this highlights the limitations of the simple analogy between God and humanity on the one hand and parent and child on the other. Yet it is many of the kenotic theologians, anxious to see the human offspring given 'space' by the divine parent, who make great play of the analogy.

There may be a certain irony in the way in which a number of male theologians have jumped onto the bandwagon of feminist perceptions of an 'empowering' God, only to end up with a typically 'male' view of the parent being disposed of by the child come of age. The presumption is that the parent and child must be in competition with each other and that the child can only come of age by winning its 'space'. God must first get out of the way for us to be free. Against that Coakley points to an idea of God 'nurturing and sustaining us into freedom'.

Coakley's approach does not undermine in any way the fundamental insight of kenotic theology, namely that human freedom presupposes divine self-limitation.

But it does undermine the assumption that this translates into a God who wills an empty space in which human beings are entirely abandoned to work out their own fate.

Much of what the kenotic theologians speak about today goes back to the writings of Dietrich Bonhoeffer in the 1930s and 1940s. It was Bonhoeffer who spoke of a God who 'allows himself to be edged out of the world' (1954: 163) and of God 'teaching us that we must live as men who can get along very well without him' (1954: 164). Though some would contend that his argument was focused on the 'God hypothesis', the idea that we can use God in order to fill in gaps in our scientific knowledge, it was soon interpreted in a far wider sense. Consider the comment by John Robinson in his widely-read book *Honest to God*, where he uses Bonhoeffer in order to claim that 'Like children outgrowing the secure moral, religious and intellectual framework of the home, in which "Daddy" is always there in the background, God is teaching us that we must live as men who can get along very well without him' (1963: 38–9). Here we move far beyond the 'God hypothesis', towards a generalized understanding of the human person in relation to his or her maker.

The gender connotations are plain to see in Robinson's quote. 'Daddy' wants the children to paddle their own canoes, whatever the cost. But is that so clearly 'Mummy's' strategy? She might prefer to talk of a lifelong partnership in which she is constantly initiating and her offspring constantly responding, and in which the space of the offspring to develop is not simply secured by parental withdrawal but by a range of approaches.

What I am suggesting is that the notion of our proceeding towards a world in which we 'get along without God' may be extended from a rejection of the 'God of the gaps' argument in science, to a rejection of every apparent connection between the human person and the God that he or she has to learn to do without. The aspects of religious life which must be made vulnerable by such a view will naturally be those surrounding rituals of worship. It is difficult to make sense of any purported holy communion with the 'absent divine father', any petitionary or other forms of prayer to the parent who rejects his importunate offspring, or any expressions of thanksgiving towards the 'Daddy' who wants his children to find their own space rather than invading his.

So interpreted (or rather misinterpreted), Bonhoeffer's call for intellectual maturity has been translated into a kind of Stoic withdrawal from God which rejects all links between the divine and human as divine apron strings to which mature 'modern' persons must refuse to cling. Yet it needs to be remembered that Bonhoeffer specifically rejected a God who came as a divine prop to supply strength in moments of human weakness, in order to argue for a God who was 'not on the borders of life but at its centre, not in weakness but in strength, not, therefore, in man's suffering and death but in his life and prosperity' (1954: 124). Bonhoeffer's rejection of a God who simply makes up for human deficiencies was intended to reinforce the idea of a God present throughout human life, a 'compatibilist' divine parent sharing the triumphs as well as the failures with their offspring.

In this context we can return to the specific question of miracles. Is the God who is 'teaching us to do without God' really compatible with those specific actions of God which this book refers to as miracles? Or would a miracle represent an unwonted interference in the lives of human beings that God has deliberately set on the path to independence, a kind of bailing out of the prodigal son which would prevent him from properly managing his own life? From the discussion around Coakley above it is clear that I would not view a miracle as such an unwonted interference.

The kenotic image of an eternally 'self-emptying' God in whom, to recall the words of von Balthasar 'the inner life of the Trinity takes its impress from the reciprocal kenosis of the divine persons in relation to each other', is a powerful expression of the freely chosen vulnerability which characterizes, as we have argued, not only the particular 'strategy' of incarnation but the eternal being of God. But does this vulnerable, compassionate, co-suffering God have to be a God who eschews miracles as acts of interfering power at variance with the freely chosen weakness of a God of love? I do not believe so. At the level of human relationships, a parent whose strategy is to leave children at the mercy of strangers and fires in order to learn from their mistakes would be arrested and charged with neglect. The normal parental strategy, certainly always with the full independence of offspring as its goal, combines constant intervention with the provision of opportunities for choice that become increasingly wider as maturity approaches.

It is impossible not to see this analogy as important to a religion whose fundamental prayer is to 'our father' (Matthew 6:9) and where Jesus seeks to reassure his listeners in the Sermon on the Mount that if they 'bad as they are', know how to give good things to their children, 'how much more will your heavenly father give good things to those who ask him' (Matthew 7:9–11). Of course God's relation to the human person is no mere extension of the human parent's relation to children. But is it clear that God's relation to the human person is closer to the first parental strategy outlined above than to the second?

The connection between miracles and authority is one that is explored throughout this book. The idea that miracles, far from being a 'proof' of Jesus' authority as some of the Deists imagined, might actually be a dangerous distraction from its true nature has been explored in the last four chapters on the miracles of Jesus and the developing discussion of miracles in Christian history. That God's self-revelation in Christ entails an acceptance of weakness and vulnerability is a fundamental article of Christian belief. But to conclude from this that God's nature would be compromised by miracles seems to me to take the argument too far. A miracle does not need to be an act of power through which the Deity shouts down any critics. It can be more like an act of quiet maternal authority which seeks only to maintain a relationship in being, not to prove its superiority.

Conclusions

This discussion of the nature of God was precipitated by consideration of the resurrection – the raising of Jesus as a miracle in the sense of a specific divine action. Can such a God, a God who 'intervenes' on specific occasions, be the sort of God who is described in a kenotic manner as eternally self-giving and self-emptying? I suggested that these two notions can be reconciled, namely a God who carries out SDA and the self-limitation which is an expression of an omnipotence of love. It should be noted that I am not here claiming to be able to make sense of the mechanism by which these special divine actions take place. But I am suggesting that such actions are consistent with the nature of a kenotic Deity.

I would argue that the God who raised Jesus from the dead was not deciding to hold fire in order to produce an even more powerful demonstration later. God was not delaying the angels who were meant to take Christ down from the cross, until they could make an even bigger splash by rolling away the stone and announcing that he was no longer held by the grave. The cross was a public event high on a hill; the resurrection a quiet restoration made known to his followers. Certainly it became the central proclamation of a religion for which there was a new sabbath, the day of resurrection, and which preached 'Jesus and the resurrection'. But no one suggested that God's miracle had proved the 'bigger' one, as Moses' miracles had proved mightier than Pharaoh's. What the resurrection established was not that God's strength was greater, but that God's weakness was destined to endure beyond man's strength.

That act of raising the dead, like the many other miracles of God, is not ruled out by the refusal of God to invade the 'space' of (let us say for once) her human offspring. She nurtures, she sustains, she inspires. Peacocke talks of a concept of God as creator which in the past has been 'too much dominated by a stress on the externality of God's creative act – he is regarded as creating something external to himself, just as the male fertilises the womb from outside' (1979: 142). Instead he asks us to consider a 'corrective to the masculine picture', which is 'God creating the world within herself'. Peacocke is happy to emphasize the 'mother God' bearing the world within her womb in order to provide an overall picture of God and humanity; yet Coakley is surely right to suggest that in the absence of any specific actions to nurture and encourage her offspring, Peacocke reverts to very 'male' imagery and assumptions about God. The world may be 'within' rather than 'apart from' God, but still Peacocke's God must refrain from any specific actions, because they would be 'inconsistent and incoherent with what the sciences show' (p. 134). In the end it is his reservations about what makes sense scientifically which determines Peacocke's view. What I have tried to show here is that for all the attraction and value of the doctrine of kenosis, it need not be incompatible with the belief in special divine actions.

The last five chapters have examined the role of miracles within Christian tradition. I have tried to approach the question both historically and doctrinally. I hope that I have been able to show in this part of the book why I feel that a definition of miracle in terms of a special action of God is the only one which will do justice to Christian thinking. For that reason I have ruled out (perhaps too summarily) in the first part of the book understandings of miracle which would have made the philosophical task much simpler, though in my view without being able to do justice to Christianity.

In the last part of the book I shall return to the problems of 'acts of God'. But I wish to do so in the context of at least touching upon the issue of miracles in a wider context than mere Christianity. In the next chapter I shall examine miracles in other religious traditions, and in Chapter 12 take a general look at miracles in the modern world.

Notes

1   The title of the classic work by D.M. Baillie (1948).
2   As was pointed out a generation ago when works like *The Myth of God Incarnate* (Hick 1977) produced something of a storm with their 'radical' reinterpretations of the doctrine of incarnation, such 'radicalism' is actually deeply conservative so far as its idea of God is concerned. The *Myth of God Incarnate* school may have seemed to be finding a way out of Christological difficulties, but it was the theological difficulties that it was arguably most determined to avoid. This point remains valid of later modifications of the original thesis, for example Goulder (1979) and Hick (1993), where it is still apparent that the 'radical' Christologists lumber us with an old-fashioned Deist deity.
3   A good guide for the perplexed is provided by Kelly (1950). For a more detailed exploration of the terms, see Stead (1977).
4   For instance by Moltmann (1981: 171–4), who sees it as a form of modalism, one that he believes inspired Barth to a questionable formulation of the Trinity as three 'modes of being' of the one God.
5   This point is well brought out by Hebblethwaite (1980).
6   See Moltmann (1981: 182), where he talks of Hegel 'picking up and deepening' the idea of each person receiving the fullness of eternal life from the other.
7   The notion of an increasing inner complexity which can be held together within an overall unity, observable as one moves higher up the evolutionary chain and (by implication) towards God is explored by Hodgson (1943).
8   Once again Kelly (1958) provides a clear exposition of the development of doctrine in the first five centuries.
9   This is Wolfhart Pannenberg's argument. See Pannenberg (1968), section 8, 'The Impasse of the Doctrine of the Two Natures'.
10 Thus Brown points out that 'this two centres-of-consciousness model [a human consciousness and a divine consciousness locked together somehow in the person of Christ] is an unnecessary construct, born of a failure to take seriously an alternative model for the Trinity' (1985: 233).
11 It is interesting to consider Moltmann's use of Jewish writers, particularly Abraham Heschel and his concept of the theology of the Old Testament prophets as a 'theology of the divine pathos' (1981), (1990: 178–81).
12 Sarah Coakley (2001: 196) associates it with the Lutheran insistence on a 'high' doctrine of the real presence.

13 See Hebblethwaite's concluding remark: 'What is the doctrine of the Trinity if not the effort so to reconstruct the doctrine of God that this "descent" may be seen as supremely, indeed paradigmatically, declaratory of what He is in himself?' (1980: 170). Hebblethwaite is here quoting D.M. MacKinnon's 1976 article on 'The Relation of the Doctrines of the Incarnation and the Trinity'.

14 Moltmann's latest thinking on kenosis can be found in 'God's Kenosis in the Creation and Consummation of the World', in Polkinghorne (2001b). Von Balthasar's ideas are discussed by both Moltmann and Coakley in the chapters they contribute to Polkinghorne (2001b).

15 'By God's own will' is an important qualification. As David Brown remarks, 'it would be a severe limitation on omnipotence to deny the possibility of abandoning it' (1985: 250).

16 It is perhaps no coincidence that Pannenberg, whose theology is focused upon the resurrection, is far more critical of a kenotic theology than Moltmann, whose theology is focused upon the cross. See Pannenberg (1968), esp. ch. 8.

PART III
MIRACLES IN A
NON-CHRISTIAN AND
CONTEMPORARY
PERSPECTIVE

Chapter 11

Miracles in Non-Christian Religions

This book has focused on the Christian tradition, an obvious limitation. Not only does this mean a failure to engage with other major religious traditions, but it also endangers the treatment of Christianity itself, which cannot be viewed apart from its own religious context, particularly that of Judaism. The tendency of Christianity to isolate itself from its religious background or (worse still) to pretend that there was nothing to Judaism after the time of Christ is something that has rightly been corrected over the last 50 years, though some would argue that there is much more still to be done.

In this chapter I shall examine some of the other major religious traditions of the world. To avoid being merely cursory, I shall try to concentrate upon aspects of these traditions which throw up interesting questions about the nature and purpose of miracles as such.

Judaism

In the chapters on the miracles of Jesus and the history of Christianity I have already touched upon the Jewish background, but at this point it can be considered in more detail. There is an important contrast between the miracles of Moses and Joshua on the one hand, and the miracles of Elijah on the other. The former represent miracles carried out on behalf of Israel against her enemies. Moses leads the Israelites out of bondage in Egypt; his outstretched hand ensures that they defeat Amalek in battle; Joshua brings down the walls of Jericho and causes the sun to stand still so that the enemies of Israel cannot escape under cover of darkness.

In the case of Elijah, on the other hand, it is the King of Israel (Ahab) who is at fault for compromising the monotheism of his people, and it is Elijah, called a 'troubler of Israel' rather than its saviour, who performs miracles to rescue his people from 'enemies within' rather than without. In this sense Elijah is the closest of the 'Old Testament' prophets to Jesus; he challenges the 'establishment' of his day; the 'hairy man' from the desert is socially inferior like the man of Galilee; he is told that his people will destroy each other bar a 'faithful remnant' of 7000, which is suggestive of the disciples and followers who in Jesus' day form 'the salt of the earth'. Unsurprisingly, when Jesus asks his disciples 'Who do men say that I am?', one of their answers is 'Elijah' (Mark 8:27f.).

Moreover with Elijah, as with Jesus, miracle-working functions as evidence of the authority of the miracle worker. When Elijah brings a widow's son back to life, she declares: 'Now I know that you are a man of God, and that the word of the Lord in your mouth is truth' (1 Kings 17:20–24). A very similar story appears in Luke's gospel, when Jesus raises the son of the widow of Nain (Luke 7:11–16). In both instances there is no stress upon the widow's faith – in the Elijah account she is positively disgruntled – but in both cases the reaction is to laud the healer. 'A great prophet has arisen among us', declare the witnesses to Jesus' miracle (Luke 7:16).

Elisha assumes the mantle of Elijah after the latter is taken up to heaven. Some of his miracles can be compared to those of Jesus too, for instance the multiplication of bread (in Elisha's case to feed a hundred) and the healing miracles. But there are differences. Elisha is capable of punitive miracles (two boys who mock his baldness are mauled by she-bears), something that is not associated with Jesus in the canonical gospels (though elsewhere, as we have seen, it is). It is also interesting that Elisha performs a posthumous miracle. When a man was left in Elisha's grave by mourners disturbed by a marauding band, the corpse came into contact with the prophet's bones and came back to life. This miracle, which clearly can bear no parallel with Jesus given Christian beliefs about the empty tomb and bodily resurrection, is, however, reminiscent of claims made about the relics of saints in Christian tradition.

The study of Judaism is particularly interesting during the period when it was more a case of Christian tradition affecting Judaism than Judaism forming the background (as Christians see it) to Christianity. Judaism of the late first century CE was clearly being influenced by the rise of Christianity and the need to respond to it.[1] Intrinsic to the formulation of this response was the question of miracles.

It should be familiar to any Christian in the twenty-first century that there were miracle-working rabbis other than Jesus (who is himself addressed and referred to as Rabbi – for example Mark 5:35) in the first century CE. The two most famous are probably Honi the Circle Drawer and Hanina ben Dosa.[2]

Hanina ben Dosa, a Galilean from Arav, who was probably active about a generation after Jesus, performed a number of nature, feeding and healing miracles. He caused rain to stop and start; in a series of small 'domestic' miracles he caused an oven to be full of freshly baked bread, vinegar to burn like oil and a house to be instantaneously repaired. These miracles are interesting because of their small-scale, private nature. The 'feeding' miracle, for instance, rather than being a way of satisfying 5000 followers (as in Jesus' miracle), is performed for Hanina ben Dosa's wife, who is too poor to bake bread and so fills the oven with kindling so that the smoke will give the impression that she is not as indigent as she really is. When a malicious neighbour guesses what is going on, ben Dosa miraculously produces the bread in order to confound the neighbour. A similar miracle, which might suggest Jesus' conversion of water into wine at the wedding in Cana but is once again at a private, domestic level, occurs when Hanina ben Dosa's daughter mistakes her vinegar jar for her oil jar, and lights the sabbath lamp from it. The lamp burns anyway, because, in the words of ben Dosa quoted in the Babylonian Talmud, 'He who commanded the oil to burn can also command the vinegar to burn' (bTa'an. 25a).

But ben Dosa performs miracles in public too. He goes in search of a troublesome snake that has been injuring people and invites the snake to bite him; it does and dies. As with many of the gospel miracles, performance of the miracle is followed by a brief saying – 'it is not the snake that kills, but sin kills' (bBer. 33a). We may note that the ability to handle poisonous snakes is something promised to those with faith in the New Testament (Mark 16:18, Acts 28:3–6). There is also a healing miracle, performed upon Rabbi Gamaliel's son, which closely follows the structure of healing miracles in the New Testament. The rabbi is asked to perform the healing, declares the boy cured (without seeing him) and those attending the sick child attest that at that moment the fever left him. The pattern is very close to that in John 4:46–53, where Jesus cures the official's son lying ill at Capernaum.

What is fascinating about these miracles of first-century Rabbinic Judaism is that they take place against a background of disapproval (or at least anxiety) on the part of the new rabbinic orthodoxy which emerges from the destruction of the Second Temple *c.* 70 CE. This event effectively shifted the realm of the sacred (and therefore the centre of religious power) from the Temple to the Torah, a 'portable Temple', and access to the holy passed out of the hands of a hereditary Temple priesthood and into those of the rabbis. Learning and piety became inextricably linked in the 'sages' whose extensive writings (the Talmud) are at once commentary on the text of the Torah, rules for living and statements of belief. Despite the prejudice that rabbinic writings are a casuistic collection of orthopractic regulations concerning the minutiae of ritual observance (a picture which owes much to the limited portrait of Pharisees in the Christian New Testament), in reality they contain numerous parables and sayings, many of which provide interesting commentary on the question of miracles.

Unsurprisingly, given the impact on Judaism of the 'sect of the Nazarenes' and the huge reputation of Jesus as a miracle-worker, Rabbinic Judaism was suspicious of miracles. There was a tradition that miracles had come to an end with the last of the prophets. Hence Rabbi Assi's remark recorded in the Babylonian Talmud (bYoma 29a):

> Why was Esther compared to the morning? To tell you that just as the morning is the end of all the night, so Esther is the end of all miracles.

Yet it did not reject them entirely; as we have seen, rabbis like Honi and Hanina ben Dosa performed them. Instead it concentrated its fire on those whose miracles are a means of self-aggrandisement (as it probably believed they were for Jesus). When Honi the Circle-Drawer draws a circle in the sand and refuses to leave it until God sends rain, God does indeed send rain. Yet Simeon ben Shetah tells Honi that he 'importunes before the Omnipresent, so he does what you want, like a son who importunes his father, so he does what he wants' (Mishna, Ta'an. 3:8). Such behaviour would be worthy of a ban of excommunication, he tells him. Rather than inviting admiration, then, Honi's miracle invites a rebuke.

Similarly, when Hanina ben Dosa heals the son of Rabbi Gamaliel, he is asked whether he is a prophet and denies it. The miracle takes place, but it does not signify the great power of the miracle-worker; on the contrary, greater power lies instead with those who are experts in the Torah.

This is the point of the extraordinary story of the oven of Akhinai (found in two versions in the Talmud: jMK 3,1 and bBM 58b–59a). Two rabbis are locked in debate over interpretations of the Law. One of them, Rabbi Eliezer, declares that 'If the law accords with my position, this carob tree will prove it.' The tree is thereby uprooted and moves its location a few hundred feet. The other scholars with him are unimpressed. He has flouted the rule of the majority on deciding points of law by the bullying tactics of performing wonders. 'There is no proof from a carob tree', the others say.

A similar reaction prevails when Rabbi Eliezer causes a stream to reverse its flow. The debate becomes even more intense when Rabbi Joshua attempts a 'counter-miracle' to stop Rabbi Eliezer destroying the walls of the schoolhouse. One rabbi wants them to fall; the other wants them to remain as they were. What happens is a compromise miracle out of deference to both rabbis. The walls are left leaning.

Rabbi Eliezer then calls forth a voice from heaven which rebukes the sages and tells them that Rabbi Eliezer is right. But even this is not enough. Rabbi Joshua quotes Deuteronomy to the effect that the Torah is on earth, not in heaven, so that even voices from above cannot challenge the interpretation given on earth. The rabbis are now in charge of determining the law and no miracle can intervene. Another rabbi, Rabbi Nathan, asks the prophet Elijah (who acts as an intermediary) what God's reaction was to this debate and receives the extraordinary reply that God laughed and said 'My children have overcome me, my children have overcome me!' Thus God is beaten at God's own game and enjoys it – a remarkable story from within a tradition for so long ignorantly portrayed as legalistic and humourless.

Thus miracles are not so much disproved or disbelieved in as demoted by Rabbinic Judaism, as are those that perform them. Those who perform miracles are frequently puffing themselves up. They are importunate. They fail to understand the nature of God's revelation in the Torah. And in one famous anecdote from the Babylonian Talmud (bShab. 53a), they are even signs of weakness rather than strength. When a man grows breasts in order to suckle his son after his wife dies, Rav Joseph comments: 'Come and see how great is this man that a miracle was wrought for him.' But Rabbi Abbaye responds: 'On the contrary, how inferior is this man that the natural order had to be changed for him.' Being a miracle-worker is almost treated as belittling; it is an emergency measure precipitated by a person's humiliating lack of natural prowess.

Whilst there are several (highly insightful) comments on the potential dangers miracles might bring in their wake, there is no wholesale repudiation of the miracles themselves. Ironically, for all their concern to repudiate the notion of the miraculous as a warrant for religious truth associated with nascent Christianity, it is arguable that they shared some of Jesus' own scepticism, not about miracles themselves but about how they might be misused (consider, for instance, Jesus' refusal to accept the demand that he produce a 'sign', and the fact that one of the temptations in the wilderness is that he throw himself off the temple and allow angels to break his fall, a suggestion against which he insists that you should not put God 'to the test' – see Luke 4:9–12). But this connection with rabbinic thinking should hardly surprise us. Jesus, himself called 'Rabbi', was steeped in the rabbinic tradition.

It would be wrong to conclude that for Judaism miracles ceased with the close of the biblical era. They continued in traditions such as those associated with the Hasidic movement in the eighteenth century, which spread among the villages and ghettos of Central and Eastern Europe, partly as a reaction to the Enlightenment, and which may be compared to that of Methodists in Britain and Pietists in Germany (Woodward 2001: 85–97). The founder of Hasidism, Rabbi Israel Baal Shem Tov (*c*.1698–1760), the 'Besht', is associated with many miraculous healings, including that of a sick child who is given 60 more years of life when his soul is 'compelled' to re-enter his body. Interestingly, the Besht has to suffer 'fiery lashes' for promising to cure the boy, because such an oath entails reversing God's intention that the boy die young (Ben-Amos and Mintz 1993: 129–31). Once again we have a miracle performed not so much to the glory of the miracle-worker as (almost) to his shame, representing as it does a challenge to God's will. The fiery lashes are almost a 'penance' for the sinful act of healing. Once more we see a sensitivity in Judaism to miracles as a potential vehicle of self-aggrandisement.

During the two hundred years in which Hasidism flourished in this part of Europe many healings were recorded. At the same time the familiar problems of authority created by miracles emerged in Judaism in conflicts between the itinerant preachers and wonder-workers, the rebbes and the local rabbis, many of whom saw the former as heretics and as a threat to their prestige.[3] Then came the events which virtually obliterated Judaism in this part of Europe. The implications of this for belief in miracles I have discussed in Chapter 5.

Islam

The picture with respect to Islam where miracles are concerned is quite a complex one. On the one hand, it is a firm tenet of Muslim belief that Muhammad was an ordinary man with a special mission from God. Allah alone is divine, unlike any of his followers or even the prophet himself. Muhammad admitted that as a man he was liable to make mistakes and did not associate himself with miracles. The sole 'miracle' was the Qur'an, which demonstrated his prophetic mission. In line with this, orthodox Islam stresses the humanity of the prophet and firmly rejects any worship of him.

At the same time some of the early biographies of Muhammad stressed his miraculous powers. The first full biography, or sira, of Muhammad was written by Ibn Ishaq about a century after Muhammad's death.[4] He describes a number of miracles surrounding Muhammad's life, as do other early biographies. A palm tree sighs as the prophet passes, a cluster of dates jumps off a tree at his command, the moon is split down the middle in order to confound his Meccan adversaries and on several occasions there are 'feeding miracles' as crowds of followers are supplied with food. Of particular importance is the 'Night Journey' to Jerusalem (according to Ibn Ishaq, Muhammad is carried there on a winged steed) followed by an 'Ascension' to paradise, in the course of which Muhammad talks to all the prophets that preceded him and is granted a vision of God (or perhaps better, a series of audiences with God, during which he negotiates down the requirement for daily prayers from 50 to 5).

Such stories reflected both popular enthusiasm for Muhammad and a desire to establish his credentials as a prophet. The connection with Judaism and Christianity is important in this context; broadly speaking, Islam claims to be the fulfilment of Judaeo-Christianity as Christianity claims to be the fulfilment of Judaism. It is unsurprising that many of the miracles in these biographies are described as impressing Jews and Christians, who are led by them to recognize Muhammad as a prophet. For example, the Christian monk Bahira is led to discover the marks of prophethood in the boy Muhammad.

Moreover, it is important to recognize that while the Qur'an very firmly sets itself against the Christian doctrines of the Trinity and the divinity of Christ,[5] it does not deny Jesus' miracles. Jesus is the leading prophetic figure in the Qur'an. He is recorded as performing miracles as a child and his miraculous virgin birth is affirmed – just as a number of miracles are described by Muhammad's biographers as attending his birth.

Though Islam, unlike Christianity, is not usually associated with a 'cult of the saints', Muslims, like Christians, venerate their saints, visit their tombs, keep relics and ask for their assistance. They do so without denying that nothing and no one may be compared to God. The tradition of asceticism and holy men which flowered in the Near East through the Christian 'desert fathers' from the fourth century CE had its impact on Islam and helped to generate Muslim ascetics and mystics, called Sufis (named after the rough woollen garments they wore to symbolize their asceticism; 'suf' means wool) (see Brown 2004: 26).

The Sufis argued that certain 'lesser miracles' (sometimes referred to as 'graces' – in Arabic 'karamat') were granted to the 'saints', including the power of prophecy, instant movement across great distances and producing objects out of nothing. Popular hagiography is full of tales of this kind. There are some healing miracles too, but the emphasis tends to be upon the supernatural knowledge which the saint has achieved. It is not difficult to see how aspects of Sufi cosmology might cause difficulties for other strands of Islam. The highest of the saints in Sufi tradition is given the title Qutb, meaning axis. He is infallible because of the oneness with God that he has experienced, and as the 'axis' around which the world turns he is mediator between the human and the divine, the 'barzakh' or interface between God and the world. Such claims do not sit easily with the emphasis upon Muhammad himself as merely human, and as Chodkiewicz (1993) points out some have seen language about the 'Seal of the Saints' as threatening to eclipse Muhammad as the 'Seal of the Prophets'. Nevertheless it is no exaggeration to say that the Sufi order has had considerable influence upon the Islamic world. There may, indeed, be some legitimacy in Daniel Brown's point (2004: 173) that its significance has been underplayed in the modern era because it has become a scapegoat for the apparent weakness of Islam vis-à-vis the West.

Certain movements of Islamic revival, such as the Wahhabis (followers of the eighteenth-century Muhammad ibn 'Abd al-Wahhab), have called for a return to the doctrines and practices of earlier generations and have denounced the veneration of 'saints' as a way of setting up rivals to God. In particular they have challenged the Sufi tradition as a 'superstitious' movement contributing to the decadence of Islam.[6]

Sayyid Ahmad Khan, a nineteenth-century Indian reformer, was determined to restore a 'pure and unadulterated Islam'. Partly through contacts with European missionaries and scholars, he decided that the Qur'an could stand alone without the 'hadith' or later traditions which claimed to transmit sayings or deeds of Muhammad. Sayyid Ahmad's position was not unlike the 'sola scriptura' (Scripture alone) principle adopted by the Protestant Reformers in opposition to what they saw as the misleading 'tradition' of the Catholic church, an analogy that earnest Anglican missionaries in nineteenth-century India doubtless delighted in suggesting to him.

Without the hadith, Sayyid Ahmad's interpretation of the Qur'an became wholly naturalistic. The Jinn, for instance, spirits created by fire and often mentioned in the Qur'an, are said to be an Arab tribe, not supernatural beings at all. The Devil is similarly demythologized as a symbol of the evil in human nature rather than a real being. As for miracles, they are in Daniel Brown's words 'a result of the pious imagination and can be entirely explained by natural causes' (2004: 204). Islam can therefore walk hand in hand with modern science because, as Sayyid Ahmad's most famous saying runs, 'Islam is nature and nature is Islam.' Both the Qur'an, as the word of God, and the world, as the work of God, are true and there is no conflict between them – a claim which recalls the tradition of 'the two books', the Book of Nature and the Bible, in Christian tradition.

Islam's stress upon the transcendence and omnipotence of God, before whom the duty of human beings is 'submission' (the literal meaning of 'Islam'), makes it difficult to affirm the authority of 'saints' in Muslim tradition. But it does not rule out miracles that are performed directly by God alone. The stress within Islam upon the all-determining will of God and the fact that nothing escapes God's power has produced debates similar to those within Christianity on 'free will' and 'predestination', with an interesting bearing on the question of miracles.

This is the point of the challenge of al-Ash'ari to the Mu'tazilites in the early tenth century CE, which was to form the basis of later Sunni thinking. Al-Ash'ari's position was controversially determinist, and led to a difficult explanation of how human beings could still be held accountable for their actions through their 'acquisition' (*kasb*) of acts created by God. As I argued in Chapter 1, al-Ash'ari is extremely interesting for his understanding of God's direct relation to the world. By this I mean that he rejects the notion of secondary causes as inhibiting God's power; everything that happens is therefore directly willed by God. The universe is not created and then left to run 'of its own accord', as the Christian scientist-theologians that we have considered believed. Instead, the universe is being recreated at every instant of time. Human action is an illusion and all change is brought about directly by God's decree.

We thereby find ourselves arriving, for theological rather than philosophical reasons, at the sort of position which Malebranche adopted in his debate with Leibniz. Malebranche could see no connection between material and immaterial substance; he therefore concluded that when, for instance, I move my arm, my act of will is the 'occasion' (hence the term 'occasionalism' to describe this philosophy) for God to move it – since only God can move arms or any other material body. Malebranche's 'occasionalism' is adopted because he cannot otherwise find a scientific explanation for movement; al-Ash'ari adopts a similar position of perpetual divine intervention because he thinks it would be insulting to God's power to adopt a different viewpoint. Each moment of history, he argues, is effectively a new creation, a direct act of God. Merely to suppose that it was brought about by preceding conditions using some theory of causation is to interpose some other agency between God and creation.

God's creation is a series of actions conceived atomistically in which whatever God wills comes into being. What God does may follow a pattern, but the pattern must never be misinterpreted as a determinant of what happens at any level, primary or secondary. A 'law of nature', precisely because of the word 'law' which seems to be prescribing how changes are to be made, violates this notion of direct divine action.

What is interesting is the reluctance of commentators to refer to this as a case of perpetual miracles. Zaehner, for instance, talks of an 'appearance of continuity and regularity and the consequent assumption that certain events will follow upon other events' as due to 'God's mercy in establishing a regular "custom" which, according to the Qur'an, he does not change'. However, Zaehner continues, God may on occasion modify this 'custom', as when God 'allows "miracles" to occur as proof of the missions of his Prophets' (1971: 186). But will this do? Malebranche did not consider that his occasionalism entailed a belief in 'perpetual miracles' from God, because a miracle, he believed, must be something exceptional. Leibniz, however, attacks this position. It doesn't matter that God moves these bodies in a law-like manner or, as Zaehner puts it, according to a regular 'custom'; the key point is that the actions are performed immediately by God. Leibniz would therefore wish to insist that al-Ash'ari's position was one of belief in perpetual divine miracles. If al-Ash'ari is assumed not to believe in miracles, it is because of a definition which assumes that a miracle must be something exceptional or rare – 'a violation of a law' , or in this case a 'custom'. But on the definition Leibniz gives (and which this book has adhered to), the concept of law is not crucial to deciding whether something is a miracle or not – a miracle, as said, is simply an action performed immediately by God (I have called it a 'special act of God'). In terms of the definition given by Leibniz, al-Ash'ari's belief in God's direction of the world redraws the nature of the debate. It is not that miracles are a violation of natural law; rather, natural law is a violation of miracles. Rather than ruling miracles out, al-Ash'ari's Islam rules out anything else.

Hinduism and Buddhism

In Hinduism there are miracles associated with Lord Krishna. In his capacity as God descended in human form to establish order on earth, Krishna can be compared to Jesus, except that in the case of Krishna (recalling the debate on kenosis in Chapter 10) the divine powers are not abandoned but concealed in his appearance on earth – and occasionally he removes the concealment. When Krishna is reported to his mother for eating dirt, he invites her to check whether this is true, whereupon she sees the whole universe in his gaping mouth.[7] Though in Luke's gospel the young Jesus appears to have a phenomenal grasp of Scripture, it is not really comparable. He remains bound by the constraints of human existence, whereas Krishna frequently transcends them. Krishna is more theophany than incarnation. He lifts up a mountain (Mount Govardhana) with one hand, kills an ogress when still a suckling infant and seduces women through his irresistibly musical voice, multiplying his form so that he can make love to several of them at once. In these miracles, many of which are the childish pranks of someone who has an unlimited power to torment and confuse, there is a strong sense of divine play which hardly registers in the West, where even the transformation of water into wine is dealt with severely as what David Brown refers to as 'flying in the face of the type of God revealed elsewhere, where miracles exhibit some deep pastoral concern' (1985: 65). Here, on the other hand, miracles are an illustration of divine play, of God enjoying being God through the world that God made.

In the case of the Buddha there are clear parallels to the life of Jesus. Both men go through a time of spiritual preparation and temptation (Jesus from Satan, Buddha from Mara). Both men have difficult relations with their families. Buddha is brought up in a palace and his father is determined to shield him from life outside. Doubtless Jesus faced similar pressures to remain at home. They both have to effectively renounce their families in order to pursue their callings, although Buddha later achieves a form of reconciliation, winning his father over with miracles. Both show extraordinary knowledge of sacred texts whilst still young – Buddha in the schoolroom, Jesus in the Temple.[8]

The Buddha achieves enlightenment and is therefore able to renounce the world, but refuses to do so in order to remain and teach others the way. This could be considered a difference from the life of Christ. The Buddha only 'appears' to be human after enlightenment – he does not suffer from pain or any limitations to his understanding, for instance. Christians might call this 'docetism' (Woodward 2001: 305) – the Buddha merely 'seems' to be human, whereas as fully incarnate Christ 'is' human and therefore suffers and dies. This raises theological issues touched on elsewhere. As so often when one tries to draw lines in the sand to distinguish religious traditions, however, it is never as simple as one thinks. The Christ who goes up a mountain and is transfigured has his own form of 'enlightenment'. When he reminds his disciples that he can summon legions of angels to his aid if he chooses, but refuses to do so (Matthew 26:53), there is a similar sense of voluntarily withholding (rather than having lost altogether) divine power. And though the Buddha does not 'die', but passes through the nine stages of meditation until he arrives at a state where (according to Anuruddha) the consciousness of sensations and ideas has passed away, that might not be so different from the 'paradise' in which the crucified Jesus reminds the 'good thief' they will both be that very day (Luke 23:43).

Both men perform miracles. The Buddha flies through the air, thereby avoiding payment to the ferryman in order to cross the Ganges. Jesus presumably could have avoided similar charges on the Sea of Galilee by walking. The Buddha wins converts by displays of miraculous power, in some of which he is pitted against various adversaries, more in the manner of Moses before Pharaoh than of Jesus. Thus he takes on the snake king of the Jatilas by matching cloud of smoke to cloud of smoke, flames of fire to flames of fire, before finally subduing their local deity and 'chief of serpents' with the words 'his fire has been subdued by my fire'. The Buddha eats a mango, plants the stone in the ground and makes a mango tree appear instantaneously. He tames a wild elephant that his first cousin Devadatta (an adversary sometimes compared to Judas in Christian tradition) sets against him. This miracle shows the distinctive compassion towards other forms of life intrinsic to a religion that believes we may ourselves be animals in a future existence. Finally, the Buddha's 'death' leads to various miracles accompanying his funeral. The body cannot be lifted in order to prepare it for cremation; then the fire under the funeral pyre will not catch. When the body has been burned, streams of water come from the sky to extinguish the funeral pyre, perhaps like the earthquake and the rending of the curtain of the temple which are described as attending the death of Jesus.

What may perhaps be marked as a difference between the miracles of Jesus and those of the Buddha is the absence in the latter case of that very strong emphasis upon healing miracles associated with the miracles of Christ. But this point must be made carefully. In one sense the whole story of the Buddha is focused upon not running away from suffering. It is his father who tries to 'beautify' the city by hiding all the 'ill-omened' ones when his son makes his first public outing. The lame, deaf, mute and otherwise afflicted are swept to one side when the chariots pass. But the Buddha does not fail to recognize (as his father wanted him to) that suffering is the common lot of humanity.

Nevertheless, the miracles do not focus on alleviating suffering through cures; the message of the Buddha is that it is possible to pass beyond suffering and need. He himself spent six years cross-legged in the open, without moving, without eating (or excreting), shrivelling up so that passers-by took him for a 'dust demon' and threw earth on him. Such deprivation goes beyond 40 days in the wilderness. It is the path to enlightenment which takes the enlightened one beyond the power of *any* suffering or deprivation. The teaching of the Buddha thus becomes in itself a cure for every illness, since it reveals the ultimate unreality of suffering and the fact that illness troubles only those who are mistakenly attached to this temporary self.

Buddhist saints achieve miraculous powers in a manner that is similar to the psychic powers gained by the yogins. The word 'achieve' is important here. For the emphasis is upon the development of spiritual insight through sustained meditation; miraculous powers are not, as at Pentecost, 'passed on' like a baton. This raises the question of whether these 'miraculous powers' are really more aptly described as extraordinary mental and physical abilities which have been acquired through training. There may be a hint of this in the ascetic traditions of the Christian saints and the Sufis, but in their case it is more an ascetic training that lays one open to the hand of God directing and performing through one. It is noteworthy that the Buddhist Scriptures refer to 'miraculous powers' and 'magical powers' interchangeably, as if being able to work miracles was the product of intense training, like the acquisition of athletic prowess (Conze 1959: 121). Magical powers, after all, are acquired by training – hence the idea of the 'magical arts'. One example suffices to make the point. It concerns achieving the power to 'dive into the earth and out of it':

> In order to achieve this, he should enter into concentration on the water-device, which begins with a contemplation of water in a bowl. On emerging from this he should mark off as much of the ground as he wishes to turn into water, and then prepare the miracle by the sustained resolve that this transformation should take place. Immediately the ground which he has marked off becomes water. And he can dive into it and out of it.
> (Conze 1959: 126)

The description suggests a manual or handbook for developing and using magical powers. Preparing a miracle is described rather in the terms one might use for preparing a meal.

The list of what these magical powers are might seem to be quite obviously beyond human resources, even after 'training' – ability to assume multiple forms, appear and disappear at will, walk through walls and mountains and on water, fly through the air, touch the sun and moon – not to mention the 'psychic' powers of penetrating the minds of others and remembering past lives, as well as understanding how the lives of others are connected to their deeds (the workings of karma). But these extraordinary powers represent the new consciousness attained through meditation; once again, as with the yogic tradition, it seems that they concern less a capacity to 'violate' the laws of nature than a capacity to see nature for what it really is. Or to put it slightly differently, the enlightened consciousness recognizes that all phenomena are themselves products of consciousness and can therefore be 'thought' into different forms. Flying through the air or walking through a mountain is like manipulating a dream; and in dreams we do not ask 'how' we managed to fly through the air or walk through a wall. We take it for granted that such things can happen.

In one story from the Mahayana tradition, the Buddha Sakyamuni is teaching from his lion throne when one of his disciples, Sariputra, asks why this world appears to be so impure. By way of answer the Buddha touches the ground with his big toe and the whole universe is suddenly transformed into a mass of precious jewels, and everyone present suddenly finds their seats transformed into thrones of jewelled lotuses. Then the Buddha restores the world to its usual 'impure' appearance. But the 'miracle', explains the Buddha, lies not in the creation of the pure world – it is always pure – but in the creation of the impure world so that impure beings will learn the lesson that all things are impermanent. The miracle is the demonstration of the emptiness and illusory character of all things so that people will strive instead for what is real.[9]

Miracles in Hinduism and Buddhism seem to be less about 'putting things right' in the world than perceiving what really exists. They have moved beyond the concern for amelioration that characterizes a woman pleading on behalf of her sick child; they want us to see that the world of sickness is not the real world. Miracles are here less the violation of natural law than the hard-earned access to a higher law.

It is easy to label this a 'world-denying' rather than 'world-affirming' perspective, and contrast it with the Christian search for grace through good works in the world, but once again the lines in the sand are not so easy to draw. Buddhism and Hinduism contain much that is world-affirming; as we have seen, one of the attractions of the Hindu God Krishna is his delight in the world and his playful enjoyment of it. And Jesus, we have to remember, enjoins his followers not to lay up treasure on earth, where it grows rusty and moth-eaten (Matthew 6:19). They should 'store up treasure in heaven' instead (Matthew 6:20). In all these traditions there is emphasis upon 'another reality' to which we should aspire.

Conclusions

This chapter has not been able to do justice to the variety and complexity within the various non-Christian traditions. It has attempted instead to bring out aspects of those traditions which might help to throw light on the question of miracles. Of necessity it has plucked different things from different areas, and this has perhaps meant that it lacks a single thread. Yet if it has shown a little of the richness and sophistication of some non-Christian religions in relation to the subject of miracles, it will have been worthwhile. Some of the themes touched upon here will be drawn together into a single argument in the conclusion to this book.

In considering Judaism, the chapter focused upon miracles during the nascent Christian era, when perhaps in response to Christian claims about Jesus there were a number of stories used to illustrate, not that miracles didn't happen, but that they did not bring glory to the miracle-worker. I have suggested that despite the context of their emergence, the stories may have connected with some aspects of Jesus' own reluctance to perform miracles.

In considering Islam, I have pointed to important strands of thinking which do highlight miracles – the biographies of Muhammad, the saints in the Sufi tradition. At the same time I suggested that the stress upon the all-powerful and transcendent God, while it might rule out miracles performed by the saints or even by Muhammad himself, arguably rules in miracles performed by God; for among those that may not challenge God's authority are not only the saints and the prophets but the laws of nature. This is what is interesting about the position of al-Ash'ari, and it forces us to consider precisely how we wish to define a 'miracle'.

In the context of Hinduism and Buddhism I mentioned the idea of miracles as God 'playing' with the world, something suggested by the story of Krishna. I then went on to consider Buddhist traditions and suggested that some Buddhist descriptions of miraculous powers seemed more like magical powers, by which I mean something that may be learned and then practised by those 'skilled' in the magical arts (this distinction has been discussed in Chapter 8 when considering the Protestant Reformation). The miracle-worker is someone who sees that phenomena are products of consciousness and can be thought into different forms.

But I concluded with a caveat concerning the 'differences' between religions. Judaism and Islam, like Christianity, have traditions which emphasize the reality of miracles as well as traditions which are sceptical about them. Where 'Indian' or 'Eastern' religions are concerned, it is easy to assume that a gulf with 'Western' religions opens up, but here again there are nuances and overlaps. It is easy, for instance, to contrast Jesus' miracles of 'healing' the sick with the Buddha's apparent claim that his teaching is itself the 'cure' for sickness, since it reveals the ultimate unreality of suffering. The truth is far more subtle than that. The Buddha, against the wishes of his family, opened himself to the suffering around him; he refused, like Dives, simply to treat the Lazarus at his gate as invisible. And Christianity arguably has an otherworldly aspect which was sometimes misappropriated to promise (as the saying went) pie in the sky when you die. It is said that among other miracles Jesus cured a withered arm and gave sight to a blind man; yet he also talked about it being better to cut off an arm or tear out an eye (thereby perhaps undoing his own work) if in so acting a person went to heaven or avoided hell (Matthew 5:29–30). One begins by thinking that two religions put different sides of an argument. One ends by thinking that in different ways each religion struggles with both sides of the argument.

Notes

1 This is the line taken by Alexander Guttmann (1947). It can be challenged because of the problems surrounding chronology where rabbinic writings are concerned. See the article by Signer (a pupil of Guttmann) in Cavadini (1999), pp. 111–26.

2 Through *Jesus the Jew* (1975) in particular, Geza Vermes did a great deal in the 1970s to restore the Jewishness of Jesus against a long tradition of setting him apart from 'the Jews', perceived as his enemies. For discussion of Honi the Circle Drawer and Hanina ben Dosa, see Vermes (1975), chs 3 and 4, and Vermes (1972).

3 There is an interesting discussion of Hasidism in particular and miracles in general in Cohn-Sherbok (1996).

4 Ibn Ishaq's biography, *Sirat Rasul Allah*, has been translated by Alfred Guillaume (1955). This is the version referred to in the text.

5 Sura 112 of the Qur'an talks of God as 'the Everlasting Refuge, who has not begotten, and has not been begotten, and equal to Him is not anyone'.

6 See Widad El Sakkakini (1982), for an account of the 'woman saint of Basra', the leading Sufi Rabia Al-Adawiyya.

7   The examples which follow are taken from *Hindu Myths: A Sourcebook* (O'Flaherty 1975).

8   There are many accounts of the Buddha's life including, it should be noted, his previous lives, with which biographies tend to begin. For a selection, see the *Buddhist Scriptures* selected and translated by Edward Conze (1959) and *The Life of the Buddha* (Foucher 1963). Leo D. Lefebure attempts a comparison between Buddha and Christ in his *The Buddha and the Christ: Explorations in Buddhist and Christian Dialogue* (1993).

9   This is a miracle from the Mahayana tradition (Buddhism, just like Christianity, has different traditions or what in Christianity would be termed 'denominations'). It can be found in the selection from the Mahayana Scriptures made by Thurman (1983: 18–19).

Chapter 12

Miracles in the Modern World

As in the case of 'other religions', so in the case of 'the modern world' we are faced with a range so vast that only a selection can be attempted. As in the previous chapter, I cannot cover every form of belief in miracles in the present day, but I can hope to illustrate ways in which the contemporary debate sheds light on some of the questions raised by this book.

If this chapter seems to emphasize rather heavily aspects of 'popular belief' in miracles, that is not because I wish to suggest that there isn't a large body of people for whom the modern world has effectively ruled them out of existence. It is because too many academics writing about miracles think that the world they inhabit is the world inhabited by everyone else. They think that there is no difference between saying that philosophers have undermined belief in miracles and claiming that they have no meaning for 'contemporary men and women'.

Just as 'pre-scientific' men and women were capable of suspicion and disbelief, so modern men and women in a 'scientific' age are capable of credulity. Bultmann's world of washing machines and wirelesses (or mobile phones) has not ceased to be a world of horoscopes, of the continuing popularity of superstitions such as touching wood and of bookshops groaning with textbooks on 'spirituality' (which make the mystery religions of ancient Rome look tame by comparison). Moreover, though some academic theologians may be embarrassed by miracles, that does not seem to be the case so far as many of the religious authorities or their followers are concerned. Some of the examples that follow concern contemporary Christian belief in miracles, but it would be unwise to underestimate their significance or to suppose that they represent simply the superstitious edges of modern Christian thinking.

Contemporary Catholic Piety

The first example – an obvious one to take – is that of Pope John Paul II, who must be assumed to represent a significant strand of Catholic thought, if not Catholic orthodoxy. A large number of people have been beatified and canonized during his pontificate, and miracles have played a part in their eligibility for that honour. The tradition of miracles associated with the saints in Catholic tradition is thereby carried through to the present day (see Woodward 1996: 184–90).

Among John Paul II's more controversial acts of beatification and canonization was that of Padre Pio, an Italian monk born in a small Italian village in 1887. Padre Pio was credited with the stigmata, the wounds of Christ, which appeared

179

on his hands, feet and side from 1918 and remained for some half a century until the time of his death in 1968, when they disappeared leaving his skin without blemish.[1]

Unsurprisingly, the claims of bearing the stigmata aroused controversy. It was not without historical precedent – St Francis of Assisi was the first of whom there is a record of the claim to be imprinted with Christ's wounds (in 1224), and there have been some 400 claims since, mostly among members of religious orders. Nor is it a claim without at least some parallels in other religions – there are claims among Muslims, for instance, of having borne wounds corresponding to those received in battle by Muhammad. But it is a claim that usually arouses suspicion. One interesting observation by critics of the tradition is that most scholars now see the likely method of crucifixion as involving nails through the wrist rather than the hand, since the wrist is better able to bear the weight of the body and prolong the torture, whereas almost all those who claimed to suffer the stigmata reported wounds on their palms and the back of their hands, not the wrists (see Harrison 1996).

The Padre Pio case was particularly controversial. During the papacy of John XXIII a series of investigations into the monk was carried out, including the bugging of his confession box. A report claimed that he used nitric acid to induce the wounds and that the so-called 'odour of sanctity' accompanying them was eau de cologne, which the monk possibly applied more for the masochistic pleasure of the sting than for purposes of deception. He was also accused of having women in his cell. The founder of Rome's Catholic University Hospital described him as a self-mutilating psychopath possessed of the devil who exploited people's credulity.

It is not the purpose of this book to reach a conclusion 'for or against' the truth of these miracles. What I am trying to do is to question what I regard as a too hastily erected barrier between the 'credulous' first century and the 'scientific' twenty-first century. I believe that generalizations like those, for instance, of Dennis Nineham in *The Use and Abuse of the Bible*, approvingly quoting C.G. Darwin, that 'London in 1750 was far more like Rome in A.D. 100 than like either London or Rome in 1950' (1978: 55), provide a misleading and unhistorical impression that there is some kind of chasm erected by science between the modern age of washing machines and wirelesses on the one hand, and the superstitious, pre-scientific past on the other. Differences there are, and they should not be forgotten, but the overall picture is much subtler than the cultural chasm portrayed by Nineham and should not be exaggerated.[2]

When we read of the reaction to Padre Pio's claims by the founder of Rome's Catholic University Hospital, we find in a modern setting precisely the same sort of arguments found in the reaction to claims about the miracles of Jesus. There is the accusation of madness, of leading the people astray and of doing the work of Satan rather than God – in Jesus' case 'casting out demons by the Prince of Demons'. In the reaction of the papacy there is the natural hostility of those in authority towards miracle-workers who might become alternative centres of power based on charismatic rather than institutional principles. Even the accusation of loose living can be compared – Padre Pio's assignations in his cell, Jesus' mixing with 'tax-gatherers and sinners'. None of this – to repeat – is to suggest any truth or falsity in the accusations made in either case. It is to suggest that whatever the imprint of two millennia of scientific and cultural progress, the nature of the reaction to miraculous claims may not have changed as much as some people like to think.

John Paul II did not share in the Vatican's suspicion of Padre Pio during the early 1960s. In 1947 he had travelled to visit the monk when a mere priest in order to have his confession heard. Later he asked the monk to pray for a friend of his with throat cancer. Wanda Polawska was later pronounced cured and lived to witness the canonization of Padre Pio in 2002 in Rome. Clearly rehabilitation of Padre Pio would not be long delayed once the former priest became Pope John Paul II in 1978.

At the same time this rehabilitation was accompanied by more investigations of the miracles associated with Padre Pio by doctors and surgeons. Some investigators stressed the power of autosuggestion, though a 'mind-over-matter' explanation, whilst it might explain a lack of perception of pain from the wounds, could hardly explain the wounds themselves. It was noted that the wounds were neither infected nor inflamed, the usual consequence of repeatedly self-inflicted injuries. It was this stability in their condition which has probably baffled medical experts most and kept them from simply identifying the monk as a self-mutilator. The results of scientific investigation were not such as to deliver some kind of binding verdict on the claims concerning Padre Pio – indeed this is very rarely the case. Rather they offered something to both sides of the argument.

The stigmata were not the only miracles associated with Padre Pio. He was also associated with bilocation – the ability to be seen in more than one place simultaneously. Most well-known of these 'bilocations' is the story of his presence in the sky over his home town producing some kind of force field that prevented Allied pilots from dropping their bombs over San Giovanni Rotondo, at the time part of Nazi-held territory. Such a phenomenon supposedly brought about the conversion to Catholicism of the American commanding general. Images of a monk suspended in the sky were also seen by many people shortly after Padre Pio's death. Naturally many claimed that these 'appearances' were the result of unusual atmospheric conditions or were a product of deliberate deception. At the same time instances of bilocation were fervently claimed by many believers, including several cardinals.

John Paul II may have encouraged the cause of Padre Pio, but there was already a cult following inspired by the monk's life. The annual figure of eight million visitors who visit the village of San Giovanni Rotondo where he lived exceeds the number who go to Lourdes. His beatification and canonization were attended by hundreds of thousands in 1999 and 2002. A new TV station was launched in 2002 in Italy dedicated to his life. Miracles are still claimed in his name. A prayer to the saint leads to a cure from cancer; in a modern equivalent of the medieval belief in relics, a lock of Padre Pio's hair held near to a sick man's face in Sicily brings him out of a coma – and so on. Meanwhile the town he lived in receives enormous economic benefits from his cult, spawning a huge business in souvenirs, statues and icons worth hundreds of millions of dollars a year, not to mention the income from pilgrims. A modern Italian or Irish town, like its medieval predecessors, knows what kind of economic miracle can be wrought by association with a popular saint.[3]

A further example from Catholic tradition is perhaps even more striking and more suggestive of the parallels between miracle claims in the first and twenty-first centuries. This is the Weeping Madonna of Civitavecchia, a poor agricultural suburb near Rome (the Rome of 2003 which is, in Nineham's view, light years from that of 100 AD) (see Kirsta 2000). La Madonina was a present to a devout electrician from his local priest in 1994. It was a simple plaster statuette of the Virgin Mary, given him to protect his home and brought from the Bosnian pilgrimage site of Medjugorje. It was one of many such 'assembly line' madonnas which could be purchased from the pilgrimage site for the equivalent of a few pounds or dollars.

Then in 1995 the electrician's daughter reported that the madonna had started crying. 'Papa! Papa! Come and look ... There's blood everywhere.' Her father saw red liquid welling up in the eyes of the statue and trickling down its cheeks and gown. The electrician reported the event to his priest at mass and it was soon a media headline. Thousands started to besiege the electrician's house. In words that recall the beginning of Mark's gospel, where Jesus' cures attract uncontrollable crowds and eventually force him to abandon the shore in a boat to avoid being crushed (Mark 3:9–10), the Scottish-born manager of the language school in Civitavecchia talked of 'a mass invasion ... they were swinging from the trees ... you couldn't move for cars, buses and people blocking the way to his home' (quoted in Kirsta 2000).

Overwhelmed by the pressure of visitors, the pious electrician returned the statuette to his local priest who then contacted the local bishop. Much to his surprise, the bishop recommended that he destroy the statue! The bishop was convinced that it was all a hoax intended to discredit local Catholics as superstitious fools. He suspected satanists and Jehovah's Witnesses.

Once again we encounter a sceptical attitude on the part of those in authority in the church. As we have already said, charismatic individuals with miracle-working powers can be a threat to institutional forms of power. In this case, of course, no such person existed, but in any case the bishop relented and took the statuette to Rome for analysis. He was led to believe that the blood would turn out to be animal blood, but in fact it was human – however, it was male blood and not the female blood one might associate with the Virgin Mary. The Vatican decided to put the bishop in charge of a theological commission investigating the case.

In a further twist to a byzantine plot, the once-sceptical bishop underwent a change in perspective and himself claimed to have seen La Madonina crying tears of blood. When the DNA test of the new bloodstains revealed them to be identical to the first, the bishop stated publicly that as male blood they must be that of Christ himself.

The political complexities of what followed need not detain us, they are too intricate and bizarre. One consistent supporter of La Madonina was the communist mayor, Pietro Tidei, who recognized the commercial potential of a miracle and was soon allocating billions of lire for infrastructural improvements – a pilgrim's hostel, parking facilities, street lights, toilets and other necessities for encouraging people to come and spend money in the deprived area he represented. It was a matter of regret to the communist mayor that he received insufficient support from the bishop in promoting his area by tying in with the big pilgrim tour operators heading from Rome to Lourdes.

On the other hand, one consistent opponent of La Madonina came in the form of the public prosecutor, who was asked to investigate a possible instance of 'pious fraud'. Meanwhile a series of TV 'exposés' sought to find alternative explanations of weeping madonnas. In one programme a popular magician shone a red laser beam onto the statue from a gallery in the church in order to show how to conjure tears of blood. In another one it was shown how statues can be fitted with special contact lenses which weep blood, or how a blood-filled syringe inside a figurine can be activated electronically by remote control. A range of other explanations have been unearthed by the Italian Committee for Investigation of Claims of the Paranormal (CICAP), including inner reservoirs, red dye under the eyes and a colourless compound that turns red when it comes into contact with ammonia vapour.

The result of the debate has been an explosion of pop science TV shows and an equal and opposite rise both in popular piety focused on La Madonina and in scepticism reaching as far as belief in deliberate fraud engineered by members of the ecclesiastical establishment.[4]

Miracles in Contemporary Hinduism

Such phenomena are not confined to Christianity. Within the last ten years there has been a wave of reports concerning statues of Hindu Gods.[5] In this case the miracle lies in the way the statue absorbs liquid rather than produces it in the form of tears or blood. Since September 1995, when eyewitnesses in India began to report accounts of statues drinking milk, there have been reports of such activity around the world, both in temples and in individual homes. Thousands of British Hindus have reported such miracles, including 10 000 who claimed to witness statues drinking milk from cups and spoons at the Vishwa Temple in South London. In an even closer parallel to Catholic miracles, nectar flowed from the feet of a photograph of Sai Baba in the shrine room of a Hindu temple in Wimbledon, South London, and holy ash came from his forehead.

Following on from Hume's comments on witnesses to miracles, we can certainly not say that these were credulous members of the community, whether in Delhi or London. Most of them were occasional rather than regular visitors to the temples, many were rich (the Hindu Gods received a lot of silver spoons to take their milk from), many worked in business and took an occasional lunchbreak in the temple, and some were in what people often take to be naturally sceptical professions like journalism. Among them was Rebecca Mae, a *Daily Express* journalist who made the interesting comment that 'as a lapsed Catholic I don't believe in stories of the Virgin Mary shedding tears. Indeed I was as sceptical as anyone – but it's difficult to dismiss something you have seen for yourself.'[6]

Of course there is no reason to suppose the rich any less credulous than the poor, the businessperson than the plumber or for that matter the journalist than the academic. Moreover there are 'explanations' of the miracle. There is the psychological explanation in terms of mass hysteria, a communal power of autosuggestion whereby people see what they want or expect to see. There is the scientific explanation in terms of 'capillary absorption', which argues that the material of the statues has some power to absorb liquid. These stand as alternatives to the account given by many Hindu worshippers that a new God had been born to save the world from evil (as if the drinking of the milk, like the star in the east at Bethlehem, heralded the coming of a saviour). Moreover, whilst Rebecca Mae is right to say that it is 'difficult to dismiss' something you have seen with your own eyes, it is certainly not impossible, or we would end up believing every conjuror's trick and conclude that women can survive being sawn in half.

What such modern miracle stories do is demonstrate that 'modern science' has not driven miracles out or curbed the enthusiasm for them. It can be used to debunk certain claims and to establish others. It may show that blood on a statue is real human blood, but it may also show that it is a dye or a different compound altogether. Though it could show whether the blood was that of the electrician or the bishop (neither was prepared to submit to a DNA test), thereby (if positive) ruling a miracle out, it could not rule a miracle in by showing that the blood was indeed that of Christ. Without twenty-four hour video surveillance in the shrine room, it cannot establish whether the ash and nectar around the photograph of Sai Baba were a plant. It can generalize (in the form of psychological science) about crowd behaviour and mass hysteria, but will find it difficult to account for every sighting, from a crowd large enough to stop the traffic in Delhi, straining to see a miracle at the hands of a marble statue of Ganesh, to the worshipper in her own home who finds her small statue in the corner of a room lapping up milk like a kitten. Science can certainly challenge (just as it can support) these miracle stories, but it cannot put paid to them. They keep on coming.

It is also clear that apart from questions of faith there are questions of economics involved. A miracle is a way of promoting downtrodden areas that wouldn't normally attract any tourism, religiously motivated or otherwise (since all tourists spend money, their motivation doesn't really matter). Here too it is easy to find parallels in New Testament times. In Acts 19:23–7 a man called Demetrius, a silversmith making silver shrines of Diana and providing employment for craftsmen in the region complains that Paul's preaching is bad for their industry and turns the whole of Ephesus against the Christian movement. But clearly the pagans of Ephesus, when they cry 'Great is Diana of the Ephesians', are proclaiming what puts their city on the map and helps to provide for its wealth rather than (or as well as) expressing an article of belief, just as a communist mayor is hardly motivated by religious belief in supporting La Madonina.

Protestant Miracles

Though it may seem as though it is pious Catholic countries like Italy and Ireland which are 'miracle-prone' in the modern world, that would be an oversimplification. Catholics, like Hindus, are not just pious in particular countries. Furthermore, despite the Freudian cliché that the future of this 'illusion' of religion is to disappear, it is clear that technology and a comfortable lifestyle do not remove the need for miracles. One of the most miracle-prone countries in the world is its most technologically advanced, the United States of America. The USA retains a predominantly churchgoing populace and a majority who believe in miracles.[7]

This belief in miracles may be partly a product of America's past, of its founding fathers and Puritan tradition, and therefore a development in reaction to rather than dependent on Roman Catholicism. In any case it is among the Protestant groups in the USA that one finds a powerful body of Pentecostalists who reject the post-biblical miracles of the medieval period (which they dismiss as 'pagan supernaturalism', an attitude discussed in Chapter 8) but believe that the miraculous taps were turned on again on behalf of the Protestants. Their sixteenth-century breakaway from the church is compared to the appearance of a 'purified remnant' of Israel under God's protection in the Old Testament. The view is that Protestantism has been preserved in a similar way from the Reformation to the present day through special acts of God (miracles) which have protected it from its enemies.

The well-known evangelist and 1988 presidential candidate Pat Robertson is an example of this belief. As a Pentecostalist he sees the receiving of the Holy Spirit at Pentecost as a receiving of the power to work miracles, one that is open not just to the original apostles but to true Christians in the modern world (see Woodward 2001: 371–5). In October 1985, when Hurricane Gloria threatened the Virginia coastline, Pat Robertson was on hand to rebuke it on television and its trajectory duly altered. Robertson also claimed that tornadoes and hurricanes were often 'punitive miracles' carried out by a God angry at such examples of lax moral behaviour in Florida as 'Gay Days' at Disneyworld. These natural phenomena therefore functioned both as instruments of God's wrath and as agents of God's mercy when Mr Robertson intervened.

It is difficult to assess the significance of high-profile people like Pat Robertson. He was, after all, a presidential candidate in 1988, and therefore hardly an insignificant figure. On the other hand, he was not elected, despite his claim to work miracles.

Other characters on the American religious landscape focus more on the benefits which God's miracles have brought to them personally. The hugely popular autobiography of Oral Roberts (1995), whose sales figures are in millions, is an example. Roberts is a well-known evangelist and son of a poor Oklahoma Pentecostalist preacher. In his book he outlines the 'twelve greatest miracles of my ministry', half of which are not cures but things like the success of his TV ministry or of the Oral Roberts university. His whole life appears in the autobiography as a series of miracles worked through him and for him. Indeed miracles cease to be exceptional events and become regular occurrences for believers. Today's avoided traffic collision, tomorrow's lucky discovery of enough money to pay the bills, all are part of the daily routine for those whose lives are effectively micromanaged by God. The bimonthly magazine published by the Oral Roberts Ministries is called *Miracles Now*. As the byword quoted in the title of Oral Roberts' autobiography has it, 'Expect a miracle.' One might almost add 'You deserve it.'

Devotees of Oral Roberts, of course, are the exception, even though their number probably runs into millions. Nevertheless, instances such as these have to be set against the perception that 'the modern world' simply cannot accept that miracles take place. On the contrary, it can, even to the point of trivializing the miraculous so that it becomes another service which believers/customers can buy into. Miracles become an additional resource or product which can be 'bought' in the spiritual marketplace.

The miracles associated with Oral Roberts and Pat Robertson have a different context to those associated with Padre Pio or La Madonina. For one thing, the miracles take place within the highly individualistic and self-oriented context of Protestantism. They are a me-enhancing bonus, an extra way in which Americans can go on feeling good about themselves. There is no ecclesiastical institution in place to review the claims made and (depending on your viewpoint) subject them to a healthy scepticism or credulously support them. The Robertson example is an interesting one for another reason, in that sometimes a 'special act of God' is a punitive miracle which serves as a reminder of God's wrath in the face of (what Robertson believes to be) human depravity, particularly homosexuality, which as contemporary Anglican experience shows is always a source of passionate pronouncements among conservative churchpeople, whether Catholic or Protestant.

Lest such attitudes are still seen as the preserve of 'religious' nations like the USA, Ireland and Italy, note the reaction only 20 years ago in Britain to the burning down of part of York Minster three days after the consecration of David Jenkins as a theologically liberal Bishop of Durham. A leader in *The Times* entitled 'Act of God' (1984) declared that it was 'hard not to be reminded of Elijah and the prophets of Baal', and the media took up the debate over whether the fire could be seen as an expression of 'divine wrath'. Here we are in 'secular', liberal-minded England, and for some reason *The Times* finds it hard not to be reminded of Elijah when lightning strikes a church roof! It is something one might expect in a sixteenth-century tract; but it is still alive and strong in the leader columns of a serious newspaper at a time of miners' strikes and detailed debates about the danger posed by cruise missiles.

In late twentieth-century Britain it was not Catholics but evangelical Protestants within the Church of England, like David Holloway, vicar of a parish church in a suburb of Newcastle upon Tyne, who made the running in arguing for a 'punitive miracle' at York Minster. Much as 60 years earlier, at the time of the evacuation from Dunkirk, people had sought to interpret days of calm as evidence of divine favour, now they were seeking to interpret less favourable events as evidence of divine wrath.

In these cases, unlike those of La Madonina and Padre Pio, there is nothing that the scientists can do by way of intervening, since no one doubts the scientifically observable natural processes by which lightning strikes a cathedral or hurricanes strike the eastern seaboard of the USA. God is here claimed to be working through rather than apart from secondary causes. In such circumstances the scientific arguments cease to be relevant, and other considerations must take their place – such as the ethical question of what sort of God might intervene in such a punitive manner.[8]

These examples of belief in miracles, which are necessarily taken from just three or four countries and one or two religious traditions, do despite their limited coverage point to a widespread belief in miracles in the modern world that is neither undermined nor underpinned by the insights of modern science. But does that mean that no impact has been wrought upon the miracles debate by two millennia of scientific progress or by intellectual movements like the Enlightenment? It would certainly be wrong to say that. The preparedness to subject miracle claims to close scientific scrutiny, for instance in the case of CICAP over La Madonina, is something that could not have taken place in an earlier age. Moreover such scientific research can and does effectively undermine claims to miracles – for instance the liquefaction of the dried blood of saints at holy festivals.[9] But what is striking is the fact that many of these miracle claims remain unaffected by scientific reasoning. If they claim miraculous coincidences like a diverted hurricane or a lightning strike on a cathedral, science can clearly offer no proof or disproof. If they are built into an individual's sense of destiny as one chosen by God, as in the case of Oral Roberts, then any number of autobiographical details can be inflated through talk of miracles. If they concern healings, then science can at most declare that the explanation of a cure is not available given the present state of scientific knowledge. The drops of blood on La Madonina are human, but they cannot be proved to be those of Christ. The stigmata of Padre Pio are unusual but can hardly be proven to have been self-inflicted or not to have been. The stories of bilocation seem fantastical and beyond anything associated even with the founder of Christianity, unless the resurrected Jesus is regarded as making simultaneous appearances to his followers – and even then, he was incapable of such things during his lifetime. Yet it is difficult to see what kind of scientific analysis could disprove such reports, or whether such an analysis might affect the eight million modern-day pilgrims who go to Padre Pio's home town every year, presumably believing in his bilocation just as they believe in their computers, their mobile phones or any other piece of machinery equivalent to Bultmann's wirelesses and washing machines.

It should also be remembered that even in our world of 'wirelesses and washing machines' there is an endless stream of claims concerning various extraordinary phenomena. Since these claimed phenomena often occur outside a specifically religious context, it is inappropriate to call them 'miracles'; they are not so much special acts of God as events which cannot be explained. We should remember Hobbes' remark in *Leviathan* that it is not enough for a miracle that an event be unusual or unprecedented (he offers the example of a talking cow). It must have a particular religious purpose – Hobbes suggests creating faith or upholding the authority of God's ministers and prophets ([1651] 1968: ch. 37).

Nevertheless such phenomena, like the miracles which are claimed from within particular religious traditions as acts of God (or of God's representatives), point – like miracles – to the ease with which the conclusions of modern science may be challenged. Three obvious examples of these claims would be crop circles, the widespread reporting of specific light effects (usually crosses and circles) on the sides and windows of houses during broad daylight, and UFOs. These will not be discussed in detail here, fascinating though they are. The point is not to defend such claims as true, but to point up their prevalence in an 'age of science'.[10]

It is important to see that the believers in such phenomena, rather than burying their heads in the sand and rejecting the insights of modern science, actually seek to employ these insights to defend and justify their own understanding. The millions of people who believe in UFOs do not deride modern science and technology; they believe that it can be made to support their cause. They echo with enthusiasm the latest speculations of the astronomers concerning life on other planets; they employ the most sophisticated camera equipment to attempt to prove their sightings genuine; they provide detailed and precise descriptions and try to establish that they have independent sources. Rather than dismissing science, they seek to embrace it, just as the Vatican sifts through complex medical reports in order to justify a healing and rejects those it sees as 'unscientific'. My point, once again, is not to defend the existence of UFOs, or for that matter miraculous healings carried out at the behest of an interceding saint. The argument is that science, however 'advanced' it may be, is ever a two-edged sword. It can debunk 'superstition'; but it can also strengthen it and lend weight to its claims.

The Return of Christ: An Imagined Account

This point about science is so important that I would like to illustrate it with an extended example, the details of which are of course purely fictitious.

Suppose somebody was to claim that they were Christ returned two millennia on. Let us imagine that this person claims to work miracles and that thousands claim to have witnessed these wonders whilst others condemn them as tricks. Let us suppose that this person has some kind of run-in with the authorities of our day, perhaps because of a radical social and political message which is extremely controversial. Then the person dies (we will presume in suspicious circumstances).

A great deal of media attention, let us say, has been focused on this 'Christ'. Some have become ardent followers, others are uninterested, a few point out that mental institutions are full of would-be Christs and a significant number of establishment figures see the 'impostor's' persona as a front for social revolution. There are fears (and hopes) of a resurrection. There are suspicions on the part of the authorities that a fake resurrection will be carried out in order to support social revolution; there are equivalent fears that the resurrection will be 'covered up' on the part of followers convinced that it will take place. Perhaps the sentiments are not so very different from what they were two millennia back. But this is the twenty-first century, and we have 'science' at our disposal...

Two doctors certify the 'Christ' dead. Then a third doctor is called to confirm the opinion of the other two. By now it is clear to everyone that the body needs to be moved. It is taken to the hospital mortuary where it is photographed and examined once again. Next of kin are called to identify the body. A few extra checks are made by doctors and questions are asked about the tagging of corpses.

It is now after midnight. But as everyone leaves the mortuary, two hospital workers are taken aside and asked to go back and remain there throughout the night. They will receive double overtime. They grumble at the request. The place is perfectly secure. What are these people afraid of? Necrophilia? Body snatchers?

The relatives ring the hospital the next day to inquire about the funeral arrangements. Whoever they speak to becomes very nervous when they ask for burial to be as soon as possible. There will have to be an autopsy. Some preliminary investigations have been made but there will need to be more. People from forensics are with the body now and their work will take a few days. Expect a funeral in a week to ten days.

The corpse is kept in the hospital for seven days, during which it is constantly watched over by at least two people. Over the course of this week it receives a number of incisions. The rib cage is opened, the stomach and various other organs are removed, and there is even an incision into the skull to examine the brain.

At the end of seven days the investigations appear to be complete, and the body is released for burial. It continues to be accompanied by two people throughout its journey to the funeral parlour and for the whole process of embalming. Great emphasis is put upon the need to keep an eye on the body. The guards are relieved every four hours and issued with caffeine tablets which they are made to take every two hours.

It is only when the lid is nailed onto the coffin, more than a week after the time of death, that the unofficial sentinels finally depart. The family has been pressured to accept a cremation, but they insist on burial. After the funeral service the coffin is carried to a grave on the edge of a housing estate in the home town of the 'Christ'. A large number of mourners follow the cortège on its last journey. A police helicopter watches the scene carefully from the skies. After the service two men remain at the graveside while the grave is filled in. They explain that they have orders to wait another three days. The gravedigger hopes they have a good book to read, since 'the people in here don't talk much'. He fixes them up with some chairs to sit on and a paraffin lamp.

This all-night vigil by the body provokes some comment on the nearby housing estate. People complain that it shows disrespect. Do the authorities expect them to come and steal the body? Can they not leave the dead to rest in peace? Children from the estate throw stones at the men beside the grave.

Meanwhile rumours circulate about a resurrection from the dead. It isn't clear whether the stories start among supporters of the would-be Christ or among other people who want to foment trouble. It is claimed that on this occasion Christ will not rise from the dead on the third day after death, but on the third day after burial. The authorities discover that any delay over interring the body has apparently been in vain, at least so far as dampening down expectations is concerned.

The two men who sit all night with the body find themselves joined by two others at dawn. The following night is 'the big one', they are told. They won't be alone to cope with the stones, the cold and the boredom. There will be lights everywhere throughout the night. All over the graveyard and part of the adjoining housing estate. It won't feel lonely at all. It will be more like a street party.

That evening a huge concentration of technical equipment is rigged up around and inside the graveyard. The adjoining housing estate, usually bathed in the orange glow of the few streetlights that haven't been vandalized or left unrepaired by the council, is suddenly awash with artificial light. There is less illumination from the floodlights at the local football ground during an evening match. Then there are the huddles of reporters, the camera crews, the microphones, the huge vans trailing cables and a mass of unrecognizable but sophisticated scientific equipment. Unsurprisingly, the local residents look harassed, and a few wish that this apparent Christ could have been buried somewhere else. They complain of being kept awake by the noise and the lights. Only a few entrepreneurs running mobile refreshment stalls look reasonably pleased with what is happening.

One piece of equipment is the centre of attention. It can detect the slightest movement in the soil to a depth of 20 feet. Not even a worm could crawl out of the ground without the machine knowing about it. It is as sensitive as the 'snickometer' used to detect the slightest brush of bat against ball in a cricket match. It can discern the first tremors of an earthquake. Its manager is particularly proud of what it can do. 'As for the rending of a temple curtain', the technician remarks, 'this little beauty could detect a fly crawling up it.'

The media and scientific circus is now in place. Many of them reflect that this is quite unlike the 'last visit', when there was none of this sophistication around. There was bound to be unbelief then, because there was so little in the way of available scientific proof. No television cameras, no tape recorders, no computers, nothing. Whereas if Christ came along now, a thousand different ways can be found of providing absolute certainty. Take the feeding of the five thousand. Someone would be there today with a camcorder. It would be on tape for all to see. One minute nothing, the next everyone stuffing themselves and baskets brimming with loaves and fishes left over at the end. No chance of disbelief now. The churches would be full within minutes. With the right scientific data you can always tell a true miracle from a forgery. It's as simple as analysing paintings or rare stones.

Everywhere there are clusters of people – for several sightseers and would-be disciples have come to see for themselves. A few dozen police are at hand too, their work cut out mediating between the invaders and the local residents. It is not like the 'original' death – a tomb in the hillside, despairing followers who had left in panic or despair, and nothing outside it but a couple of drowsing guards, sleeping off their dinners on what they probably considered pointless sentry duty beside the grave of some Galilean madman.

In the morning the sun rises onto a scene that looks as drab as Las Vegas at dawn. All the sparkling lights of the night before are shown up in a dull artificial glow. Faces look worn after the long vigil of the night. There is litter everywhere, chased around by the dogs of the estate. The children have grown tired of admiring sophisticated worm detectors or trying to get themselves onto television, and the television crews have grown tired of chasing away the children. By mid-morning most of the people there have decided it's time to go. They've started to hate the place. Besides, it's clear that nothing's happened. The guards get up and leave as well. For the first time peace and privacy seem to have a chance of descending on the grave.

By mid-morning, however, there are reports in the media that Christ has risen a second time from the dead. A few others who had also claimed to be Christ (for every celebrity breeds imitators) now declare that the real Christ has appeared to them and has wished them well in their endeavours to save the world. Others claim to have seen Christ too. A family in Birmingham claims to have had dinner with the risen Christ. Of course they took pictures of the event.

Arguments break out concerning the authenticity of these reports. Calls are made for anyone encountering the risen body to take a photograph proving that Christ is no longer dead. For instance, Christ could be pictured holding up that day's newspaper, a technique sometimes used by kidnappers to prove that a hostage is still alive. Or Christ could be asked to telephone the media. Anyone with information that could lead to proof that Christ has risen from the dead is asked to contact a hotline. By the end of the day it has been besieged with calls from people saying that they have seen Christ.

Before long there are pictures of Christ holding up today's newspaper. But are they of *the same person*? Is this the glorified body of Christ, looking naturally different from Christ's earthly body, or is it somebody else's unglorified body looking like Christ? And what could this other one be, the one from the dinner in Birmingham? Is it perhaps an over-exposed picture of Christ taken long before death, now paraded as a halo of light around Christ's glorified self?

The only thing anyone can clearly recognize is that in the face of these claimed appearances the authorities are growing worried. It is not only the public hysteria, the way in which everyone seems to encourage everyone else until they are all nearly out of control (the death of Princess Diana had a similar effect, and for a while that produced a dangerous threat to the institution of monarchy). So far as the opponents of this purported Christ are concerned, all the dangerous nonsense spouted while the person was alive is now being given a new lease of life after death. It is claimed that many of the 'visions' being reported have been invented by supporters to help foment civic disorder. Something has to be done to defuse these infectious resurrection stories. And there is only one way of doing that. Dig up the body. Show it for what it is. A rotting corpse.

Since the carnival has only just left, the feelings of local residents are stirred up further when it returns a day later. This time there is a more serious incident. Incensed by the renewed disturbance, and by the plan to disinter, people from the estate invade the graveyard and refuse to let the grave be touched. Only after a considerable scuffle are they cleared out of the way by police. The grave ends up cordoned and curtained off, like a deathbed in a hospital ward.

Later that day there is film of the coffin being lifted to the surface. Meanwhile there are urgent discussions about whether a rotting corpse can be shown on television. After all, it will have to be a close-up. Perhaps it could be 'improved' in some way without it being at all unclear who it is – there is mention of a precedent in the form of the sons of Saddam Hussein. The pictures can be shown late in the evening, after the nine o'clock watershed when children are supposedly in bed.

When the coffin is finally brought to the top and the lid opened, an angry shout emerges from behind the curtain. Nothing there.

There is immediate suspicion that the body has been stolen. A number of people from the local housing estate are arrested and questioned. At first they are treated mildly. It is understandable that this disturbance of the dead has troubled them. So they moved the body somewhere private, where it could truly rest in peace. It is easy to sympathize with this. Just tell us where the body is... Then requests become demands. Moving bodies and desecrating graves is a very serious offence. But no one provides any information and everyone denies having been near the grave.

Eventually it is officially confirmed that the body has been 'removed' from the grave. Police are investigating. Several people from a nearby housing estate have been taken for questioning. Charges will be brought. By now it is being argued that the body snatchers are supporters of the fanatical views of the Messiah. They were determined to preserve the legend by disinterring the remains and hiding them. A search of the area is under way...

A close examination is made of the empty coffin and a police spokesperson interviewed. Were there fingerprints? No. The grave robbers had been careful. Professionals, in fact. So not residents of the local housing estate? That couldn't be ruled out. Were there any signs of disturbance when the coffin was dug up? That is difficult to say, since they weren't looking for any at the time. Well, were there signs of the lid having been opened already? Were there any signs whatever of the grave having been disturbed when they went to dig up the body? Were they ruling out the possibility that someone else had exhumed the body before them? No, they didn't rule it out. In fact that was a line of inquiry which they were actively investigating.

Over the next few days there is endless speculation in the media. It is generally agreed that when the lid of the coffin was nailed down a body was inside it, but there is now some doubt about whether there was a body in the coffin that was laid into the ground. The men who were paid to guard the body were hired by people who feared that the Christ would somehow get up off the mortuary slab and walk away during the days immediately following death. When the lid was nailed down more than a week later, and the coffin placed in the hearse, they didn't continue to watch it second by second as the funeral procession got under way. A surreptitious exchange was not absolutely impossible.

Then there were the guards themselves. Hospital employees initially, who might well be low-waged employees sympathetic to the social teaching of Christ. Later on other people from a private security firm were brought in, but even they might contain people who couldn't be trusted. A thorough investigation is made into the background of everyone involved in the whole security operation, and it is found that at least two people had attended rallies at which Christ spoke, whilst one of the hospital workers had been on strike. Were such people absolutely trustworthy?

Then there is the question of an early exhumation. The authorities claim not to have noticed whether the grave had been disturbed, which is implausible but not impossible. Less difficult to believe is the possibility that sympathizers from the nearby estate might want to come and claim the body, either out of solidarity with the movement Christ represented or in order to perpetuate it with a supposed miracle. The hostility between them and those who invaded the area after the burial was palpable. There had been a scuffle over disinterring the body. Perhaps they'd been afraid that their action in exhuming the body would be discovered if the coffin was dug up, and that had been the real motive for trying to prevent its being disturbed.

What I am suggesting by way of (an, of course, entirely hypothetical) illustration is that even modern science may not provide the means to place beyond doubt what happened to a contemporary 'Christ' who died and then perhaps rose again. There might be an attempt to prevent a 'repeat resurrection' being faked, but it would not be difficult for a 'new tradition' to change the circumstances of that resurrection taking place (third day after burial rather than after death). There might be attempts to watch over the body after burial, but the claims to a sighting of the risen Christ could occur anyway – and could 'encourage' other sightings. These sightings could not be proved genuine or false, even with modern scientific methods. The body could be disinterred. Here I suggest a scenario where it isn't there but even so doubts remain. It might have been stolen or it might never have been in the coffin in the first place. Another scenario, of course, would be that the body *is* there. Even this is not necessarily decisive. We should remember that there are Christians who claim that resurrection is not bodily and therefore that Christ could rise even if his corpse remained rotting in the grave.[11]

It seems to me that human error and unreliability, shifting interpretations and the sheer difficulty of covering every eventuality and dealing with unpredictable human responses make it perfectly plausible that a claim about Christ's rising from the dead in the twenty-first century would be as much a source of controversy (with scientific evidence wielded on either side of the argument) as it was in the first century. Is this footage real or a forgery? Is this a cure or a spontaneous remission or a false diagnosis? Is it really walking on water caught on this video camera here, or is it a clever fake, one film superimposed upon another? The believers would challenge the unbelievers for explanations, while the unbelievers would challenge the believers for 'proof'. Neither side could prove the other wrong.

Conclusions

In the end it is not science which makes the difference. There are issues of authority and of economics involved, which may be decisive, as in the case of the communist mayor of Civitavecchia, a worthy heir to the pagans of Ephesus. There is the using of miracles in order to bolster personal beliefs or prejudices (depending on your point of view) or to shore up a personal self-image of success. There are the usual stories of ecclesiastical power-broking and infighting (extraordinary in the case of La Madonina, and desperately in need of a comic genius to dramatize them). There is the force of popular piety, which sometimes seems more encouraged in its beliefs than plunged into self-doubt by scientific revelations of deceit, as if the true believers can now show themselves in conditions of adversity. From the opposite perspective there is the sort of powerful moral argument against 'acts of divine wrath' which was advanced at the time of the York Minster fire, and the passionate defence of 'punitive miracles' as an expression of a divine wrath, an outlook which is neatly tailored to the sense of moral outrage felt by characters like the eccentric Vicar of Jesmond in Newcastle upon Tyne.

This chapter has tried to show how easily – despite the Enlightenment and the development of scientific reason – modern-day arguments about miracles can call to mind those of the first century, and how easily people today can find themselves replaying the concerns, passions and sceptical dismissals of others two millennia ago.

Notes

1   Woodward (1996) discusses the Padre Pio case. There is also an interesting discussion of Padre Pio's life in the *Fortean Times* 162 (September 2002).

2   There are even those who argue that the Bible is closer to us now than it has been culturally for centuries. See the discussion in Brown (1985), p. 32.

3   Thus the small town of Knock in Ireland, which became famous when 15 people claimed to witness an apparition of the Virgin Mary in 1979, now receives a million and a half visitors annually and has an international airport. When the low-cost airline BMI Baby decided to include flights to Knock in its schedule, the local newspaper reported that the airline 'had faith in miracles'. The meaning of this sentence was presumably that they had faith in the power of miracles to ensure an economically viable throughput of pilgrims.

4   'Ecclesiastical conspiracies', whether true or false, can work in opposite directions. There can be a 'conspiracy' to advocate a miracle, but there can also be a 'conspiracy' to deny one for fear of making a charismatic individual too powerful in relation to the establishment. On the charismatic vs institutional theme, which so often recurs in the history of religion, see Zimdars-Schwartz (1991) in relation to encounters with the Virgin Mary.

5   This phenomenon was reported in many different parts of the world on 21 September 1995. It received worldwide media attention.

6   *Hinduism Today* ran a series of articles analysing the claimed miracles and media response in its issues for November and December 1995 and January 1996. Though it

took the view that the miracles were genuine, it did make the interesting point that it was often the Indian press which was the most sceptical, while the British press contained comments like those of Rebecca Mae!

7   A *Newsweek* poll of 1 May 2000 established that a majority of Americans claimed to believe in miracles. Some very much less technologically advanced countries poll lower percentages.

8   See the Archbishop of York's arguments in *The Guardian*, 31 July 1984. The issue is briefly discussed in Wiles (1986), ch. 1.

9   One of the most common areas in which the scientific argument gets very intense on both sides is that of the miraculous liquefaction of the blood of saints, often during religious ceremonies on their feast days. See, for instance, the discussion of St Januarius in Epstein and Garlaschelli (1992).

10   Crop circles alone have spawned a wealth of literature. See Pat Delgado (1992) and Nicolas Montigiani (2003), who traces interest in the phenomenon back to a 'mowing devil' referred to in Hertfordshire in 1678. Both works are determined to be as 'scientific' as possible. Crop circles are linked to belief in UFOs, of course, since it is frequently argued that they are signs of an 'alien presence' or landing.

11   See the still fascinating divergence of opinion on the issue between Lampe and Mackinnon (1966). Lampe feels that the empty tomb is not an essential ingredient of Christian belief in the resurrection of Jesus. Mackinnon disagrees. See Chapter 9 of this book.

Chapter 13

Summary and Conclusions

Many different themes have been covered in the course of this book. If there is a justification for such wide-ranging coverage, it is that miracles do not represent a minor and perhaps embarrassing aspect of religious belief. Within Christianity alone they involve central theological and philosophical issues concerning the relation of God to the world, the way in which God acts and the goodness of God. They are also central to the understanding of the Bible and the history of the Christian religion. Despite my obvious selectivity, both between religions and within Christianity itself, I hope to have been able to show that the question of miracles is not unimportant.

In conclusion, I want to draw together three key themes concerning the nature of miracles. These could be summed up in terms of the following three questions. First, what are miracles? Second, how do miracles happen (if they do)? Third, why do miracles happen (if they do)?

What are Miracles?

In the first chapter of this book I defined a miracle as 'a special or immediate act of God, as opposed to God's continuous work of creating and sustaining the world. The result of this act will be beneficial and religiously significant.'

I said nothing in my definition about 'violating' or 'breaking' a law of nature. There were two reasons for this. One reason is that it seems to me that we often talk about a 'miracle' when there is no violation of a law of nature involved. I am thinking of the 'coincidences' which are the stock-in-trade of popular parlance concerning miracles. Holland's example of the child trapped on the railway line or Lewis' example of the nine days of calm sea at Dunkirk are illustrative of these 'miracles' which do not violate any law. Yet I have argued that the idea of thanking God for calm seas and trains halting in the nick of time surely implies that God did something to make things happen this way. God may not have done anything that nature couldn't in principle do – yet, on this occasion, it was God that did it (or so the believers in 'coincidence miracles' claim). There was a 'special or immediate act of God', and therefore according to my definition a 'miracle', even though it could be argued that it was not one which violated any law of nature.

The second problem I have with miracles as 'violations of the laws of nature' lies in the fact that the 'laws of nature' are constantly changing and at any one time there will be disagreement between scientists over what they are. In the seventeenth century some people saw the weapon-salve as scientific; others saw it as totally unscientific and thus, if efficacious, it could only be so because of a miracle. In Chapter 9 I mentioned Michael Perry's theory, in *The Easter Enigma*, that in his post-mortem state Jesus causes the disciples to project images of him. The resurrection thus ceases to be unique and ceases to be a miracle. It turns into an example of various psychic phenomena which, for those who believe in them, are scientific and obey certain laws. I also mentioned the way in which Leibniz, unable to accept the idea of action at a distance, preferred to see miracles where Newton's disciple Samuel Clarke saw science. In Chapter 11 I suggested that the 'miraculous powers' of the yogins might be more aptly described as extraordinary mental and physical abilities which have been acquired through training. These powers represent the new consciousness attained through meditation. They concern less a capacity to 'violate' the laws of nature than a capacity to see nature for what it really is. I suggested that the enlightened consciousness recognizes that all phenomena are themselves products of consciousness and can therefore be 'thought' into different forms. Certainly this may be a naive and ignorant reading of Buddhist traditions, about which I know little. Even if it is, the point can still be made that what to one person is against all laws of nature, to another person is an illustration of laws which not everyone can perceive or aspire to.

This is why in the chapter on Hume I tried to take issue with his scepticism. For Hume prepares us, in his long discussion over the reliability of witnesses, for a scenario where an event takes place which hasn't really happened – people have simply lied or been deceived. This, however, is not necessarily the problem. The problem needn't be that people have lied or been confused over what happened. They may agree about what they have seen, but disagree about how to interpret it. Is it a miracle, or is it the workings of an as-yet-undiscovered law? Does a cancer patient recover because spontaneous remissions illustrate something that medical science has yet to discover, or because of an immediate act of God? There need be no tricks or dishonesty involved over 'what happened' – a terminally ill patient walked out of hospital fully recovered. The issue concerns how that is to be interpreted. It seems to me that there can be no certainty (since we obviously cannot anticipate what medical science will know in a century's time) that a miracle has taken place. At the same time, however, there is no certainty that a miracle has *not* taken place.

I therefore offer a definition focused not upon 'unnatural acts' – acts which violate laws of nature – but upon special or immediate acts of God. I am left with the problem of how these 'acts of God' work – which I shall address in the second part of this conclusion – but I do not have to be worried about their relation to the laws of nature. I think that there is a common misunderstanding of 'primitive' human beings existing in a lawless environment of 'pre-scientific' anarchy, where they would 'believe anything', which is patronizing and wrong (but the people of a bygone era are the one group in society who cannot rise up to protest their case). At the same time there is a common misunderstanding of contemporary human beings as sophisticated and not given to 'primitive' superstition, a belief which is equally at odds with reality, as I have tried to show in Chapter 12. Having no laws of nature did not prevent most contemporaries of Joseph from treating him as a cuckold; having technology everywhere around them does not prevent millions of contemporary pilgrims from believing in statues of the Virgin Mary that weep tears of blood or Hindu statues that drink milk.

How do Miracles happen?

In Chapters 3 and 4, I ruled out the idea that there are 'holes in the web', gaps in the closed continuum of cause and effect through which some specific divine initiatives could slip. I rejected the idea that more recent developments like chaos theory or the uncertainty principle allowed space for SDA. But I also argued that this search for 'holes in the web' was misplaced anyway. If it was going to be possible to speak about SDA, it would not be because God could occasionally be given a slot in the system from which to launch divine initiatives.

The point has often been made – and is widely though not universally accepted – that where human actions are concerned two different forms of language can coinhere. Thus I can say that 'I waved my hand', in language describing an action that I intended to carry out. And I can give a technical description of changes in my body involving nerves and muscles which describe the same event. Unsurprisingly, some have rushed to find a way of describing God's actions in the same terms, with the physical universe as God's body and miracles as (presumably) actions taken by that 'body'. I rejected this notion. I could make no sense of the world as God's body. But I could also see that people were reluctant to talk about God as a 'disembodied' or 'unembodied' agent. They didn't see how acts of God could be affirmed where there was no 'instrumental substructure' to God's actions in the world, no 'causal joint' in the famous phrase of Austin Farrer.

I ended those two chapters with the remark that many contemporary scientist-theologians have a stronger sense of God as Creator of a universe which, after all, they are able 'professionally to admire', than of the separation between God and humanity represented by the myth of the Fall. Such a doctrine seems to play little part in their affirmation of God's all-around presence. They are constantly pointing out that their 'theism' or (in Peacocke's case) 'panentheism' emphasizes that God is not set apart from the human person as mere spectator, mere observer, mere indifferent Deist deity – the sort of being that John Robinson began to hack away at half a century ago in *Honest to God*, when he attacked the notion of a 'God up there' and started ladling out indigestible spoonfuls of something called 'the ground of our being'.

Yet whilst of course the detached observer of Deism cannot be affirmed, is there not something in the notion of separation expressed by the doctrine of the Fall, which genuinely throws light on the relations of God and humanity, not just in terms of ethics but ontologically? In all this search for causal joints and instrumental substructures, as in the whole approach of Thomism, transcendental or otherwise, there is an attempt to deny the ineradicable separation between human and divine which is not a question of divine indifference but of the conditions of human perception and thought.

Kant was the philosopher who provided the double-edged remedy to Hume's rampant empiricism. He made it clear that the mind imposes upon the material of experience its own forms of cognition. This gives us confidence that what we find in reality will conform to a manageable pattern – precisely because it is we who have imposed the pattern. At the same time, however, this means that we cannot know things as they are in themselves, apart from the knowing subject. Kant gives us the confidence to work with phenomena, but only by highlighting the fact that they are but phenomena, but appearances. We are empowered by Kant, because we can work confidently with our assumptions of space and time, or cause and effect (though these concepts have been modified over the last three hundred years, of course); but we are also trapped by Kant, because he is the philosopher who makes it clear that we can't jump out of our cognitive skins. Work confidently, he seems to be saying, but work as mortals.

Of course Kant's philosophy is more complicated than that. In the transcendental dialectic of the *Critique of Pure Reason*, for instance, he struggles with ways in which, despite the limits to our knowledge, we may maintain concepts like 'self' and 'God' as 'ideas of reason' with a regulative role.[1] Nevertheless, the fundamental point about Kant's 'Copernican Revolution' in philosophy remains crucial. Yet it troubles many theologians. Latching on to the austere bachelor lifestyle of Kant himself (though his dinner parties were always convivial), his reluctance to attend church for anything other than official ceremonies and his dislike of hymn-singing and prayer (a shameful activity, he seems to have thought, or at the very least an embarrassment), they assume that Kant was doing more than reacting against his Pietist upbringing or asserting the primacy of the ethical. They assume that he has falsely isolated the human from the divine, cutting it off from streams of contact between the divine and human mediated by ritual, emotion and aesthetic intuition, streams which would flow again in the Romantic movement of the early nineteenth century.

However, Kant did not feel constrained by his philosophy to deny miracles. In his *Lectures on Philosophical Theology*, he argues that 'every event given in the world is directed by God's supreme will'. The divine direction, however, is partly 'orderly' (*ordentlich*) and partly 'extraordinary' (*ausserordentlich*), a distinction which could be compared to that between SDA and GDA. Kant's definition of 'miracle' is similar to my own. He writes that 'any event which is produced immediately by the divine will is a miracle, an effect of God's extraordinary direction' (Kant 1978: 155). Miracles, he suggests, should neither be expected nor denied.

Kant warns of how a 'lazy reason' might 'derive anything from God as its immediate cause when sharper reflection might convince us that it was only a natural effect' (1978: 155). This is always a temptation, either because of a 'lazy reason' or because of pious longing for a miracle. Indeed, I have argued that we can never be sure that whatever we witness isn't a natural effect whose cause we have not yet managed to discover. At the same time, he suggests, miracles may occur – even as an answer to prayer, though Kant rightly warns against the use of prayer 'as a means to getting our own way' (1978: 155). He is more worried about the moral dangers of petitionary prayer than its theoretical possibility.

Nothing more effectively puts paid to the Deist 'observer' than Kant's philosophy. The God 'up there' is dismissed completely; God cannot be a part of the universe, an object in space in time, however grand. But Kant's philosophy also excludes the idea that God must be provided with some kind of toehold, some tear in the web, in order to act in the world. Such an approach puts a specific divine cause alongside other causes, in much the same way that the 'God up there' becomes a superior object ranked alongside (if also above) other objects.

When a miracle occurs, it isn't as if space needs to be found for God to get in. It isn't as if room has to be found for the divine cause to squeeze in among all the other causes. Nor, if a miracle takes place, is there a gaping hole in the explanation of an event. If a terminally ill child recovers from cancer, there is no logical requirement to pronounce a miracle. Surprises like this happen in medicine all the time, because it is still learning about illness and how to treat it – there are gaping holes everywhere, and the explanations that fill them often create new ones in their place.

Kant recognizes that we have to interpret reality in terms that make sense to us, and this involves making use of cause and effect. A miracle affirms that an event cannot be made sense of in these terms – the only terms in which we can make sense of anything. Therefore we have to say that it is something that we cannot make sense of at all. A miracle is never like a conjuring trick which can be followed up with a behind-the-scenes explanation of 'how it works'. A miracle can never be explained, however sophisticated our scientific awareness becomes. There is no 'causal joint' and there is no 'mechanical substructure'; to contradict an older but still highly pertinent work (Farmer 1935: 155–7), God does not get in on the 'underside' of events.

There is nothing observable in the event itself – however striking it may be – that compels us to call it a miracle. It certainly doesn't have to be called that – in some cases it can be called a coincidence, in others the working of an as yet undiscovered law. Moreover, as Hume reminds us, we may question the honesty or accuracy of the witnesses to an event. In the excursus on a 'modern Christ' who claimed to rise from the dead, I tried to show that even in a modern technological age uncertainty about what has happened will remain.

But just as there is nothing in the event itself to demand that it be explained as a miracle, so also there is nothing in the nature of any event which can stop it being a miracle. It doesn't have to be something in the 'microworld' where cause and effect do not apply, or something which the laws of nature cannot explain. It can neither be said that a miracle 'cannot happen' nor that a particular event 'can only be' a miracle.

Why do Miracles happen?

In the definition of 'miracle' which I offered, I spoke of a special act of God which was beneficial and religiously significant. Hobbes's talking cow is therefore excluded as a marvel rather than a miracle; acts which are not those of God, and acts which are deliberately designed to harm are also excluded from the definition. However, though I argued that miracles are beneficial I rejected the idea that they occur at the point where human need is greatest. The danger of the 'miracle of Dunkirk' view is that it sees God plugging the gaps where human capacity fails – an alternative version of the 'God of the gaps' approach. God does not perform miracles in the manner of a UN intervention force, muscling in where human evil threatens to get out of hand. Nor is God like a protective parent, intervening when there is real danger of harm to God's human offspring.

Undoubtedly, the problem of why God acts when God does has led some to prefer the idea that there are no SDAs. Certainly if miracles were sticking plaster to cope with the world's wounds, then God could be accused of treating minor cuts and ignoring gaping wounds in the human patient. But I have argued that this is not the purpose of miracles.

Others have incorporated a rejection of miracles into the principles of a 'kenotic' theology, according to which God deliberately limits Godself in order to provide 'room for' human freedom. Although I feel that the principles of a kenotic theology are correct and important, I do not see why they should necessarily rule out miracles. I am more sympathetic to Sarah Coakley's position that even a God who loved us and 'gave us space' might tweak our ears now and again.

By stressing the 'religious significance' of miracles, I have emphasized the importance of miracles as 'signs', following the New Testament habit of bracketing together 'signs and wonders'. The act of God must be (from the perspective of the human observer) a sign of God. Both 'sign' and 'wonder' are words that refer directly to the perspective of the observer; the observer is morally and aesthetically affected by what takes place, and also has to interpret its significance. But I have rejected any definition of 'miracle' which defines it in terms of the subjective response of the believer. There is always an act of God to which response has to be made.

We can see the concern for a proper 'reading of the signs' in the miracles of Jesus. His miracles do not only relieve human need; they announce the coming of the kingdom of God. When the disciples of John ask Jesus whether he is 'the one who is to come, or are we to expect some other?', Jesus answers 'Go and tell John what you hear and see: the blind recover their sight, the lame walk, the lepers are made clean, the deaf hear, the dead are raised to life, the poor are hearing the good news – and happy is the man who does not find me a stumbling-block' (Matthew 11:2–6).

The mention of a stumbling block is important. Since this is a kingdom which comes not in power but in love, the danger is that the herald will distort the message being heralded. The healing miracles are presented as events requiring proper interpretation. I have suggested that it is very easy to misinterpret miracles as crude demonstrations of superior force, and I have argued that Jesus is keenly aware of this – hence the presentation of the Devil encouraging him to throw himself off the parapet of the temple, one of the three temptations in the wilderness (Matthew 4:5, Luke 4:11–12). The Devil reminds him that angels will support his fall – angels who, as Jesus elsewhere says, could have been summoned to prevent his arrest (Matthew 26:53). Yet he submits to arrest and tells his disciples to put away their swords. They are not to expect miracles. Not even the crowds who taunt him can force one. He goes to his death.

Jesus heals the importunate and the persistent, responding to a need that he cannot ignore, angered by the suffering he sees and determined to relieve it, but always seeking to have these actions properly understood. Here the 'kenotic' theologians surely do understand a sense in which God's love may be compromised by acts of power which try to stamp the overwhelming authority of the Christian God upon the world, like it or not.

This is not to say that there isn't another element of Jewish and Christian tradition where miracles clearly are acts of power. In this tradition God is the supreme weapon of mass destruction. The weapon can be summoned to aid Moses or Joshua against the enemies of God's people; it protects the apostles against their enemies in a hostile Roman Empire; it confounds the pagans who stand at the gates of Rome and threaten to destroy a 'Christian Empire'; it destroys demons and keeps the people of the Middle Ages from disease and starvation; it is the 'superior' magic against Pharaoh or pagans or the wrong denomination of Christians. This tradition cannot be wished away; yet it is also very hard to find any consistency between this tradition and that of Christ's miracles as signs of a Kingdom that refuses to force itself upon the world.

Indeed I would argue that these two traditions concerning miracles cannot only be observed sitting uneasily together in the Bible, but are evident throughout the later history of Christianity. In the sections on the history of Christianity, I have tried to show that it is impossible to ignore the way in which belief in miracles has been exploited by individuals and groups wanting personal, political and economic power in society. Miracles always raise questions about who has authority in the religious community. They always have an economic implication and a socio-cultural resonance. In Naguib Mahfouz's novel *Midaq Alley*, we read of a 'cripple maker' who creates beggars. He is giving people a livelihood. 'They came to him whole and left blind, rickety, hunchbacked, pigeon-breasted, or with arms or legs cut off short' ([1947] 2001: 55). It is the reverse of the gospel story where people come to Christ crippled and leave whole. But the 'Doctor' in Mahfouz's story, written in British-occupied Egypt shortly after the war, shows compassion in his own way, responding to the economic needs of those who have to eke out a living in the streets of Cairo. A miracle of healing, in such circumstances, would be unthinkable without the economic conditions which would make it a genuine benefit.

I have tried to illustrate some of the political, social and economic factors involved both in the past and in the present in order to suggest how important it is to understand the meaning of miracles, and not simply focus on the question of 'what happened'. Without understanding how the miracle operates as a sign – without understanding its 'significance' – it may be counter-productive; it may feed the ego of a man like Oral Roberts who asks us to 'expect' miracles. Ironically, such is the discomfort one feels with the way in which miracles are often used in the modern day as a means of domination that writing a book like this can have a curious effect. One sets out with gritted teeth to make the case for miracles in a secular age. One ends up wanting to debunk many if not most of the miracles paraded about in what, for all its technology, is fittingly described as a new age of superstition.

Conclusions

By way of conclusion, I should like to return to the sceptical tradition concerning miracles within Rabbinic Judaism. The tradition warns against miracles, less as a physical impossibility than as a possible source of corruption – as the rabbis believed they had been for those who had turned to the 'sect of the Nazarenes'. Yet, as I have also pointed out, the tradition did not reject them entirely. Rabbis like Honi and Hanina ben Dosa performed miracles. The tradition concentrated its fire on those whose miracles are a means of self-aggrandisement (as it probably believed they were for Jesus). When Honi the Circle-Drawer draws a circle in the sand and refuses to leave it until God sends rain, God does indeed send rain. Yet Simeon ben Shetah tells Honi that he 'importunes before the Omnipresent'. Rather than inviting admiration, then, Honi's miracle invites a rebuke. A miracle is a mark of failure, requiring a change in the natural order to accommodate some need, as in the story of the man who grew breasts to suckle his son. The story of the oven of Akhinai shows that experts in the Torah have greater power than miracle workers. Yet in all this the occurrence of miracles is not denied.

The events which virtually obliterated Judaism from Europe were a reason for many people to give up belief in miracles. They were ruled out not by there being some event, like Jesus' resurrection, which could be explained without a miracle (that has always been the case), but by there taking place events which demanded a miracle that did not happen. The problems this raises have to be faced. If we believe in miracles, this means that no miracles at Auschwitz doesn't mean no miracles at all. It means that miracles do not appear where human suffering or need is greatest. It means that comfortable notions of God looking after God's children have to be modified. In a cruel confirmation of the rabbis' own wisdom, it means that miracles are not a way of coping with life's difficulties.

Yet I suggested that for all their desire to distance themselves from nascent Christianity, there was ironically some parallel between the rabbis' scepticism about miracles and that of Jesus himself. He too could see how dangerous a capacity to work miracles might be for the miracle-worker; he was certainly afraid of being misunderstood because of his miracle-working abilities. He too, a rabbi from unworthy Galilee, might have echoed the sages of Rabbinic Judaism when they said:

> The height of folly is to place reliance upon miracles; the depth of wisdom is to know that miracles take place.
>
> (Neusner and Neusner 1996: 171)

Notes

1 See the section on the Transcendental Dialectic in the translation of Kant's first Critique by Norman Kemp Smith (1929).

Bibliography

Baillie, D.M. (1948) *God was in Christ: An Essay on Incarnation and Atonement*, London: Faber and Faber.

Baker, J.A. (1975) *The Foolishness of God*, London: Fontana.

von Balthasar, Hans (1990) *Mysterium Paschale*, Edinburgh: T. & T. Clark.

Barbour, Ian G. (2001) 'God's Power: A Process View', in John Polkinghorne (ed.) *The Work of Love: Creation as Kenosis*, London: SPCK.

Barr, James (1977) *Fundamentalism*, London: SCM Press.

Barr, James (1983) *Holy Scripture: Canon, Authority, Criticism*, Oxford: Oxford University Press.

Barrow, J.D. and Tipler, F.J. (1986) *The Anthropic Cosmological Principle*, Oxford: Oxford University Press.

Bartsch, H.-W. (ed.) (1972) *Kerygma and Myth*, London: SPCK (first published by Reich und Heidrich, Hamburg, 1948–55).

Ben-Amos, Dan and Mintz, Jerome R. (eds and trs) (1993) *In Praise of Baal Shem Tov: The Earliest Collection of Legends about the Founder of Hasidism*, Northvale, NJ: Jason Aronson.

Bonhoeffer, Dietrich (1954) *Prisoner for God*, New York: Macmillan.

Bonhoeffer, Dietrich (1971) *Letters and Papers from Prison*, London: SCM Press.

Brown, Daniel (2004) *A New Introduction to Islam*, Oxford: Blackwell.

Brown, David (1985) *The Divine Trinity*, London: Duckworth.

Brown, Peter (1978) *The Making of Late Antiquity*, Cambridge, Mass.: Harvard University Press.

Brown, Peter (1981) *The Cult of the Saints: Its Rise and Function in Latin Christianity*, Chicago: University of Chicago Press.

Bultmann, Rudolf (1972) 'New Testament and Mythology', in H.-W. Bartsch (ed.) *Kerygma and Myth*, London: SPCK.

Cavadini, John C. (ed.) (1999) *Miracles in Jewish and Christian Antiquity*, Notre Dame, Ind.: University of Notre Dame Press.

Chodkiewicz, Michel (1993) *Seal of the Saints: Prophethood and Sainthood in the Doctrine of Ibn al-'Arabi*, tr. L. Sherrard, Cambridge: Islamic Texts Society.

Coakley, Sarah (1997) 'Feminism', in C. Taliaferro and P. Quinn (eds) *A Companion to Philosophy of Religion*, Oxford: Blackwell.

Coakley, Sarah (2001) 'Kenosis: Theological Meanings and Gender Connotations', in J. Polkinghorne (ed.) *The Work of Love: Creation as Kenosis*, London: SPCK.

Cohn-Sherbok, Daniel (ed.) (1996) *Divine Intervention and Miracles in Jewish Theology*, New York: Edwin Mellen Press.

Conze, Edward (ed. and tr.) (1959) *Buddhist Scriptures*, London: Penguin.

von Dam, Raymond (1993) *Saints and their Miracles in Late Antique Gaul*, Princeton, NJ: Princeton University Press.

Davies, Brian (1993) *An Introduction to the Philosophy of Religion*, Oxford: Oxford University Press.

Davis, Stephen (ed.) (2001) *Encountering Evil: Live Options in Theodicy*, Louisville, Ky.: Westminster John Knox Press.

Delgado, Pat (1992) *Crop Circles: Conclusive Evidence?*, London: Bloomsbury.

Dilley, Frank (1983), 'Does the "God who acts" really act?', in O.C. Thomas (ed.) *God's Activity in the World*, Atlanta: Scholar's Press.

Ehrman, Bart D. (1999) *After the New Testament: A Reader in Early Christianity*, Oxford: Oxford University Press.

Epstein, Michael and Garlaschelli, Luigi (1992) 'Better Blood through Chemistry: A Laboratory Replication of a Miracle', *Journal of Scientific Explanation* 6: 233–46.

Farmer, H.H. (1935) *The World and God*, London: Nisbet.

Farrer, A. (1966) *A Science of God?*, London: Geoffrey Bles.

Farrer, A. (1967) *Faith and Speculation*, London: A. & C. Black.

Flew, Antony (1961) *Hume's Philosophy of Belief*, London: Routledge and Kegan Paul.

Flint, Valerie J. (1991) *The Rise of Magic in Early Medieval Europe*, Oxford: Clarendon Press.

Fiddes, Paul (1988) *The Creative Suffering of God*, Oxford: Clarendon Press.

Foucher, A. (1963) *The Life of the Buddha according to the Ancient Texts and Monuments of India*, tr. Simone Brangier Boas, Middletown, Conn.: Wesleyan University Press.

Frei, Hans (1974) *The Eclipse of Biblical Narrative*, New Haven: Yale University Press.

Freud, S. (1961) *Complete Psychological Works*, London: Hogarth Press.

Geach, Peter (1969) *God and the Soul*, London: Routledge.

Geach, Peter (1977) *Providence and Evil*, Cambridge: Cambridge University Press.

Gibbon, Edward (1909) *Decline and Fall of the Roman Empire*, London: Methuen.

Gilkey, Langdon (1961) 'Cosmology, Ontology and the Travail of Biblical Language', *Journal of Religion* 41: 194–205.

Goulder, M. (ed.) (1979) *Incarnation and Myth*, London: SCM Press.

Griffin, David Ray (2001) 'Creation out of Nothing, Creation out of Chaos and the Problem of Evil', in Stephen Davis (ed.) *Encountering Evil: Live Options in Theodicy*, Louisville, Ky.: Westminster John Knox Press.

Guillaume, Alfred (1955) *The Life of Muhammad: A Translation of Ibn Ishaq's Sirat Rasul Allah*, Karachi: Oxford University Press.

Guttmann, Alexander (1947) 'The significance of Miracles for Talmudic Judaism', *Hebrew Union College Annual* 20: 363–406.

Hall, Lindsey (2003) *Swinburne's Hell and Hick's Universalism*, Aldershot: Ashgate.

Harrison, Ted (1996) *Stigmata: A Medieval Mystery in a Modern Age*, London: Penguin.

Hebblethwaite, Brian (1979) 'Predestination and Divine Foreknowledge', *Religious Studies* 15, December.

Hebblethwaite, Brian (1980) 'Recent British Theology', in Peter Toon and J.D. Spiceland (eds) *One God in Trinity*, London: Samuel Bagster.

Hebblethwaite, Brian (2000) *Evil, Suffering and Religion*, London: SPCK.

Hebblethwaite, Brian and Henderson, Edward (eds) (1990) *Divine Action: Studies Inspired by the Philosophical Theology of Austin Farrer*, Edinburgh: T. & T. Clark.

Hick, John (ed.) (1977) *The Myth of God Incarnate*, London: SCM Press.

Hick, John (ed.) (1993) *The Metaphor of God Incarnate*, London: SCM Press.

Hick, John (1996) *Evil and the God of Love*, New York: Harper and Row.

Hobbes, Thomas (1968) *Leviathan*, ed. C.B. Macpherson, Harmondsworth: Penguin (first published 1651).

Hodgson, L. (1943) *The Doctrine of the Trinity*, London: James Nisbet.

Holland, R.F. (1989) 'The Miraculous', in Richard Swinburne (ed.) *Miracles*, London: Macmillan.

Hooker, Morna (1991) *The Gospel According to Mark*, London, A. & C. Black.

James, M.R. (1924) *The Apocryphal New Testament*, Oxford: Oxford University Press.

Jantzen, Grace (1984) *God's World, God's Body*, London: Darton, Longman & Todd.

John of Salerno (1958) *Life of St. Odo of Cluny*, trans. Dom Gerard Sitwell, OSB, London: Sheed and Ward.

Johnson, David (2000) *Hume, Holism and Miracle*, Ithaca, NY: Cornell University Press.

Kant, I. (1929) *Critique of Pure Reason*, tr. Norman Kemp Smith, London: Macmillan.

Kant, I. (1978) *Lectures on Philosophical Theology*, tr. Allen W. Wood and Gertrude M. Clark, Ithaca, NY: Cornell University Press.

Kasper, Walter (1984) *The God of Jesus Christ*, London: SCM Press.

Kaufman, Gordon (1968) 'On the Meaning of "Act of God"', *Harvard Theological Review* 61: 175–201.

Kaufman, Gordon (1972) *God the Problem*, Cambridge, Mass.: Harvard University Press.

Kaufman, Gordon (1983) 'On the Meaning of "Act of God"', in O.C. Thomas (ed.) *God's Activity in the World*, Atlanta: Scholar's Press.

Kelly, J.N.D. (1950) *Early Christian Creeds*, London: A. & C. Black.

Kelly, J.N.D. (1958) *Early Christian Doctrines*, London: A. & C. Black.

Kierkegaard, S. (1962) *Philosophical Fragments*, Princeton, NJ: Princeton University Press.

Kierkegaard, S. (2001) *Fear and Trembling*, Princeton, NJ: Princeton University Press.

Kirsta, Alex (2000) 'The Crying Game', *The Guardian*, 9 December.

Lampe, G.W.H. and MacKinnon, D.M. (1966) *The Resurrection*, London: Mowbray.

Langford, M. (1981) *Providence*, London: SCM Press.

Larmer, Robert (1988) *Water into Wine?*, Montreal: Queen's University Press.

Larmer, Robert (1996) *Questions of Miracle*, Montreal: Queen's University Press.

Lawton, J.S. (2002) *Miracles and Revelation*, Cambridge: James Clarke.

Lefebure, Leo (1993) *The Buddha and the Christ: Explorations in Buddhist and Christian Dialogue*, Maryknoll, NY: Orbis Books.

Lessing, G.E. (1957) *Lessing's Theological Writings*, ed. Henry Chadwick, Stanford, Calif.: Stanford University Press.

Levine, M.P. (1989) *Hume and the Problem of Miracles: A Solution*, Dordrecht: Kluwer.

Lewis, C.S. (2002) *Miracles*, London: HarperCollins (first published 1947).

Livingston, James C. (1971) *Modern Christian Thought from the Enlightenment to Vatican II*, London: Macmillan.

Locke, John (1958) *The Reasonableness of Christianity*, Palo Alto, Calif.: Stanford University Press.

Lohse, Bernard (1966) *A Short History of Christian Doctrine*, Philadelphia: Fortress Press.

Mackie, J.L. (1982) *The Miracle of Theism*, Oxford: Clarendon Press.

McKinney, R.W. (ed.) (1976) *Creation, Christ and Culture*, Edinburgh: T. & T. Clark.

MacKinnon, D.M. (1976) 'The Relation of the Doctrines of the Incarnation and the Trinity', in R.W. McKinney (ed.) *Creation, Christ and Culture*, Edinburgh: T. & T. Clark.

McLain, F. Michael (1990) 'Narrative Interpretation and the Problem of Double Agency', in Brian Hebblethwaite and Edward Henderson (eds) *Divine Action: Studies Inspired by the Philosophical Theology of Austin Farrer*, Edinburgh: T. & T. Clark.

Macquarrie, John (1977) *Principles of Christian Theology*, New York: Scribner's.

Mahfouz, Naguib (2001) *Midaq Alley*, Cairo: The American University in Cairo Press (first published in Arabic in 1947 as *Zuqaq al-Midaqa*).

Marx, Karl (1957) *On Religion*, Moscow: Progress Publishers.

Marxsen, Willi (1968) 'The Resurrection of Jesus as a Historical and Theological Problem', in C.F.D. Moule (ed.) *The Significance of the Message of the Resurrection for Faith in Jesus Christ*, London: SCM Press.

Moltmann, J. (1974) *The Crucified God*, London: SCM Press.

Moltmann, J. (1981) *The Trinity and the Kingdom of God*, London: SCM Press.

Moltmann, J. (1990) *The Way of Jesus Christ*, London: SCM Press.

Moltmann, J. (2001) 'God's Kenosis in the Creation and Consummation of the World', in J. Polkinghorne (ed.) *The Work of Love: Creation as Kenosis*, London: SPCK.

Montigiani, Nicolas (2003) *Crop Circles: Evidence of a Cover-Up?*, Frankfurt am Main: Carnot Press.

Moore, Robert (1997) 'Between Sanctity and Superstition: Saints and their Miracles in the Age of Revolution', in Miri Rubin (ed.) *The Work of Jacques le Goff and the Challenge of Medieval History*, Woodbridge: Boydell Press.

Moule, C.F.D. (1966) 'St Paul and Dualism: The Pauline Conception of Resurrection', *New Testament Studies* 12: 106–23.

Moule, C.F.D. (ed.) (1968) *The Significance of the Message of the Resurrection for Faith in Jesus Christ*, London: SCM Press.

Neusner, Jacob and Neusner, Noam M.M. (1996) *The Book of Jewish Wisdom: The Talmud of the Well-Considered Life*, New York: Continuum Press.

Nineham, Dennis (1978) *The Use and Abuse of the Bible*, London: SPCK.

O'Flaherty, W.D (ed. and tr.) (1975) *Hindu Myths: A Sourcebook*, London: Penguin.

Paley, William (1838) *The Works of William Paley*, Oxford: Oxford University Press.

Pannenberg, W. (1968) *Jesus God and Man*, London, SCM Press.

Peacocke, A.R. (1979) *Creation and the World of Science*, Oxford: Clarendon Press.

Peacocke, A.R. (1998) 'Biological Evolution – A Positive Theological Appraisal', in R.J. Russell, W.R. Stoeger and F.J. Ayala (eds) *Evolution and Molecular Biology: Scientific Perspectives on Divine Action*, Notre Dame, Ind.: University of Notre Dame Press.

Peacocke, A.R. (2001a) 'The Cost of New Life', in J. Polkinghorne (ed.) *The Work of Love: Creation as Kenosis*, London: SPCK.

Peacocke, A.R. (2001b) *Paths from Science Towards God*, Oxford: Oneworld.

Perry, Michael (1959) *The Easter Enigma*, London: Faber & Faber.

Pinnock, C.H. (ed.) (1994) *The Openness of God: A Biblical Challenge to the Traditional Understanding of God*, Carlisle: Paternoster Press.

Plantinga, Alvin (1986) 'Is theism really a miracle?', *Faith and Philosophy* 3: 109–23.

Polkinghorne, John (1991) *Reason and Reality*, London: SPCK.

Polkinghorne, J. (1998) *Belief in God in an Age of Science*, New Haven: Yale University Press.

Polkinghorne, John (2001a) 'Kenotic Creation and Divine Action', in J. Polkinghorne (ed.) *The Work of Love: Creation as Kenosis*, London: SPCK.

Polkinghorne, John (ed.) (2001b) *The Work of Love: Creation as Kenosis*, London: SPCK.

Puccetti, Roland (1967) 'The Loving God – Some Observations on John Hick's *Evil and the God of Love*', *Religious Studies* 2: 255–68.

Remus, Harold (1997) *Jesus as Healer*, Cambridge: Cambridge University Press.

Richardson, Alan (1941) *The Miracle Stories of the Gospels*, London: SCM Press.

Roberts, Oral (1995) *Expect a Miracle: My Life and Ministry*, Nashville, Tenn.: Thomas Nelson.

Roberts, R.H. (2002) *Religion, Theology and the Human Sciences*, Cambridge: Cambridge University Press.

Robinson, John (1963) *Honest to God*, London: SCM Press.

Rosenzweig, F. (1985) *The Star of Redemption*, Notre Dame, Ind.: University of Notre Dame Press.

Roth, John K. (2001) 'A Theodicy of Protest', in Stephen Davis (ed.) *Encountering Evil: Live Options in Theodicy*, Louisville, Ky.: Westminster John Knox Press.

Rowland, C.C. (1982) *The Open Heaven: A Study of Apocalyptic in Judaism and Early Christianity*, New York: Crossroad.

Rowland, Christopher (1988) *Radical Christianity*, Cambridge: Polity Press.

Rowland, C.C. (2003) *Revelation*, London: Epworth.

Rowland, C.C. and Corner, Mark (1990) *Liberating Exegesis: The Challenge of Liberation Theology to Biblical Studies*, London: SPCK.

Rubin, Miri (ed.) (1997) *The Work of Jacques le Goff and the Challenge of Medieval History*, Woodbridge: Boydell Press.

Russell, R.J., Stoeger, W.R. and Ayala, F.J. (eds) (1998) *Evolution and Molecular Biology: Scientific Perspectives on Divine Action*, Notre Dame, Ind.: University of Notre Dame Press.

Ruthven, Jon (1993) *On the Cessation of the Charismata: The Protestant Polemic on Postbiblical Miracles*, Sheffield: Sheffield Academic Press.

Saunders, Nicholas (2002) *Divine Action and Modern Science*, Cambridge: Cambridge University Press.

Sayers, Dorothy (1941) *The Mind of the Maker*, London: Methuen.

Schleiermacher, F.D.E (1978) *The Christian Faith*, Edinburgh: T. & T. Clark.

Segundo, J.L. (1976) *The Liberation of Theology*, New York: Orbis Books.

Selby, Peter (1976) *Look for the Living: The Corporate Nature of Resurrection Faith*, London: SCM Press.

Signer, M. (1999), 'Restoring the Balance: Musings on Miracles in Rabbinic Judaism', in John Cavadini (ed.) *Miracles in Jewish and Christian Antiquity*, Notre Dame, Ind.: University of Notre Dame Press.

Simon, Ulrich (1979) *A Theology of Auschwitz: The Christian Faith and the Problem of Evil*, Atlanta: John Knox Press.

Smart, Ninian (1962) *Historical Selections in the Philosophy of Religion*, London: SCM Press.

Smith, Morton (1998) *Jesus the Magician: Charlatan or Son of God?*, Berkeley, Calif.: Ulysses Press.

Spinoza B. (1862) *Tractatus Theologico-Politicus*, trans. Robert Willis, London: Trübner & Co.

Spinoza, B. (1989) *Tractatus Theologico-Politicus*, Leiden: Brill Academic Press.

Stead, G.C. (1977) *Divine Substance*, Oxford: Oxford University Press.

Swinburne, Richard (1970) *The Concept of Miracle*, London: Macmillan.

Swinburne, Richard (ed.) (1989) *Miracles*, London: Macmillan.

Swinburne, Richard (1996) *Is there a God?*, Oxford: Clarendon Press.

Swinburne, Richard (2003) *The Resurrection of God Incarnate*, Oxford: Oxford University Press.

Taliaferro, C. and Quinn, P. (eds) (1997) *A Companion to Philosophy of Religion*, Oxford: Blackwell.

Taylor, A.E. (1946) *The Christian Hope of Immortality*, London: Macmillan.

TeSelle, Eugene (1990) 'Divine Action: The Doctrinal Tradition', in Brian

Hebblethwaite and Edward Henderson (eds) *Divine Action: Studies Inspired by the Philosophical Theology of Austin Farrer*, Edinburgh: T. & T. Clark.

Thomas, Keith (1973) *Religion and the Decline of Magic*, London: Penguin.

Thomas, O.C. (ed.) (1983) *God's Activity in the World*, Atlanta: Scholar's Press.

Thurman, Robert (1983) *The Holy Teaching of Vinalakirti: A Mahayana Scripture*, University Park, Penn.: Pennsylvania State University Press.

The Times (1984) 'Act of God', 10 July.

Toon, Peter and Spiceland, J.D. (eds) (1980) *One God in Trinity*, London: Samuel Bagster.

Towler, Robin (1984) *The Need for Certainty*, London: Routledge

Tracy, Thomas (1984) *God, Action and Embodiment*, Grand Rapids, Mich.: Eerdman's.

Tracy, Thomas (1990) 'Native Theology and the Acts of God', in Brian Hebblethwaite and Edward Henderson (eds) *Divine Action: Studies Inspired by the Philosophical Theology of Austin Farrer*, Edinburgh: T. & T. Clark.

Tweyman, S. (ed.) (1996) *Hume on Miracles: Responses to Hume's Essay on Miracles*, Chicago: St. Augustine's Press.

Vailati, Ezio (ed.) (1997) *The Leibniz–Clarke Correspondence*, Oxford: Oxford University Press.

Vanstone, W.H. (1977) *Love's Endeavour, Love's Expense*, London: Darton, Longman & Todd.

Vermes, G. (1972, 1973), 'Hanina ben Dosa: A Controversial Galilean Saint from the First Century of the Christian Era', *Journal of Jewish Studies* 23: 28–50; 24: 51–64.

Vermes, G. (1975), *Jesus the Jew*, London: Collins.

Voltaire (1927) *Works*, New York: Walter Black.

Ward, Benedicta (1990) 'Monks and Miracles', in John C. Cavadini (ed.) *Miracles in Jewish and Christian Antiquity*, Notre Dame, Ind.: University of Notre Dame Press.

Warfield, B.B. (1918) *Counterfeit Miracles*, New York: Charles Scribner's.

Weber, Max (1961) *General Economic History*, New York: Collier.

Weber, Max (1965) *The Sociology of Religion*, New York: Collier.

Widad El Sakkakini (1982) *First Among Sufis: The Life and Thought of Rabia Al-Adawiyya, the Woman Saint of Basra*, tr. Nabil Safwat, London: Octagon Press.

Wiles, Maurice (1986) *God's Action in the World*, London: SCM Press.

Wiles, Maurice (1999) *Reason to Believe*, London: SCM Press.

Williams, Bernard (1973) *Problems of the Self*, Cambridge: Cambridge University Press.

Wollheim, Richard (1963) *Hume on Religion*, London: Fontana.

Woodward, Kenneth L. (1996) *Making Saints: How the Catholic Church Determines Who Becomes a Saint, Who Doesn't and Why*, New York: Simon and Schuster.

Woodward, Kenneth L. (2001) *The Book of Miracles*, New York: Touchstone.

Wrede, Wilhelm (1971) *The Messianic Secret*, tr. J. Greig, Cambridge: James Clarke (first published 1901).

Wright, G.E. (1952) *God Who Acts*, London: SCM Press.

Wright, N.T. (2003) *The Resurrection of the Son of God*, London: SPCK.

Zaehner, R.C. (ed.) (1971) *The Concise Encyclopaedia of Living Faiths*, London: Hutchinson.

Zaehner, R.C. (1974) *Our Savage God*, New York: Sheed and Ward.

Zimdars-Schwartz, Sandra L. (1991) *Encountering Mary: From La Salette to Medjugorje*, Princeton, NJ: Princeton University Press.

Index